MILTON, MATERIALISM, AND EMBODIMENT

Medieval & Renaissance Literary Studies

General Editor

Rebecca Totaro

Editorial Board

Judith H. Anderson	Jonathan Gil Harris
Diana Treviño Benet	Margaret Healy
William C. Carroll	Ken Hiltner
Donald Cheney	Arthur F. Kinney
Ann Baynes Coiro	David Loewenstein
Mary T. Crane	Robert W. Maslen
Stephen B. Dobranski	Thomas P. Roche Jr.
Wendy Furman-Adams	Mary Beth Rose
A. C. Hamilton	Mihoko Suzuki
Hannibal Hamlin	Humphrey Tonkin
Margaret P. Hannay	Susanne Woods

Originally titled the *Duquesne Studies: Philological Series* (and later renamed the *Language & Literature Series*), the **Medieval & Renaissance Literary Studies Series** has been published by Duquesne University Press since 1960. This publishing endeavor seeks to promote the study of late medieval, Renaissance, and seventeenth century English literature by presenting scholarly and critical monographs, collections of essays, editions, and compilations. The series encourages a broad range of interpretation, including the relationship of literature and its cultural contexts, close textual analysis, and the use of contemporary critical methodologies.

Foster Provost	Albert C. Labriola	Richard J. DuRocher
EDITOR, 1960–1984	EDITOR, 1985–2009	EDITOR, 2010

MILTON, MATERIALISM, AND EMBODIMENT

ONE FIRST MATTER ALL

Edited by
Kevin J. Donovan
and Thomas Festa

DUQUESNE UNIVERSITY PRESS
Pittsburgh, Pennsylvania

Copyright © 2017 Duquesne University Press
All rights reserved

Published in the United States of America by
DUQUESNE UNIVERSITY PRESS
600 Forbes Avenue
Pittsburgh, Pennsylvania 15282

No part of this book may be used or reproduced,
in any manner or form whatsoever,
without written permission from the publisher,
except in the case of short quotations
in critical articles or reviews.

Library of Congress Cataloging-in-Publication Data

Names: Donovan, Kevin Joseph editor. | Festa, Thomas editor.
Title: Milton, materialism, and embodiment : "one first matter all" / edited by Kevin J. Donovan and Thomas Festa.
Description: Pittsburgh, Pennsylvania : Duquesne University Press, 2017. | Series: Medieval & Renaissance literary studies | Includes bibliographical references and index.
Identifiers: LCCN 2016054226 | ISBN 9780820707020 (cloth : alk. paper) | ISBN 9780-271092959 | Subjects: LCSH: Milton, John, 1608–1674 — Criticism and interpretation. | Materialism in literature. | Monism in literature.
Classification: LCC PR3592.M38 M55 2017 | DDC 821/.4 — dc23
LC record available at https://lccn.loc.gov/2016054226

∞ Printed on acid-free paper.

CONTENTS

ACKNOWLEDGMENTS   VII

Introduction: "One First Matter All"
   Kevin J. Donovan and Thomas Festa   1

PART ONE: MATERIALITY AND THE SENSES

1. The Fragrance of the Fall
   Lauren Shohet   19

2. Sound as Matter: Milton, Music, and Monism
   Seth Herbst   37

PART TWO: HUMAN EMBODIMENT

3. Milton on the Move: Walking and Self-Knowledge in *Paradise Lost*
   Ryan Hackenbracht   59

4. Radical Relations: The Genealogical Imaginary and Queer Kinship in Milton's *Paradise Regained*
   Erin Murphy   81

PART THREE: ANGELIC EMBODIMENT

5. Milton's Strange Angels
   Rebecca Buckham   111

6. Dark Looks and Red Smiles: Homeric Gesture and
   the Problem of Milton's Angels
   Lara Dodds   137

PART FOUR: MILTON'S MATERIALISM REDUX

7. Orson Pratt, Parley Pratt, and the Miltonic Origins
   of Mormon Materialism
   John Rogers   157

8. "The Scanning of Error": *Areopagitica* and 3-D–Printed Guns
   David A. Harper   189

NOTES   211
ABOUT THE CONTRIBUTORS   239
INDEX   243

ACKNOWLEDGMENTS

"Say, Muse, thir Names then known, who first, who last": from the first to the last contribution to this essay collection, the book has been a collaborative effort, a product of the work and support of many individuals and institutions. It gives us great pleasure to thank Kristin A. Pruitt and Charles W. Durham, who in 1991 created the biennial Conference on John Milton held in Murfreesboro, Tennessee, and then edited eight collections of essays that grew out of those meetings. We must also warmly acknowledge the encouragement and support of Mary C. Fenton and Louis Schwartz, who edited the next three collections selected from the Murfreesboro conference before entrusting us with the task. To speak briefly of the material circumstances that created this essay collection, then, the chapters that became the "one first matter" of this book began life at the 2013 Conference on John Milton, sponsored by the English department at Middle Tennessee State University, where shorter or related earlier versions of these essays were presented. We thank MTSU for its material support of the project. Beyond Murfreesboro, we owe enormous gratitude to the team at Duquesne University Press, especially Susan Wadsworth-Booth, the editor-in-chief, and Rebecca Totaro, general editor of the Medieval and Renaissance Literary Studies series for the press. Thanks as well to the anonymous readers for the press, who offered many helpful suggestions that greatly improved the collection.

INTRODUCTION

"One First Matter All"

KEVIN J. DONOVAN AND THOMAS FESTA

In recent decades, it has become increasingly common to find students of early modern English literature taking an interest in materialism as a theoretical and historical subject of study. Thus, for example, literary historians have undertaken analyses of topics such as Spenser's paradoxical treatment of materiality in his allegorical Faeryland; Donne's ambivalent relations to a mechanistic cosmos, the decay of nature, and the threats posed to traditional belief by the new science; and Cavendish's deployment of animality and materialist natural philosophy in *The Blazing World*.[1] Embodiment and materiality have of course long been topics of great interest in studies of Shakespeare, not least because the plays have always been performed.[2] Add to these literary-critical preoccupations the current philosophical emphasis on vitalism — sometimes called the "new materialism" or "object-oriented ontology" — and the scholarly trends indicate a timely and significant watershed for the humanities in general and early modern literary studies in particular.

The history of early modern materialism has grown in importance with the resurgence of vitalism as a modern philosophical approach. Seeking to challenge Kant's "Copernican Revolution" of subject-oriented philosophy and its aftermath, thinkers as diverse as Gilles Deleuze, Bruno Latour, Quentin Meillassoux, Jane Bennett, and Timothy Morton have returned to ontological questions that arose with particular force during the seventeenth century, especially on the topics of monism and materialism, in order to rethink the status of objects from the vantage of ecology, gender, and politics.[3] A rapprochement is needed between historical investigations into materialism as understood in the early modern period and the ecocritical concern for the nonhuman in contemporary vitalist materialism, or what Jane Bennett calls "thing-power materialism": "Thing-power materialism figures materiality as a protean flow of matter-energy and figures the thing as a relatively composed form of that flow."[4] The point of retelling the ontological story with special attention to objects, for Bennett and other modern vitalists, is neither to deny nor minimize the roles of human subjectivity and social construction in constituting an individual human being's relationship to the material world, or indeed the human body's historical and cultural situatedness as a bio-political object. Rather, "thing-power materialism, as an adventurous ontological imaginary, offers a picture of matter as so active, intricate, and awesome, that it's no disgrace to be made up wholly of the stuff oneself."[5] The decentering of human subjectivity, in other words, allows for a recognition of the human being as a materially constituted body entangled in a network of physical objects pulsing with vital energy. Another way of saying this might be to say that vitalism, in both its modern and early modern manifestations, seeks to acknowledge and celebrate a dignity, resistance, and vitality in the nonhuman world with which the human is enmeshed. Not merely a backstory or strand in a new historical genealogy, early modern vitalism, therefore, may be said to possess a special resonance with current theoretical and political concerns emerging from shared attention to the material world for its own sake.[6] Even as modern vitalists urge a thoroughgoing materialism that opposes idealism and metaphysics, their concentrated focus on the animating energy and interconnectedness of the natural world intersects with the seventeenth century monist materialist belief in unity of matter and spirit and discovers precursors in that pre-Kantian movement.

Such ecological themes of stewardship and care for the nonhuman, respect for the sanctity of that which has not been accounted within the domain of the subject, come to the fore in Milton's writings since, as Abdiel insists in *Paradise Lost*, "God and Nature bid the same."[7] Readers of Milton have long known that his works have an important, if idiosyncratic, place in the story of early modern materialism, precisely because of his particular form of vitalism. Thomas Newton, in the first variorum edition of *Paradise Lost* in 1749, summed up vast swathes of critical resistance to Milton's heterodoxies in this comment to *Paradise Lost* 5.478: "Our author should have considered things better, for by attributing his own false notions in philosophy to an Arch-Angel, he has really lessen'd the character, which he intended to raise. He is as much mistaken here in his metaphysics, as he was before in his physics.... For Milton, as he was too much of a materialist in his philosophy, so was too much of a systematist in his divinity."[8] The critic's eye is sharp, even if his gloss is heavy handed. First, Newton's bias needs to be set aside: the condescending tone, the righteous dismissal of the philosophy, the ideologically driven judgment of aesthetic failure. Once we've stripped away the superficial prejudices of another era, however, the depth of Newton's insight becomes startlingly clear. Milton was a materialist in his philosophy. His theology was systematic. The physics and the metaphysics of *Paradise Lost* are of a piece. Ironically, it was the coherence of Milton's vision that so disturbed this early critic, above all the systematic way in which the poet intertwined his materialism and his theology.

Not surprisingly, given the vehemence of Newton's objections, the passage has stayed close to the center of controversy in Milton studies ever since. The implications of Raphael's speech ripple outward to mark other books of the epic. In the infamous grumblings of Samuel Johnson (who, like Newton, objected to Milton's unorthodox monism), "he has unhappily perplexed his poetry with his philosophy.... The confusion of spirit with matter which pervades the whole narration of the war of heaven fills it with incongruity."[9] In spite of such stringent critical denunciations, the archangel Raphael's after-dinner speech to the first human being has lost none of its explanatory power in contemporary criticism. For, in the passage from which we have chosen the subtitle of this essay collection, Milton's systematic materialism fuses physics and metaphysics — even to the point of eradicating any meaningful distinction between the two.

As is spelled out in the chapter "On Creation" in *De doctrina Christiana*, Milton's theology and his science are one, since the origin of matter is not nothing, as was traditionally believed, but God's own substance. In the traditional view, *creatio ex nihilo*, only God existed before creation, but God created everything else from nothing. As Augustine puts it in perhaps the most canonical formulation of the idea in orthodox Christianity, "In the beginning, that is from yourself, in your wisdom which is begotten of your substance, you made something and made it out of nothing. For you made heaven and earth not out of your own self."[10] Therefore, as Augustine argues in response to the question of where evil had come from if not God, evil arises from the perversion of a good creature's will, and "the evil will arises not from the fact that the man is a natural creature, but from the fact that he is a natural creature made out of nothing."[11] Against this view, Milton argues that since God *is* substance, all substance must ultimately derive from him, *creatio ex Deo*: "For indeed that original matter is not to be thought of as an evil or worthless thing, but as a good thing, a seed bank [*seminarium*] of every subsequent good. It was a substance, and derivable from no other source than from the fountain-head of all substance; at first unarranged and disorganized [*indigesta modo et incomposita*], but afterwards God arranged [*digessit*] it and made it beautiful."[12] In the theological treatise, Milton first describes the original matter botanically, as a "seed bank," and then twice uses forms of the highly suggestive Latin word *digerere*, the root of "digestion," for God's arrangement of this chaotic substance at Creation. God digests the first matter from his own substance, thus ordering the fertile ground from which the seeds of goodness spring into a created universe.

In the context of the dialogue between Raphael and Adam in *Paradise Lost*, these figures of speech become literal, even as the distinction between literal and figurative, like the one between matter

and spirit, vanishes in a complex mimesis of the speech's monism.
The poetry ranges along a graduated continuum of figuration and
concreteness, its language thereby embodying the dynamic scale of
being-in-the-cosmos that is its content. The nested metaphors (if that
is what they are) of alimentary, alchemical, and botanical transmutation provide the finest illustration of Milton's cosmology, ontology, and ecology anywhere in his poetry. Lush figuration becomes
transfiguration:

> O *Adam*, one Almightie is, from whom
> All things proceed, and up to him return,
> If not deprav'd from good, created all
> Such to perfection, one first matter all,
> Indu'd with various forms, various degrees
> Of substance, and in things that live, of life;
> But more refin'd, more spiritous, and pure,
> As neerer to him plac't or neerer tending
> Each in thir several active Sphears assignd,
> Till body up to spirit work, in bounds
> Proportiond to each kind. So from the root
> Springs lighter the green stalk, from thence the leaves
> More aerie, last the bright consummate floure
> Spirits odorous breathes: flours and thir fruit
> Mans nourishment, by gradual scale sublim'd
> To vital Spirits aspire, to animal,
> To intellectual, give both life and sense,
> Fansie and understanding, whence the Soule
> Reason receives, and reason is her being,
> Discursive, or Intuitive; discourse
> Is oftest yours, the latter most is ours,
> Differing but in degree, of kind the same.   (PL 5.469–90)

As the comments of Newton and Johnson show, readers of *Paradise Lost* have long understood this passage as directly communicating Milton's own philosophical ideal. If the negative attention such acute readers have paid to the passage were the only indication of its importance, we would do well to scrutinize it with great care. Nonetheless, despite its gorgeous poetry and challenging philosophy, Raphael's speech never received full consideration until William Kerrigan, in the groundbreaking chapter on Milton's materialism in his Freudian study of *Paradise Lost*, made the extraordinary claim that "the success of the epic depends to a large extent on the kind of poetic effect that is the best defense of the ontological moments in Book 5." Kerrigan argues that the speech is one of the few "privileged passages" in which Milton "was able to root the entirety" of his poem "with logical and emotional force." As he says, "One. First. Matter. All. These four words alone, fully heard, comprehend a great poem with much to say. To have them before us in a meaningfully syntactic sequence is to be made momentarily giddy with the plasticity of huge meaning, able to present itself to us with harrowing abstraction." For Kerrigan, the biological fact of Milton's blindness — which derived from poor digestion, according to seventeenth century medical thought — led to psychological conditions necessitating a "private theodicy." This task in turn made heretical monism of matter and spirit an especially attractive guarantor of the potential for redemption in the material language of poetry as well as the diseased physical body.[13]

Regardless of whether readers today will be convinced by these psychoanalytic conclusions, Kerrigan was surely right to draw our attention again to this passage as Milton's elegantly refined way of leading us back to first principles. In the genealogy of contemporary Milton criticism, it was in fact Kerrigan's student, Stephen M. Fallon, who most influentially contextualized the passage and its implications for the epic in terms of seventeenth century intellectual history. "In Raphael's speech," says Fallon, "the plant begins as a metaphor for the steps of the hierarchy of matter only to become a synecdoche for the process by which creatures ascend the hierarchy.... The roles of digester and digested are interchanged.... The logic of the plant simile asks us to see man as digested by the world."[14]

In the unfallen world where Raphael speaks of this ontological mobility for humankind, the "tract of time" by which human bodies may be metabolized, refined, or sublimed "all to spirit" is marked by decisive acts of free will and choices, and this is certainly what Raphael is getting at when he says that each kind has been "plac't" in its own sphere "Till body up to spirit work, in bounds / Proportiond to each kind" (5.478–79). All are in their "several active spheres assigned," ontological spaces conceptually and sonically rhyming with "each kind," but it is the *work* of ascent through rational volition that Milton emphasizes in the play of the phrase "in bounds / Proportiond to each kind," since these "bounds" are both proportionate leaps forward and justly delineated boundaries.[15] The work of humankind, therefore, is moral and physical, volitional and intellectual, as Fallon argues: "Moral choices in *Paradise Lost* have implications for choices about where one wishes to be placed along the continuum of the one first matter."[16]

According to Milton's heretical monism, the "bright consummate floure" is undoubtedly consummate in the sense of being perfect, unified, and complete. As everyone who has ever read the epic must know, this "spiritous," perfected blossom will inevitably suffer as a result of the Fall. While the metaphor of the "gradual scale" transforms, in Fallon's terms, into a synecdoche of the process of ascent, the idealism of the passage should be tempered by our realization of the tragic inevitability of the Fall. Where "one wishes to be placed along the continuum of the one first matter," as Fallon describes it, may no longer be relevant in the determination of where one finds oneself in the hierarchy. Nonetheless, perhaps it is true, as Leah Marcus suggests, that Milton's use "of a natural flower to convey the continuum suggests that it is imbedded in natural process and may therefore be available to fallen humanity as well."[17] At any rate, synchronic idealism gives way to diachronic history. Regardless of whether we quite agree with John Leonard that "Adam and Eve are on probation in the Garden until they have proved their worthiness to *ascend*," the fact remains that they will not do so, no more than the rest of us, as a result of their lapse.[18]

From this vantage, Raphael's natural philosophy may take on a distinctly political cast. Ontology encodes politics; or, rather, Milton displaces politics onto ontology. According to John Rogers, in his brilliant reading of Milton in the context of seventeenth century vitalism, this reconfiguration of the idealism of Milton's political theory in post-Restoration England emerged in response to the period's pressure to articulate in natural philosophy a formal base upon which a superstructure of political organization could be founded. "If we do not see in Raphael's natural philosophy the homogeneous saturation of all matter with spirit that we have come to identify with midcentury vitalism," argues Rogers, "that is because we do not see in the post-Restoration Milton a consistent faith in a liberal political philosophy derivable from such a vision of matter."[19] Even as the fall of the commonwealth and the apostasy of the English people recapitulate the Fall of Adam and Eve and the consequent history of apostasy and idolatry among the Israelites as detailed in Michael's account to Adam in books 11 and 12, so the enthusiastic idealism represented in Raphael's monistic materialism suffers a corresponding degradation in the wake of the failed revolutionary experiment. As Rogers explains, "The theory of popular empowerment that Milton had felt compelled to bury, ten years earlier, in its strictly political avatar reemerges in both *Paradise Lost* and *Christian Doctrine* as a vitalist theory of matter. When Milton describes in these late works the propagation and extension of divine spirit throughout the entire mass of the original matter, we can see a recrudescence of the radical philosophy of organization he had embraced in the great treatises of the vitalist period, *The Tenure of Kings and Magistrates* and *The Defence of the English People*."[20] Milton's monist materialism in this way enfolds the political thought of the earlier prose, digests it, we might say, as a means of renegotiating the experience of defeat in the Restoration. If the dialectics of history have forced Milton to recognize the negation of his ideal state, the idealism may nevertheless survive as part of a new synthesis. Ironically, the ideal of ontological transmutation, of bodies working up to spirit, reemerges in sublated form as the primordial matter.

Of course, this materialist turn in Milton's thought has religious as well as political implications. The conceptual alliance between monism and monotheism, while never explicitly fleshed out in Milton's writings, is intuitively suggested by the archangel Raphael when he says that "one Almightie is, from whom / All things proceed, and up to him return."[21] Likening "spiritual to corporal forms" may simply be a means of accommodating speech to limited human cognition, but what if, as Raphael asks about his narrative method for the war in heaven, "Earth / Be but the shadow of Heav'n, and things therein / Each to other like, more then on earth is thought" (5.573–76)? To say this is to reverse the conventional flow of linguistic accommodation and to suggest how completely the materialist cosmos of *Paradise Lost* does not distinguish physical from metaphysical. Put another way, "the doctrine of the Incarnation, of God becoming flesh," according to Gordon Teskey, "does not for Milton lead to a *theophany*, a 'revelation of God,' but to an *anthropophany*, 'a revelation of the human.' ... It is the revelation of the human as having taken into itself the full authority of a transcendent God."[22]

What this vision of the universe as created *ex Deo* rather than *ex nihilo* means for Milton's theology may not be fully, explicitly connected in his writings to anti-Trinitarianism, yet the heresies are as logically continuous as they are conceptually analogous. Regardless of whether we prefer the term "Arian" to describe Milton's invectives against the orthodox, post-Nicene conception of the Trinity, this heresy may be deduced from monist materialism. In other words, it follows from Milton's materialism that the Son of God would share the same substance as the Father, but this does not mean that they share the same essence. Consider once again the quotation from Augustine that exemplifies the traditional doctrine, *creatio ex nihilo*, here quoted more fully: "In the beginning, that is from yourself, in your wisdom which is begotten of your substance, you made something and made it out of nothing. For you made heaven and earth not out of your own self, *or it would be equal to your only-begotten Son and therefore to yourself*."[23] Milton's materialism coheres around precisely this issue, admitting the logic that Augustine must deny in order to maintain his commitment to the Trinity. The first logical break in Augustine's thought — God couldn't have made the universe out of himself or it would be the same as the Son — Milton would have accepted without perceiving a contradiction. The created, subordinate deity depicted in both *De doctrina*'s chapter on the Son of God and in the epic's representation of the initiating moment of the Son's begetting in office in book 5 is of the same one first matter as the rest of the universe precisely *because it is all God's substance*. Of course, the Son of God is also "the bright consummate floure" of creation, matter turned all to spirit, the process perfected in the tract of time. After all, Milton's monistic materialism admits of hierarchy. What Milton would never have accepted in Augustine's formulation is the next logical leap, the Trinitarian insistence on the essential identity of Father and Son, and therefore the logical incompatibility of a created universe sharing the Son's substance and therefore being the equal of the Father himself. The specter of pantheism Augustine conjures in order to dismiss this line of reasoning sounds more like Spinoza than Milton, though these two seventeenth century thinkers are probably closer in their thought than either is to Augustine: "Except for God, there neither is, nor can be conceived, any substance, that is, thing that is in itself and is conceived through itself. But modes can neither be nor be conceived without substance. So they can be in the divine nature alone, and can be conceived through it alone. But except for substances and modes there is nothing. Therefore, everything is in God and nothing can be or be conceived without God, q.e.d."[24] From theology, to politics, to philosophy, as the essays collected in this book show in various ways, no corner of Milton's thought was untouched by his mature commitment to heretical materialist monism, and this has affected the reception of his major works down to the present day.

Miltonic embodiment and the significance of the senses in Milton's works are particular concerns of several of the contributors to this volume. The first two essays focus on experience embodied in the senses of hearing and smelling. Drawing on a range of studies on the phenomenology of scent, from modern olfactory science to philosophers and psychologists ranging from Plato to Deleuze to Oliver Sacks, Lauren Shohet's "The Fragrance of the Fall" shows that scent has the power "to dissolve boundaries of time, agency, space, and ontological category" in *Paradise Lost*. Differences between pre- and postlapsarian experience, between innocence and experience, between figurative and literal, here and there, then and now, source and adaptation are all complicated by the poem's representations of fragrance. Scent's "potential to shrink, expand, and overlayer timeframes" and cosmic states is shown to raise interpretive issues fundamental to the poem's theology and philosophy. Seth Herbst's essay "Sound as Matter: Milton, Music, and Monism" reexamines the representation of music in Milton's *Paradise Lost*, explicitly relating Milton's ideas about music to his monism. Whereas Stephen Fallon's influential account of Milton's monism found a monistic metaphysics to be entirely absent from his writings before the divorce tracts, Herbst finds "unexpected traces of monist thinking" appearing in Milton's poetry as early as the Nativity ode, specifically in his thinking about music, a subject that has been neglected in accounts of Milton's materialist philosophy. Herbst shows that seemingly Platonist or figurative descriptions of music's effect on the souls of hearers in *Paradise Lost* and in earlier works such as the ode and *Of Education* can be better understood as literal expressions of Milton's philosophical monism. "Adam's description of sound makes use of conceptual terms that suggest it functions as a physical, material object." In *A Mask*, Milton shows music "as ethically charged — produced by and expressive of good or evil — while consistently and vividly evoking sound as a real, not metaphoric, acoustic phenomenon." In these early works, by thinking of music as both a material acoustic phenomenon and an intellectual phenomenon, "a metaphor for a creature's relationship with God," Milton could begin to come to terms with paradoxes that would inform his mature poetry and theology.

The next four essays deal in various ways with the poetic and ethical significance of embodied thought. Ryan Hackenbracht, in "Milton on the Move: Walking and Self-Knowledge in *Paradise Lost*," shows that the "pedestrian" physical activity of walking is invested with more significance than at first appears. In *Paradise Lost* Milton's representation of bodily motion draws on Homer and Virgil as much as on biblical tradition to rework and enlarge the genre of epic for his Protestant readership. In contrast to the sinful and vainglorious striding of Sin and Death, modeled on the striding of Homeric heroes,

Milton "relocates peripatetic value in the humble and quiet walking of Adam and Eve," both before and after the Fall. Ultimately Milton "reinvents the epic motif of walking by aligning it with the Protestant virtues of obedience, humility, and trust." In "Radical Relations: The Genealogical Imaginary and Queer Kinship in Milton's *Paradise Regained*," Erin Murphy also discusses Milton's politics and poetics of embodiment. In his brief epic, she argues, Milton relinquishes the materiality of biological reproduction for a grounding of identity in ties that could be seen as spiritual but which are ultimately political and resonate with gender politics in our own day. Her essay explores the ways in which the poem's representations of the relations among birth, textuality, identity, and political power resonate with broader issues of the genealogical imagination that were current following the restoration of the Stuart monarchs. Murphy finds the poem emphasizing a connection between sonship and kingship while simultaneously erasing or downplaying the role of genealogy in Milton's primary sources, the Gospels of Matthew and Luke. Both identity and temporality are represented as unstable in *Paradise Regained*: Jesus's identity as Son of God appears both provisional and performative. The poem thus provides an "anti-genealogical exploration of kinship" that challenges the logic of hereditary monarchy. And the poem's "opaque return to the mother" in its closing lines "leaves open the question of how this radical reimagining of family will inform the politics to come." Mary's maternal identity is denaturalized and performative in the poem in ways that have significant affinities to Hobbes's account of maternity in *De cive*. The brief epic, she asserts, presents a vision of family relations that "helps define a conception of the human that undergirds the postdynastic contractual citizen."

The next two essays shift from human embodiment to angelic embodiment. Rebecca Buckham, in "Milton's Strange Angels," discusses Adam's encounter with Raphael as a "cross-species encounter" that raises ethical questions about representations of the nonhuman that are salient in current ecological criticism. Buckham acknowledges the theological and philosophical significance of Milton's monistic materialism, which enables the dialogue between

Raphael and Adam in book 5, but finds significant disparity between the two beings as well. Raphael's claim that angelic and human substance differ only in degree rather than in kind fails to account for the radical otherness that the angel and Adam encounter in each other. Thus *Paradise Lost* not only invites us "to think or to believe something about angels, but also to encounter them" in all their strangeness in a way that is analogous to our thinking about other species of primate, challenging us to avoid the risk of anthropocentrism. Also resisting the impulse to elide the differences between angels and humans in *Paradise Lost*, Lara Dodds in "Dark Looks and Red Smiles: Homeric Gesture and the Problem of Milton's Angels" reexamines a topic that a number of commentators on *Paradise Lost* over the years have found embarrassing or scandalous: the blush attributed to Raphael in book 8 when he tells Adam that angelic spirits experience a form of erotic desire and lovemaking. She locates this issue within "a broader discourse of coloring in *Paradise Lost*," one that includes "dark looks" as well as pale and red visages. In their expressive facial expressions, both "the fallen and unfallen angels share a *habitus* built from the gestures of the Homeric heroes" that distinguishes them from Milton's human characters, so that "it would be wrong to assume" that the angels' "changes in color occur in the same way or for the same reasons that humans blush or blanch." The motif of dark looks that recurs in the *Iliad* and the *Odyssey* to indicate characters' feelings of anger, scorn, or indignation reappears in Milton's representations of the angels as warriors. Likewise the "contracted brow" displayed by the archangel Raphael before he reproves Adam for uxuriousness is derived from this same Homeric motif. Milton reworks the gestures of Homeric heroes so that they legibly "articulate principles of similarity and difference with respect to materiality [substance and spirit], species, and gender," allowing Adam "to negotiate participation in the 'one first matter' of a monistic universe with the distinctive subjectivity allowed by one's form, species, or gender."

The final two essays examine issues involving Milton's materialism in specifically American political and historical contexts. In "'One Elementary Simple Substance': Orson Pratt, Parley Pratt, and the Miltonic Origins of Mormon Materialism," John Rogers returns to his recurring interest in the influence of Milton on early Mormon readers and leaders. *Paradise Lost* was widely read and discussed by a variety of nineteenth century Americans from varying levels of literacy, who made use of stylistically simplified adaptations. Rogers shows that "antithetical" or "satanic" (in Blake's sense) readings of *Paradise Lost* influenced the emergent theology, metaphysics, and cosmogony of early leaders of the Latter Day Saints. Milton appealed to the Latter Day Saints in part because his conscious Hebraism accorded with Mormons' own embrace of an Old Testament scriptural mode. In addition, Milton's defense of polygamy in *De doctrina* served as a direct source for early Mormon defenses of "celestial marriage." Furthermore, Milton influenced early Mormon writers by the substance of his metaphysics, particularly his rejection of the orthodox view of creation *ex nihilo*. Milton's account of the Creation in chapter 7 of *De doctrina Christiana* influenced Mormon metaphysics in its account of "a seamless continuum between a material earth and a spiritual heaven." Furthermore, early Mormons, Rogers argues, were influenced not only by the arguments in *De doctrina* but by the poetic expression of Milton's materialism in *Paradise Lost*. Rogers's essay particularly focuses on one of the Mormon prophet Joseph Smith's earliest disciples, Orson Pratt, whose treatise *Great First Cause, or the Self-Moving Forces of the Universe* (1851) enunciates a view of the liberatory potential of material beings to aspire to more rarefied and spiritual levels of being, which goes even further than Milton. Pratt rejects Milton's view of matter created *ex Deo*. Even further, he argues that God is a creature, "a belated effect of matter's capacity to combine and unite itself into meaningful formations." Like Philip Pullman in *His Dark Materials*, Pratt derives "the doctrine of the contingent and created God" from "a rigorously antithetical, satanic reading of *Paradise Lost*."

David A. Harper, in "'The Scanning of Error': *Areopagitica* and 3-D Printing," examines the strange story of a recent "political appropriation" of *Areopagitica* in a manifesto by a gun activist who cited Milton's tract in defense of his disseminating "free, downloadable plans for

[a] print-at-home gun." *Areopagitica*'s argument against the law passed in 1644 requiring that books be licensed before publication apparently was deemed by Cody Wilson to provide an intellectual precedent and justification — or, as Wilson called it, a "spiritual analogue" — for his project of facilitating "the endless, unregulated production of guns." Harper demonstrates various ways in which Milton's protest against a particular kind of regulation of printed books is ill suited to a defense of unregulated "printing" of firearms. Milton does not, of course, argue for a totally unregulated press, and Harper precisely situates *Areopagitica* in its particular topical contexts, delineating the range of state sanctions against totally unregulated printing that Milton is happy to endorse. Likewise, Milton's defense of copyright is clearly contrary to the animus against state-enforced copyright expressed in the dystopic fiction that inspired Wilson, and his distrust of the ignorant masses hardly suggests sympathy with Wilson's project of putting firearms in the hands of anyone with access to a printer. Harper also notes Milton's "association of gunpowder with evil, and absolute evil at that" in poems written both early and late in his career. The analogy between the printing of books in Milton's day and producing guns on 3-D printers today falters as well when we consider the difference between the production of original ideas that Milton celebrates and the mass production of mechanical copies, which is the essence of the 3-D printer. Furthermore, Harper shows that while Milton's vitalist materialism complicates "the distinction between objects" such as guns and "speech acts," Milton's insistence that books can be held to account for their consequences, as well as his insistence that the value of books resides in their ability to give birth to ideas and reason undermines any claims of affinity between Milton's tract and Wilson's manifesto.

The essays gathered here clearly demonstrate the far-reaching implications for Milton studies of a renewed focus on Milton's materialistic monism and its implications for the embodied experience of Milton's characters as well as his readers. From the works' original composition to their reception over time, from the seventeenth century to our own day, issues of embodiment and materialism are shown to complicate and enrich Milton's meanings. We hope that this collection will stimulate further research into the implications of Miltonic monism for the interpretation of Milton's work, including political, phenomenological, religious, and gender-oriented approaches to Milton's writings. Ultimately these essays should contribute to a more far-reaching understanding of vitalist materialism in modern as well as early modern literary culture.

PART ONE

MATERIALITY AND THE SENSES

CHAPTER 1

The Fragrance of the Fall

LAUREN SHOHET

However determinedly aloof Milton's Satan might hold himself from the *visual* delights of Eden, that *"Assyrian* Garden, where the Fiend / *Saw* undelighted all delight" (*PL* 4.285–86; emphasis added), he does not even assay a pretense of distancing himself from its fragrances.[1] Recalcitrant and resolutely belligerent, Satan nonetheless is moved by Eden's "vernal aires, / Breathing the smell of field and grove" (4.264–65). *Paradise Lost* makes Eden the stage for Satan's great psychomachia: whereas in hell the newly fallen angel had briskly dismissed recollections of heavenly pleasures ("Is this the Region, ... That we must change for Heav'n, this mournful gloom / For that celestial light? *Be it so*" [1.242–45; emphasis added]), Eden finds his internal debate between submission and defiance protracted, as, "much revolving" (4.31), Satan plays out an extended interior catechism, cyclical in reasoning, that produces a soliloquy some 80 lines in length (4.32–113). In Eden, Satan repeatedly revisits decisions — "his face / Thrice chang'd" as he affirms, reconsiders, and reaffirms his rebellious resolution (4. 114–15) — and consonant with this is an Edenic capacity for pleasure, reversion to an earlier privilege, contrary to his definitive renunciation of all God-given gifts in the hell of books 1 and 2. In Eden, Satan's whiff of "purer aire" still "to the heart inspires /

Vernal delight and joy" (4.153–55). Responding to Edenic odors in ways that revisit his previous condition, temporarily amenable to reconciliation or solace as he takes in the odors "able to drive / All sadness but despair" (4.155–56), Satan indicates the ability of smell in *Paradise Lost* to travel across, loop through, and indeed to dissolve boundaries of time, agency, space, and ontological category.[2] Odor conveys the complex experiences of "both/and" rather than "either/or" that permeate the epic's distinctive theology and aesthetics.

Early modern studies have only recently begun to consider the phenomenology of smell, notably in Jonathan Gil Harris's discussion of Shakespearean gunpowder, Holly R. Dugan's work on early modern perfume, and Holly Crawford Pickett's study of post-Reformation polemical responses to incense.[3] Tracking scent may yield consequences as far-reaching as Bruce R. Smith's study of Renaissance sound, which revealed how differently selves are constituted aurally — in more permeable, imbricated relationships to environments — than they are visually.[4] Perhaps even more thoroughly than sound, smell interweaves self and other, subject and object, agency and passivity, producer and receiver, event and representation, past and present. Smell sponsors distinct ways to imagine subjectivity and epistemology, as the deeply associative operations of fragrance reshape perception of spatial, temporal, and agential relationships. Olfaction, then, offers a deeply useful way into the early modern vitalist questions that this collection undertakes to plumb, and the poetics of smell hereby focuses what Thomas Festa and Kevin Donovan in this volume's introduction cast as the epic's "complex mimesis of...monism."

Paradise Lost uses fragrance to convey the ineffable. In addition, moments of olfactory connection shift scale, interweave history and the transhistorical, and overlayer different ontological and textual realms as they transform their receivers' experiences of time, place, and being. The epic offers smell as a counterpoint to the verbal, which — perhaps particularly in its poetic dimensions, since rhythm depends upon duration — is "tedious" in the sense of "occupying time." (This sense notably concludes "On the Morning of Christ's Nativity," when time recommences after its supernatural suspension and the poem remarks, "Time is our tedious Song should here have ending" [239]). Since temporality does not constrain the divine, words can frustratingly delay or impede divine communication with created beings; as the angel Raphael laments, "Immediate are the Acts of God...but to human ears / Cannot without process of speech be told" (*PL* 7.176–78). Smell, by contrast, is immediate. Perhaps this is why the book of Revelation describes the "prayers of saints" as "odours" (Rev. 6.8): communications of the holy surmount mediation and delay. In *Paradise Lost*, smell's immediacy becomes not only a key to linking past and present for human psyches, but also a means to address the heuristic difficulties of fallenness. However we evaluate the degree of Pelagian thought in the poem, the epic's prefigurations, reflections, and reduplications of both temptation and Creation scenes yield notions of the Fall more complex than a simple, single, unidirectional instant. Both temporally and in other registers, scent offers a lexicon for multivalent, supple, sometimes recursive relationships between innocence and experience that intersect significantly not only with the phenomenology of smell (as represented in the poem and as studied by modern-day science) but also with the theological and narratological complexity of undertaking theodicy through the poetics of "sacred Song" (*PL* 3.29).

Fragrance Unbound

Prominent among the barely imaginable pleasures of the prelapsarian garden of Eden are its fragrances. When the Father sends Raphael to Eden, the episode begins with smell.[5] Scent accompanies and indeed identifies Raphael, as he "shook his Plumes, that Heavn'ly fragrance filled / The circuit wide." Accordingly, "Strait knew him all the Bands / Of Angels under watch" (*PL* 5.286–88). Then, as this celestial being enters the earthly garden, the narrative introduces Eden by its odiferous profile. Raphael comes into this "blissful field" "through Groves of Myrrh, / And flowring Odours, Cassia, Nard, and Balm" (5.292–93) in what John R. Knott describes as a "boundary crossing into a place where an extravagant fragrance suggests a condition of bliss too great to be contained."[6]

Later, Adam's story of his first sentient moments similarly recalls that "all things smil'd, / With fragrance and with joy my heart oreflow'd" (PL 8.265–66). Overflowing fragrance evokes the abundance of Edenic joy; it also typifies the way smell transcends categories. Adam's memory, that is, transubstantiates fragrance into fluid (if we take "oreflow" to ontologically describe the properties of what he observes), or the synaesthesia of smell and touch or sight (if we take it to hermeneutically focus on his own perception). Extending the categorical interweaving, this originary experience of fragrance is sparked by "all things smil[ing]" (8.265), registering Edenic "things" enjoying affect. In Eden, apparently, odor can flow, and things can feel. Prelapsarian bliss is distinctive both in its intensity and its holistic constitution. The poem frequently represents Eden with figures of synaesthesia. When Edenic "Birds thir quire apply" (4.264), and "aires, vernal aires, / Breathing the smell of field and grove, attune / The trembling leaves" (4.264–66), the repeated word "aires" can apply flexibly to either the choir of birdsong or to breezes, mixing avian and ambient sources of melody. Indeed, the terms "quire" and "leaves" both belong in twin lexica of music and textuality (and if the poem does not ask us to imagine birds singing from sheet music, the evocation of postlapsarian practice invites imaginative comparison of trained human singers to prelapsarian natural warbling). The line instantiates another kind of blending as well, since "breathing" indicates the aires both inhaling and exhaling scent. The rhetorical operations of synaesthesia convey the characteristically unbounded somatic experience of odor: both quotidian experience and modern science tell us that smelling overlaps with tasting, and fragrance characteristically permeates its environment more thoroughly than other sensed phenomena, perhaps because it often is perceived less consciously.[7]

In these Miltonic passages, fragrance operates expansively, spilling into and then out of Adam's heart in response to the blurring of insensate and sentient in "smiling" "things." Other descriptions, conversely, show fragrance contracting distance, with smell rendering far reaches instantaneously at hand. When gentle gales in Eden "whisper whence they stole" their "balmie spoiles" of "native perfumes" (*PL* 4.158–59), strictly reading the language of "stealing" connotes not that the perfumes merely index their origins but, rather, that the adventurous wind has abducted them thence to Eden. At the same time, a broader reading of the figure — one aligned with common-sense knowledge that sniffing a scent does not consume it — leaves that origin "there" whence it came at the same time that the distant place becomes manifest "here" where it is perceived. Fragrance does not transcend or mitigate or contract space, perhaps, so much as "fold" or "pleat" it (in the terms Deleuze develops from Leibniz), making "there" and "here" temporarily proximate but intact and available for reseparation or recombination — just as past and present time pleat together for Satan when he whiffs Edenic air.[8]

Odor's role in Eve's temptation shows scent crossing other kinds of boundaries as well. Smelling blurs the distinction between engagement and disengagement; it would be quite different for humans to have been instructed not to *smell* the fruit.[9] Taking a moment here to consider what it means to embrace or refuse different sensory encounters illuminates the distinctiveness of odor in ways that carry beyond sense experience to its spiritual implications. As is well known, Satan presents the fruit's allure to Eve's every sense: even as "in her ears the sound / Yet rung of his perswasive words" (*PL* 9.736–37), she also "gazes" on that fruit "which to behold / Might tempt alone" (9.735–36), and its "smell / So savorie" (9.740–41) "inclines" her to "touch or taste" (9.742). Among these many attractions, the Father's injunction that humans are not "to taste that onely Tree / Of knowledge" (4.423–24) answers to an agentive crispness particular to taste. The boundary between putting something in the mouth or declining to do so is clearer, and more voluntary, than homologous sensory engagements. Scenting, glimpsing, and hearing proceed from simple proximity to the sensed object: sound, sight, and odor normally are perceptible through passive awareness. Touch occupies a middle ground, with some encounters between skin and and its stimulant being more passive (feeling a warm breeze) and others more willfully chosen (reaching out to touch). Likewise, the means of closing off the senses varies: sight and taste are easily cut off by closing the eyelids or lips; ears and noses can be more effortfully and less completely blocked off; touch is variably involuntary (when sensing ambient environmental qualities like temperature) or voluntarily sought.

Thus, abstaining from tasting the fruit as a "sign of... obedience" (4.428) accords with other boundaries that create opportunities for pious obedience, like the gated border of Eden (4.131, 178) that the God of *Paradise Lost* limns as a clear demarcation, un-onerously but not obliviously transgressed. Avoiding the fruit's fragrance, by contrast, would seem inimical to fully aware — which is to say devout — presence in the garden. The fruit can be smelled by fallen and unfallen alike, fragrance intertwining pre- and postlapsarian experience along a continuum, or perhaps "pleating" the time before and after the Fall, unlike the binary operations of "mortal tast" (1.2). Indeed, scent somewhat surprisingly infiltrates Eve's dream. Among the sensory temptations encountered when the serpent leads Eve to the tree, only odor permeates her imaginative preview of the Fall. When Eve tells Adam her dream of Satan's holding the fruit to her mouth, she reports that "the pleasant savourie smell / So quick'nd appetite, that I, methought, / Could not but taste" (5.84–86), without mentioning the fruit's visual, tactile, or gustatory qualities. Although sleep studies report that everyday dreamers seldom experience smell, *Paradise Lost* presents it as the only one of what Adam calls the "five watchful Senses" (5.104) so present in Eden that it enters into dreamscapes.[10] Joe Moshenska considers *Paradise Lost*'s exploration of how touch "among all the senses has the potential to perturb or deform the world" and how, in the "establishment of intimate physical relationships" in the epic, "mutuality and reciprocity can lapse into hierarchical domination," a possibility "most fully explored in the role which touch plays in the Fall itself."[11] By contrast, our smelling does not impact the world. Odors act upon us. *Paradise Lost* mines these characteristics to convey subtleties of agency, culpability, and foreknowledge in the experiences of Eve's scenting the fruit: in dream and in waking, as preview and as event.

Sent Scents

In addition to pleating space and time on earth, smell can communicate from one cosmic realm to another. Prayer "fl[ies] up" to the Father in heaven, "clad / With incense" (*PL* 11.15, 17–18), conveying offerings like the smoke of animal sacrifice that it will ritually replace in postlapsarian liturgical practice. And fragrance is the medium through which the Son effects the reconciliation between humanity and the Father that these prayers seek. The Son brings the "smell of peace toward" a newly repentant "Mankinde" (11.38) and clothes Adam and Eve's supplications in redolent incense so that they may pass "dimensionless through Heavn'ly doors: then clad / With incense, where the Golden Altar fum'd" (11.17–18). Arrived in heaven, odor continues to synaesthetically cross sensory categories. The Son presents fragrant prayers to the Father's vision — they "c[o]me in sight / Before the Fathers Throne" (11.19–20) — and the Son announces them with the imperative "See Father" (11.22). Taste joins the array when the Son remarks the "pleasing savor" (11.26) of repentance's fruits. Duly received into heaven, fragrance's capacity to cross boundaries conveys the mystical ontological blending of agents required for the transaction of grace: the Son proposes to the Father that the latter "all [humanity's] works on mee / ... ingraft ... / Accept me, and in mee from these receive / The smell of peace toward Mankind" (11.34–38). The unusual directionality of smell here ("*toward* Mankind," when smell is usually ambient rather than vectored) draws attention to the opposite pulls of the word "receive" (the smell gathered into by the Father) and the phrase "toward Mankind" (going out from the Father). Smell's pervasive, shared, interpenetrating reception conveys mysteries of the Trinity.[12]

Less happily, scent also crosses from earth to hell, alerting Death to his postlapsarian portion. No sooner is Adam fallen than, in distant hell, Death "snuff'd the smell / Of mortal change on Earth" (10.272–73). The diction of this passage underscores smell as foundational for Death's knowledge: he "upturn[s] / His Nostril wide into the murky Air, / Sagacious of his Quarry from so farr"

(10.279–81) — "sagacious" meaning both "canny" and, in early modern usage, "keen of scenting." This book 10 passage not only communicates instantly across the "prodigious," as-yet-unbridged chasm of chaos (10.302); it also neatly pleats narrative time, abruptly reminding the reader of ravenous Death and foul Sin hungrily flanking the adamantine gates of hell, where the narrative had left them ominously poised "in counterview" (10.231) long before in book 2.

In addition to diegetic pleating, *Paradise Lost* poetically uses smell's capacity to bring together disparate moments in time as well as space — poetic opportunities that, I shall argue, fold in hermeneutic and theological dimensions as well. Both the description of Satan's grateful reception in book 4 of "gentle gales / [that] Fanning thir odiferous wing dispense / Native perfumes" (*PL* 4.156–58) and Death's sagacious sniff of mortal change in book 10 are followed by similes that multiply the connections effected by fragrance. According with epic's habits, book 4 addresses the challenge of conveying the inexpressible — here, the olfactory delights of Eden's "native perfumes" — with a simile. Eden's "purer air" (4.153) greets Satan,

> As when to them who sail
> Beyond the *Cape of Hope*, and now are past
> *Mozambic*, off at Sea North-East winds blow
> *Sabean* Odours from the spicie shoar
> Of *Arabie* the blest, with such delay
> Well pleas'd they slack thir course, and many a League
> Chear'd with the grateful smell old Ocean smiles.   (4.159–65)

Scent links the prelapsarian smellscape with the land breezes carrying Arabian particles over the ocean, in images conveying scent from line to line with serial enjambments. This passage not only connects Eden to the geographically removed southern part of Africa, but also to the postlapsarian maritime world of sailors plying the spice trade. Within that quotidian world, the figure spatially conjoins the distant points of Sheba (Yemen), Mozambique, and the Cape of Good Hope. In addition to these spatial connections, the deictic marker "now" in the second line quoted above temporally flings the reader into the present time of the simile's sailors.

These extensions and connections are already copious. And they continue to multiply as the passage continues, as smell sponsors further compressions and dilations of place, time, and textual horizon:

> So entertaind those odorous sweets the Fiend
> Who came their bane, though with them better pleas'd
> Then *Asmodeus* with the fishie fume,
> That drove him, though enamourd, from the Spouse
> Of *Tobits* Son, and with a vengeance sent
> From *Media* post to *Aegypt*, there fast bound.   (4.166–71)

Litotically describing Edenic breezes as more pleasing to Satan than smoke was to the bridegroom-slaying demon Asmodeus whom Tobias repelled by burning fish parts, this passage moves from the narrative present of *Paradise Lost* to the time of the apocryphal book of Tobit, from prelapsarian Eden to biblical-era Persia. Smell moves the imagination across space and time. Adducing to further spatial extension, the book of Tobit allusion invokes a tale of diaspora: the eponymous Tobit is an exile in Nineveh, his son Tobias is divinely guided still further away to wed the oft-widowed Sara in Media, and the lustful demon Asmodeus is driven by smell all the way to Egypt. Resonances between *Paradise Lost* and this deeply enfolded narrative nugget — this allusion following from a simile — multiply its creases yet further. Raphael will be Tobias's guide, as he is Adam's; Tobias requires the angel because he inhabits the fallen world produced by Adam's failure to heed Raphael. The "fishie fume" (4.178) thus wafts into the text of *Paradise Lost* as a temporally twisty a posteriori preview of what will have happened when the fiend does indeed prove, as predicted, the odorous sweets' "bane" (4.168) — even as the poem also registers their persistent pleasures. The contradiction between the claim that Satan will obliterate Edenic fragrance and the scents' continued gracious effect creates a kind of polychronicity, with prelapsarian and postlapsarian coexisting.

The scent of carrion Death sniffs at the moment of "mortal change" (*PL* 10.273) is also followed by a simile:

> So saying, with delight [Death] snuff'd the smell
> Of mortal change on Earth. As when a flock

> Of ravenous Fowl, though many a League remote,
> Against the day of Battel, to a Field
> Where Armies lie encampt, come flying, lur'd
> With scent of living Carcasses design'd
> For death, the following day, in bloody fight. (10.272–78)

When *Paradise Lost* here deploys the conventional trope of the beasts of battle — that motif drawing with chilling accuracy on the way carrion-eating beasts and fowl follow marching armies to war — the simile invokes a literary history yet to be written (rather like what Lara Dodds's essay in this volume demonstrates to be the epic's "Homeric" angels) in order to dramatize this originary moment of mortality itself. Skillfully deploying the rhetorical arsenal that poetry will create (will have created?) to describe fatal encounters redoubles the extant timeframes, from prelapsarian/postlapsarian to prelapsarian/mortal/immortal. The simile's effects stretch beyond the temporal to the theological when scent proleptically "lures" predators with carcasses-to-be. This produces a vivid objective correlative for the poem's difficult questions about free will, foreknowledge, and agency: if the carcasses are "designed" for death, what free will do they retain? If animal carrion-eaters — and the spectral Death — know more of the soon-to-be-carcasses' fate than the persons animating them, how should we understand this privilege?

Smell and Semiotics

In attempting to describe an unfallen world, *Paradise Lost* confronts the limitations of fallen human language. Harder still, conventional strategies for conveying the remarkable carry the risk either of minimizing the radical change of the Fall (Pelagianism), or of implicitly circumscribing free will by imputing an always-already fallenness to prelapsarian circumstances when rhetorical figures like similes associate them with the fallen world. (Perhaps this is why the epic's narrator suddenly, and surely rather belatedly, worries in book 10 whether "great things to small may be compar'd" [10.306]). This semiotic challenge of mismatch between postlapsarian signifier and unfallen signified intersects with the theological challenge of assessing the Fall's magnitude. A famous example of this problem surrounds the poem's word "wanton," particularly in the context of Eve's "wanton ringlets" (PL 4.306) and the garden's "wanton growth," whose branches "require / More hands than [Adam's and Eve's] to lop" (4.628–29). As critics have asked, if Eve's hair already connotes indiscipline upon her creation, was she ever truly sufficient to stand? And if the fecundity of the garden overwhelms the first couple's capacity, how robust was their Edenic condition from the beginning?[13] Diane McColley finds in these questions a postlapsarian inadequacy to attend to a radically prelapsarian state. For McColley, critics who deconstructively read "wantonness" as inherently fallen heedlessly inscribe their own understanding onto a very different world. Many readers, however, remain unconvinced that this account erases the inherent vulnerability in the poem's constitution of Eve.

Rather than weigh in on one side of this debate or the other, the kind of polychronous semiotics elicited by smell allows for multiple understandings of terms like "wantonness" — responses that can be simultaneously prefallen and postlapsarian. Hereby the poem can acknowledge the impossibility of a fallen reader fully understanding prelapsarian "wantonness" — and yet somehow to apprehend it nonetheless, at least by degree. Another, somewhat less remarked, appearance of "wanton" that follows on the description of Raphael's first entrance into the garden illustrates this particularly well. In fact, this passage at once sets a scene for polychronous reading, draws attention to its rhetoric of comparison, and concerns fragrance — bringing together three of the strategies I am arguing the epic uses to construct a reverberatingly multilevel semiotics that suspends demands for full rational integration. The passage reads:

> Thir glittering Tents [Raphael] passd, and now is come
> Into the blissful field, through Groves of Myrrhe,
> And flouring Odours, Cassia, Nard, and Balme;
> A Wilderness of sweets; for Nature here
> Wantond as in her prime, and plaid at will.   (5.291–95)

Even as Raphael encounters Edenic smells of myrrh and flowers, a deictic "now" irrupts from the past-tense narrative, throwing the reader into immediate relation to the scene described. At the same time, the conventional narrative past tense persists, which multiplies the frames of reading. Furthermore, as the poem enumerates Eden's floral scents, it reports that Nature "wantoned as in her prime." As just discussed, in book 4, the vexed term "wantoned" thematizes semiotic questions for its reader, activating perception of multiple timeframes, before and after the Fall. Here, the curious phrase "*as* in her prime" works similarly. Surely the first days in the garden *are* Nature's prime. The apparently supererogatory "as," asserting something to be like itself, draws attention to strategies of understanding and representation, and thereby thematizes evaluation of their adequacy. If, alternatively, we are to understand that Nature was not in fact new for some substantial period of time between the Creation and Raphael's arrival — that instead Raphael finds Nature *like* what it once had been, at a moment long enough ago to bear remark — that possibility too sponsors consideration of different scales and standards of time.

Smell and Cognition

Smell traditionally has been considered the most animal of the senses, but the uses of allusion and simile in *Paradise Lost* also consider olfactory capacities specific to humans. These concern scent's potential to shrink, expand, and overlayer timeframes (prelapsarian, postlapsarian, historical, present, future) and cosmic states (unfallen, fallen, foreknown, redeemed.) In its beasts-of-battle simile, the poem acknowledges nonhumans' preeminent sense of smell, describing how odor can draw "ravenous Fowl" dwelling "many a League remote" (*PL* 10.274) from its source, and noting that Death similarly scents his "Quarry from so farr" (10.281). In these figures, beasts and the spectral Death are more proficient than humans in detecting scent across distance. But human readers engaging the figure command more smell-sponsored capacities across time. Language and literary tradition connect the reader's moment of reading to historical battles and the epic traditions that record them — perhaps also to the scriptural promises that recuperate them. Humans may not sniff events "many a league" remote, but as readers they prove sagacious of happenings many an era, and many a book binding, away.

The superiority of animal smell seems to be one reason the Western philosophical tradition often devalues it. Anthropologists write that Western modernity takes smell as "the sense of madness and savagery," contrasted with sight as the "pre-eminent sense of reason and civilization."[14] Eighteenth- and nineteenth-century accounts by Albrecht von Haller, Captain James Cook, and others maintain that "the sense of smell is more highly developed among savages than among civilized men," in Alain Corbin's summary phrase.[15] Nineteenth century ethnography casts "the suppression of the sense of smell" as "one of the defining characteristics of "civilized man."[16] Smell also arouses suspicion because of its diffuseness, its liminality, and its resistance to verbalization. Plato remarks upon the difficulty of verbally distinguishing smells: odors "have no name, and they have not many or definite and simple kinds, ... only ... painful and pleasant."[17] Richard Brathwaite's 1620 *Essaies upon the Five Senses* decries smell as "the unnecessariest of all other *Sences*."[18] Kant finds both smell and taste "subjective": experienced inside the body (within the oral or nasal cavities) and, for Kant, yielding more information about the perceiving subject than the thing itself, since encounters with scent generate "more an idea of our enjoyment of the object than knowledge of the external object."[19] Anthropologists Constance Classen, David Howes, and Anthony Synnott suggest that Western modernity devalues odors because they "cannot be readily contained, they escape and cross boundaries, blending different entities into olfactory wholes[, and] such a sensory model can be seen to be opposed to our modern, linear worldview with its emphasis on privacy, discrete divisions, and superficial interactions."[20]

In the world of *Paradise Lost*, however, smell becomes valuable precisely for its diffuseness and ability to bridge different realms, conditions, and cosmic orders. For a postlapsarian sensibility to apprehend heaven or to imagine a human world before the Fall, the liminality that may be inimical to reason is indeed salutary. Fragrance can "open the portals of the elements and the heavens whereby man can glimpse through them the secrets of the Creator," in the words of sixteenth century occult philosopher Cornelius Agrippa von Nettesheim.[21] In Siculus Diodorus's natural history (a likely source for *Paradise Lost*'s descriptions of aromatic Africa), the fragrance of spice trees can "even ravish...the Senses with delight, as a thing divine and unutterable."[22] Modern-day phenomenological investigators share this notion of smell's transcending the rational and the verbal. Psychologist Avery Gilbert remarks upon the "magical" feel of scent memory, a perception Gilbert ascribes to the difference between studied recall based on "deliberate effort," on the one hand, and "odor memories [that] accumulate automatically, outside of awareness," on the other.[23] Because "we don't remember remembering" scent memories, smell seems wondrous when it triggers a sudden, vivid recollection of the distant past.[24] This kind of involuntary association may not be a valued epistemology for Cartesian/Baconian modernity, but it offers opportunities for the mystical aims of theodical epic.

Smell, Time, and Theodicy

The central problem of logic for *Paradise Lost* is, of course, the difficulty of "justify[ing] the wayes of God to men" (*PL* 1.26). The epic's justification hinges on the Father's distinction between sequence and causality, which he advances fervidly, but not — to all readers — persuasively, in book 3.[25] Acknowledging that Satan will "assay / If [Man] by force he can.../...pervert" (3. 90–91), the Father proclaims the outcome of Satan's effort in a confident future tense in the very next hemistich: "and shall pervert" (3.91). At the same time, God denies that "Predestination over-rul[es] / [Creatures'] will" (3.114–15), concluding of disobedience that "if I foreknew, / Foreknowledge had no influence on their fault" (3.117–18). But the Father's "if" here reopens, for suspicious readers, the very possibility he has just declared definitively resolved.

When the question of free will versus foreknowledge comes to a head in Eve's temptation, the poem avails itself of scent, and the multilayered semiotics of "both-and" that have come to be associated with it, to play out the complexes of past/present/future and of causality/agency/self-determination in ways that accommodate their multiple relationships — those cohabitations that can seem uncogent, or at least uncomfortable, in the Father's logical defense. When Satan approaches Eve to seduce her from obedience, he finds her "Veild in a Cloud of Fragrance" (9.425). The equipoise of this fragrant cloud image contrasts with two perhaps troublingly directional images of visual desire offered before and after this fulcrum moment. Beforehand, when Eve quits Adam and Raphael's colloquy in book 8, her attendant "pomp of winning Graces" "from about her sho[o]t Darts of desire / Into all Eyes to wish her still in sight" (8.61–63). Then, after the Fall, Eve's "Eye dart[s] ... contagious Fire" (9.1036) in response to Adam's newly lascivious "amorous intent" (9.1035). The similarity of these two scenes of desire, one ostensibly prelapsarian and one fallen, raises familiar questions about Eve's constitution: is there a fundamental contrast between the armed "winning Graces" associated with Eve (but not part of her) before the fall and her postlapsarian weaponized eye (a bodily component)? Or does Eve seem problematically enticing throughout? When, between these two narrative moments, Satan finds Eve capaciously, odoriferously, and ambiently "Veild in a Cloud of Fragrance," only "half spi'd" (9.426), she is neither the center nor the origin of directional darts of visual desire (as she is both earlier and later). With this extratemporal fragrant veil, the poem can encompass (or avoid) both culpability and innocence, both predisposition and self-determination.

The "Cloud of Fragrance" proceeds to sponsor the blendings and reduplications so often associated with moments of smell in *Paradise Lost*, to ends consonant with similar passages, but perhaps even more pointed as the setup to this decisive moment in the story. The cloud emanates from and enfolds Eve, her flowers, and Eve herself (as "fairest unsupported Flowr" [9.432]).[26] Ensuing similes for Satan's reaction to the "delicious" "Spot" (9.439) of the fragrant garden link it with analogues both literary ("feign'd" [9.439]) and scriptural ("not Mystic" [9.442]). The poem compares Eden with the "Gardens / ...of reviv'd *Adonis*" (9.439–40) in Ovidian verse (ironically invoking the site of Adonis's reanimation to describe the place where Eve will consign humans to mortality), then offers a redoubled, re-mediated gesture toward ekphrastic representation of gardens within an inset scene of poetic recitation in the *Odyssey*, referring to gardens remarked by "renownd / *Alcinous*, host of old *Laertes'* Son" (9.440–41). Requiring that the reader parse multiple versions of sources and their progeny (Laertes and Odysseus, Menelaus's feast and Alcinous's entertainment, verbal account and represented image), these lines snag the reader's attention, disrupting diegetic momentum with riddling demands to disentangle the allusive reference. These demands highlight the serpentine tangle of generations both dynastic and literary, as "thick-wov'n" as the "Arborets and Flowers" (9.437) of the fragrant garden bed itself. Retaining its focus on scent in this decisive moment as Satan approaches Eve, the poem compares Satan's response to the fragrant cloud

> As one who long in populous City pent,
> Where Houses and thick Sewers annoy the Air,
> Forth issuing on a Summers Morn to breathe
> ....
> The smell of Grain, or tedded Grass, or Kine,
> Or Dairie. (9.445–51)

Whereas identifying "old Laertes' Son" required the reader to cast attention backward in his or her own literary history—but forward from the Edenic moment being described—to Homer, Satan's response looks forward to the present moment of Milton's reader, familiar with early modern urban sewage.

Such figures construct a way for a limited, fallen perception to imagine the ineffable by superimposing temporal frames of reference slightly askew to one another, like an illusion of curvature created from many straight lines. Smell facilitates this strategy of accreting slightly but significantly noncoincident moments by what psychologist Rachel Herz calls the "resistance to being overwritten" of odor memories that is much stronger than for visual or verbal recollection. Herz reports that "the first association made to an odor interferes with the formation of any subsequent associations," and, in *Paradise Lost*, the durability of the older view creates depth when newer experience joins it without supplanting the earlier version (as we saw in Satan's response to Eden's "purer air" in 4.153).[27]

Smell can transport humans immediately back in time. When psychologist Maria Larsson researched memory cues in geriatric subjects, she found that "smell cues evoked thoughts of early childhood, under the age of 10," whereas, for the same elderly population, verbal and visual cues linked to adolescent memories.[28] These smell memories were, despite their comparative antiquity, "exceptionally rich and emotional," and Larsson's subjects were "much likelier to report the sudden sensation of being brought back in time."[29] If mediation and disguise are signature changes accompanying the Miltonic Fall — with the Fall, "signs" emerge in communication both human (Adam acknowledges to Eve "in our Faces evident the signes / Of foul concupiscence" [*PL* 9.1077–78]) and divine (God will in the postlapsarian world leave "of his presence many a signe" [11.351]) — the unmediated quality of smell links it strongly to a prelapsarian condition. Responses to smell are direct: "sudden and unexpected," as Herz's subjects report.[30] Scent cues are processed in the amygdala, the "wellspring of emotion in our brain," and "pure emotion is the most immediate and central component of [scent] memory"; "what happened, who was there, where it was — becomes filled in only later."[31] Folding time, whisking the perceiver immediately back to an earlier condition without space for demurral or reflection, scent replaces consciousness (whether Satan's, Marcel Proust's, or Milton's postlapsarian reader's) in a bygone era.

Smell and Polychronicity

But odor is essential for fully inhabiting the present as well. A patient of Oliver Sacks who lost his sense of smell reports that without the "rich unconscious background to everything else" normally supplied by smell, his "whole world was suddenly radically poorer."[32] In *Paradise Lost*, too, smell's immediate presence is as significant as its summoning of distant times. Scent operates in concert with other cues and contexts — the visual, the rational, the verbal, the allusive — that fill in additional frameworks, none fully supplanting the others. Hereby the connection of realms sponsored by scent posits "both/and" responses to questions that can seem intractable to "either/or" formulation. Polychronous, scent lets us practice both fallen and unfallen apprehension. Olfaction thus addresses in a different register the theological problems that the Father in book 3 articulates with exquisite, but not always transparent or convincing, forensic scrupulousness. Smell likewise addresses narrative problems of how to represent free will and divine foreknowledge as coexisting, or how to grasp predestination and foreknowledge from both the copious divine view and the more limited human one, or how fallen poetic language can convey prelapsarian experience.

Olfaction's distinctive capability to render "then" in the "now" capaciously allows for simultaneous perception: as then and now, as fallen and unfallen, as satanically infected misperception and as clear-eyed witnessing. In a 2008 article summarizing research on smell aptly titled "The Nose, an Emotional Time Machine," journalist Natalie Angier remarks upon its polychronous capabilities: "Olfaction is an ancient sense, the key by which our earliest forebears learned to approach or slink off. Yet the right aroma can evoke such vivid, whole body sensations that we feel life's permanent newness, the grounding of now."[33] Might Angier's "permanent newness" be a Miltonic "Paradise within" (12.587)?

CHAPTER 2

Sound as Matter
Milton, Music, and Monism

SETH HERBST

I want to begin with an intuition: in a universe that is completely material—where every object, animate or inanimate, is composed of physical stuff—even music must be made of matter. It is a radical idea, that sound could be reified as substance, but one that arises logically from the interweaving of narrative and cosmology in *Paradise Lost*. Music is constantly produced and heard in a universe where everything that exists is fashioned from the substance of God.[1] To read Milton's epic is to be confronted with the powerful sense that music participates in a chain of material being. But is this intuitive sense borne out by the logic underlying Milton's representation of music in the poem?

The question turns out to have significance not only within *Paradise Lost* but also in the larger narrative of Milton's intellectual development. One crucial strand of that narrative is the evolution of Milton's thinking about body, soul, and matter. This strand of thought has been of particular interest to Miltonists over the past few decades. In what has been accepted as the standard account, Stephen Fallon argues that Milton's monist materialism developed gradually over the course of his life. In Fallon's analysis, Milton's writings reveal incremental stages between an adherence to orthodox dualism in the early poems and the final, heterodox concept of monism staked out in *De doctrina Christiana* and realized in *Paradise Lost, Paradise Regained,* and *Samson Agonistes*. The great progression toward monism in Milton's thinking, Fallon argues, occurs in the divorce tracts of the 1640s.[2]

It will be one of my central assertions in the following pages that traces of Milton's monist materialism were already in evidence as early as 1629, the date of the Nativity ode. Fallon's dismissal of the early poetry as unequivocally dualist is, in my estimation, too categorical an assessment.[3] I want to suggest instead that the early poems bear significant if unexpected traces of monist thinking, and that reassessing them in this light can contribute to a more nuanced, nonlinear sense of Milton's complicated intellectual development.

As important as that project, however, is the surprising nature of the traces themselves. While Fallon and others have offered imaginative accounts of the role monism plays in Milton's poetic ontology and cosmology, no critical attention has, to my knowledge, offered the possibility that Milton's monism also animates his thinking about music.[4] Music is a constant, central, and highly developed theme in Milton's poetry, from the early Nativity ode and "At a Solemn Musick" to *Paradise Lost* and *Paradise Regained*. If my opening intuition holds water — if Milton's representation of music in *Paradise Lost* can indeed be shown to bear the influence of his monism — then the depiction of music in the early poems will provide a comparative index of Milton's monist thinking. If, that is, Milton's representation of music in his later poetry can be classified as "monist," and his earlier representations of music correspond to his later representations, then we have solid evidence for monist tendencies earlier in Milton's career than previously realized. To assess that possibility, I will first analyze music as it is represented in *Paradise Lost,* and then, with that benchmark in mind, turn to Milton's earlier poetry for comparison. My analysis will evaluate two dimensions of music as Milton represents it: ontology, or the nature of its being, and agency, the nature of the action it achieves. My goal throughout will be to allow monism and music to illuminate one another.

"Thir Songs Divide the Night": Milton's Material Music

What might "monist music," music operating under the rules of animist materialism, sound like? Is there solid evidence for an extension of Milton's materialist philosophy into the aesthetic realm of music and music making? Stephen Fallon helps us begin our inquiry. In tracing the development of Milton's monism, Fallon briefly attends to the subject of music in Milton's 1644 prose tract *Of Education*. In what seems a clear echo of Platonic theory, Milton suggests that hearing or playing music after exercise or meals has a beneficial effect on students. Fallon's concern in drawing on this passage is to demonstrate that Milton is approaching, but not yet fully espousing, a materialist conception of the soul. Citing physically suggestive phrases in Milton's account of music, such as "*composing their travail'd spirits*" and "send their *mindes* backe to study *in good tune*," Fallon deduces that Milton has at least begun to think of the soul as a physical entity:[5] "While editors normally point to Plato and Aristotle [as the basis for Milton's portrayal of music's effects], a more pertinent parallel is Francis Bacon, who...attributed those effects to music's power to move (literally) the corporeal spirits....Like Bacon, Milton follows Plato and Aristotle on the effects of music but suggests that the medium of the effect is corporeal motion."[6] Fallon's persuasive mode of analysis can be productively extended to *Paradise Lost*, where, as we shall see, music *moves* the souls of the angels and of Adam and Eve.

In book 4, when Eve asks Adam why the stars shine during the night, Adam replies with a discursive explanation that concludes by evoking the nocturnal music of angels:

> Millions of spiritual Creatures walk the Earth
> Unseen, both when we wake, and when we sleep:
> All these with ceasless praise his works behold
> Both day and night: how often from the steep
> Of echoing Hill or Thicket have we heard
> Celestial voices to the midnight air,
> Sole, or responsive each to others note

> Singing thir great Creator: oft in bands
> While they keep watch, or nightly rounding walk,
> With Heav'nly touch of instrumental sounds
> In full harmonic number joind, thir songs
> Divide the night, and lift our thoughts to Heaven.[7] (PL 4.677–88)

Adam here proclaims that the angelic music of "ceaseless praise" continually operates to "lift our thoughts to Heaven." This effect occurs "both when we wake, and when we sleep." At first blush, this description seems to be a textbook instantiation of Platonic musical theory: Milton imagines heavenly music of praise as inducing a kind of psychosomatic effect on human rational processes. But a more complex reading emerges when it is recalled that for Milton "thoughts" connote more than rational processes. The word "thoughts" is in fact a Miltonic synonym for "soul": as Raphael later tells Adam, "the Soule / Reason receives, and *reason is her being*" (5.486–87; emphasis added). If Milton's monism holds that the body consists in the soul, it also stipulates that the soul consists in rational thought. In operating on *thoughts*, then, music is operating on the substance of the soul, and its effect is physical: it "*lift(s)*" our thoughts to Heaven." What first strikes the reader as figurative language expressing the Platonic agency of music (lifting the thoughts to heaven) emerges on closer scrutiny as a rigorously monist image, the erection of the corporeal soul into a form "neerer tending" to God (5.476). The agency of music already accomplishes in part what Raphael suggests God may someday fully realize: the conversion of humanity's substance into the more refined, freer ethereal substance of angels.[8]

So far, so good: it might reasonably have been expected that within the monist universe of *Paradise Lost* Milton would utilize the agency of music with respect to the soul to emphasize the material ontology of the soul. But there is more, and this is where Milton's distinctive intellectual approach can be felt more palpably. In Adam's account, Milton also extends his animist materialism to encompass sound itself. How? Adam's description of sound makes use of conceptual terms that suggest it functions as a physical, material object.

Adam notes with an aficionado's ear that the angels sing in a complex choral configuration, "sole, or responsive each to others note." The sonic picture implies an extraordinary formal complexity, in which individual melody can either stand alone as monophony or seamlessly intertwine with other monophonic strands to create a rich polyphony that Adam calls "full harmonic number" (*PL* 4.687). This complex pattern of recombination makes use of the conceptual framework of geometry, implying musical parts as independent shapes that can be integrated into a unified larger shape. But if music has the property of shape, or *form*, it also has the property of *accident*— external texture that gives form material presence: Adam describes the rich timbral variegation of angelic music, as "instrumental sounds" are often added to the a cappella "celestial voices" (4.686, 682). By giving it the philosophical properties of form and accident, Milton suggests that music behaves as a physical object. Milton's choice of a physical verb for the interaction of music with its environment emphasizes this sense of musical sound as a material object: "thir songs / *Divide* the night" (4.687–88; emphasis added).

Both in its effectual agency and in its own ontology, music as Adam describes it comports with Milton's animist materialism: the agency of music on the soul confirms the soul's material nature, while music itself takes on a material ontology, to the point where sound itself can act as physical matter in "dividing" the night. Indeed, given the agency of music with respect to the soul, its material ontology should come as no surprise. For if music has a physical effect on what Milton conceived of as the substance of the soul, then must not music itself be a material phenomenon? In other words, if Milton's logical thinking is rigorous and his materialist universe is comprehensively imagined, then for music to have a material effect on the material substance of the spirit, it must, at least in some dimension, be imagined as itself consisting of matter.

Other accounts of music in *Paradise Lost* confirm and amplify this reading. Wherever music is heard, it is both conceptualized as a physical, material object and, as such, has a profound effect on the substance of its listeners' souls. This effect can be either good, as when the angelic music lifts the thoughts of Adam and Eve to heaven, or bad, as with the infernal music produced by the fallen angels in hell:

> Others more milde,
> Retreated in a silent valley, sing
> With notes Angelical to many a Harp
> Thir own Heroic deeds and hapless fall
> By doom of Battel; and complain that Fate
> Free Vertue should enthrall to Force or Chance.
> Thir Song was partial, but the harmony
> (What could it less when Spirits immortal sing?)
> Suspended Hell, and took with ravishment
> The thronging audience.   (2.546–55)

The music of complaint produced by the lounging demons is described in conceptual terms consistent with Adam's description of angelic music. Like angelic music, this infernal music is imagined as a kind of physical object: it has both accident — for example, the timbral variegation of harps accompanying the Spirits' voices — and form: the impressively progressive harmony that "suspended Hell."[9] But while its accident is similar to that of unfallen music — the demons produce "notes Angelical" — in its specific form infernal music differs from the heavenly song. Unlike angelic music, infernal music is not properly choral; instead, it is "partial," produced in disjunct parts that, while they do combine in "harmony," remain musically exclusive from one another — as the "sole" yet "responsive" singers of the heavenly chorus did not.[10] With its "notes Angelical," the music of the demons has the accident of heavenly music and might seduce the unwary listener into believing it to be such; but its underlying form, not immediately apparent to the ear, makes clear that infernal music is ontologically very different from the music of the unfallen angels.

As a physical, material object, infernal music should, like angelic music, have a material effect on the soul, but since its ontology is formally different from that of angelic music, we would also expect infernal music to demonstrate a different agency. Milton does not disappoint us. Infernal music does not "lift" the thoughts of the fallen angels to heaven. Instead, it "took with ravishment / The thronging audience" (*PL* 2.554–55). This action offers a precise contrast to Adam's statement of the effect of angelic music. "Ravishment" here means specifically "ecstasy; delight...the fact of being entranced or captivated" (*OED* 2.a). In a monist universe, where a living being's body is congruent with its soul, to be taken with ravishment means for one's soul to be *imprisoned* by sensual delight. This imprisonment ushers the soul from free rationality into enslavement by the senses. Good angelic music raises the soul into free rationality, lifting *thoughts* (a synonym, we recall, for the soul) to heaven and thus refining man's substance to a slightly more ethereal, angel-like consistency; fallen angelic music, however, abases the soul into nonrational pleasure and by implication hardens the corporeal substance of the fallen angels into an imprisoning container. Even as these fallen angels complain that fate has subjected their power of free will to God's tyranny or to pure chance ("Others...complain that Fate / Free Vertue should *enthrall* to Force or Chance" [2.546–51; emphasis added]), they *choose* to abandon themselves to an imprisoning hedonism. The irony is clear: the angels freely chose to fall just as they now freely choose to produce music that enthralls their "Free Vertue."

The parallel accounts of heavenly and infernal music suggest two important, related conclusions about the phenomenon of sound in a universe governed by animist materialism. The first is ontological: in Milton's universe, the basic phenomenon of sound behaves like the primordial matter on which the original act of Creation was performed. As we recall from God's speech in book 7, when God retired himself from infinitude, what was left behind was chaotic matter, bereft of his goodness and subject to "Necessitie and Chance" (*PL* 7.172; see also 7.165–73). When God sends the Son out to shape the matter of chaos into the universe and its contents, chaotic matter becomes once again *good*. Of course, it is possible for matter, which is morally neutral, to be either good or bad. Human beings were originally good until their fall, after which, according to Milton in *De doctrina Christiana*, their matter became corrupt; on Milton's account, man's material corruption is transmitted from parents to child as original sin.[11] The contrasting music of the good angels and the fallen angels suggests that making music is an act of creation that shapes the morally neutral matter of sound into either good or bad form.

Once sound has been shaped creatively into either good or bad music, that music also possesses, as we have seen, a further power to shape other matter. This is the second conclusion about the nature of sound, and it elucidates the agency of music: if music making is a creative act that echoes the supreme act of divine Creation, then music itself, once created, retains in its material nature a further creative potency to influence other matter by adjusting it toward good or evil. This creative power to affect other matter operates not only on living beings such as Adam and Eve but also on the geographic substance of the natural world around them: "Witness if I be silent, Morn or Eeven, / To Hill, or Valley, Fountain, or fresh shade / Made vocal by my Song, and taught his praise" (5.202–04). Thus sing Adam and Eve in their glorious morning orison. Their creative production of sound as good music — a song of praise — influences the matter of the landscape in which they stand: the landscape responds to their song. This response is no mere echo. Instead, in Adam and Eve's account, the "Hill, or Valley, Fountain, or fresh shade" take on the animacy of living beings. "Vocal" means specifically "Endowed with a voice, possessed of utterance; exercising the power of speech or of uttering sounds" (*OED* II.4.a). Adam and Eve are claiming that their song causes the matter of the landscape to take on the capacity to utter coherent sounds, and, further, that in so doing the putatively inanimate landscape completes what is properly a rational activity: learning how to praise God. It might be objected that Milton is merely allowing Adam and Eve to engage in a bit of fancy personification as they describe what is in fact the echo of their voices. Certainly Milton is not arguing that Adam and Eve's song takes on the creative power of God so as to render their natural surroundings an animate, rational creature. But I think, if we recall Fallon's concept of animist materialism, that Milton is indeed suggesting a more profound effect than an echo. What is implied is that Adam and Eve's song of praise slightly refines the material substance of the landscape so that it tends nearer to God.

Milton provides a formal mimesis for this refining power of good music. In Adam and Eve's 56-line morning orison (5.153–208), the word "praise" occurs as a line ending no fewer than six times (5.172, 184, 191, 196, 199, 204). The rime-riche effect is further amplified by a variety of line-ending words that produce close slant-rhymes with the word "praise" — for example, "flies" (176), "rise" (185, 188), and "shade" (203) — some of which present their own rime-riche pairings (e.g., "rise"). For a poet who famously rejects the "jingling sound of like endings" as "the troublesom and modern bondage of Rimeing,"[12] this passage is a notable departure and as such represents a calculated effect. Even as Adam and Eve claim their Song has the power to transform the matter of the natural world around them, Milton ratifies their claim by allowing their song to transform the normative blank-verse terrain of his poem. Like the diegetic landscape, the material substance of the poem is itself refined so that its line endings, usually nonrhyming, begin to rhyme. Like the diegetic landscape, the poetic landscape is quite literally "taught his *praise*" (emphasis added). The mimetic effect achieved by rhyme demonstrates for the reader the creative power of music to give new shape to other matter.

That power, a hallmark of music in Milton's monist universe, is precisely what the younger poet emphasizes in his account of divine music in the "Ode on the Morning of Christ's Nativity" (1629): "Ring out ye Crystall sphears" (125), the speaker implores,

> Once bless our human ears,
>   (If ye have power to touch our senses so)
> And let your silver chime
> Move in melodious time;
>   And let the Base of Heav'ns deep Organ blow,
> And with your ninefold harmony
> Make up full consort to th'Angelike symphony.
>
> For if such holy Song
> Enwrap our fancy long,
>   Time will run back, and fetch the age of gold,

> And speckl'd vanity
> Will sicken soon and die,
>   And leprous sin will melt from earthly mould,
> And Hell it self will pass away,
> And leave her dolorous mansions to the peering day.[13]

The speaker here imagines the power of celestial music to effect a beneficial material change in the substance of the fallen world: "speckl'd vanity" will sicken and die even as the "earthy mould" will be purged of the corruptions of sin; the entire geography of hell will be dissolved into sunlight. This material potency anticipates the creative agency of music as Milton later imagines it in his materialist epic universe. It does not, however, fully conform to that model. The speaker in the Nativity ode suggests that he is only imagining the material agency of celestial music, and that this imaginative vision (rather than any physical consequences) is actually what the music brings about: "For *if* such holy Song / *Enwrap our fancy long,* / Time will run back" (emphasis added). Milton has begun to conceive of music as possessing material creative agency, but at this early stage in his intellectual development he remains tentative about that materialist conception and so relegates it to a poetic flight of "fancy."

Similarly, Milton's mature musical ontology is present here in qualified terms. At first blush, it seems that Milton conceptualizes music as physical, having both form and accident. In formal terms, the "ninefold harmony" of the crystal spheres is complemented by the further harmonic strand of "Heav'ns deep Organ"; the result is the "full consort" of "th'Angelike symphony." As for accident, Milton uses the synesthetic epithet "*silver* chime" (emphasis added), which appeals to the sense of sight to convey the accidental texture of music. But somehow music in the Nativity ode does not quite take on the physical, material immediacy that is its distinctive feature in *Paradise Lost*. The reason, I think, is that unlike the extraordinary, freshly imagined musical imagery of *Paradise Lost*, Milton here resorts to stock images drawn from Ptolemaic cosmology and poetic cliché.

In *Paradise Lost*, Milton asks the reader to imagine the exciting formal possibility of a chorus at once "sole" and "responsive each to others note" (4.683). Here, however, the poet resorts to borrowing the well-known Ptolemaic concept of the music of the nine spheres. Not only is the image generic; "ninefold harmony" is an evocative epithet rather than an attempt to describe a real harmonic form. Similarly, "silver" is a cliché rather than original descriptor for the sound of music, and is again evocative rather than specifying a precise musical sound. Without the mature Milton's bolder inventiveness, this music does not, in its form and accident, quite take on the physical presence that evokes music as matter in *Paradise Lost*. Finally, it is also crucial to note that, as with its material agency, the acoustic picture of celestial music is qualified as an imaginative vision within the poem — a product of fancy.

In that very act of qualification, however, Milton actually forces himself more boldly to anticipate a crucial aspect of his later monism. As Fallon notes, Milton's conception of the body/soul formation is explicitly dualist in the Nativity ode: the speaker refers to the body as "a darksom House of mortal Clay" (14), a house in which the disjunct soul lives.[14] But in his account of a vision induced by music, the young poet introduces a physiological mechanism that implies the connection of body and soul. The speaker first describes the sensory apprehension of music — "Once bless our human *ears*, / (If ye have power to touch our *senses* so)" (emphasis added) — and then wonders what might happen if "such holy Song / Enwrap our *fancy* long" (emphasis added). The auditory sensory stimulus on the body's senses seamlessly enwraps our *fancy* — that is, the imaginative faculty of the soul.[15] If a sensory stimulus on the body has a direct effect on the soul, then is not some material connection between body and soul implied? The physical verb for music's interaction with fancy, "enwrap," is highly suggestive. What I am proposing is not that Milton is here consciously monist in his conception of the body and soul but, rather, that as he thinks about music and depicts it in his early poetry, he begins to anticipate not only his mature materialist conception of the universe, but also concrete aspects of the monist philosophy at the center of his materialism.

That anticipation is even more pronounced in another early lyric, "At a Solemn Musick" (c. 1631–33). Here, the agency of divine music on the soul is imagined in terms strikingly similar to Adam's account, written some 30 years later:

> Blest pair of *Sirens*, pledges of Heav'ns joy,
> Sphear-born harmonious Sisters, Voice, and Vers,
> Wed your divine sounds, and mixt power employ
> Dead things with inbreath'd sense able to pierce,
> And to our high-rais'd phantasie present,
> That undisturbed Song of pure concent. (1–6)

Milton's speaker here adjures the allegorical figures of heavenly music, Voice (sound) and Verse (text), to present their intertwined "divine sounds" to human beings on earth. Hearing this "undisturbed Song of pure concent" has a remarkable effect on human beings: it raises high their *phantasie*, a word synonymous with "fancy" in the Nativity ode.[16] If Fallon were to analyze this passage, he would likely note that Milton here describes the operation of music on the soul in terms at least as suggestively physical as those in *Of Education*—but a full decade earlier. In fact, the language of the lyric more precisely corresponds to Milton's later monist vision: just as Adam notes that heavenly songs *"lift* our thoughts to heaven" (*PL* 4.688; emphasis added), the speaker of "At a Solemn Musick" claims that heavenly song *raises*, or erects, the mental faculties.

As in *Paradise Lost*, music in "At a Solemn Musick" also possesses the material agency to animate entities that are not alive. In *Paradise Lost* that power is formulated as making the inanimate landscape "vocal" (5.204); in the early lyric, the formulation is an allusion to the Orpheus myth, in which the bard could bring rocks and other inanimate natural objects to life: "Wed your divine sounds, and mixt power employ / Dead things with inbreath'd sense able to pierce" ("At a Solemn Musick," 3–4). The power to pierce the matter of "dead things" with "inbreath'd sense" is more than an allusion to Orpheus;

it is a statement of the creative agency of music that anticipates the terms Milton will use in *De doctrina Christiana* for the divine act of Creation itself: God's *breathing* of life into the matter of his creatures. Once again, my claim is that the imaginative work of rendering music in poetry encourages the young Milton to think about both music and the soul in ways that correspond to a philosophical system he would not formally enunciate for several decades.

So much for the agency of music in "At a Solemn Musick." As for its ontology, Milton again closely anticipates his mature vision. Just as in *Paradise Lost*, music is evoked in conceptual terms that suggest a physical object with both form and accident. The form of the "melodious noise" (18) of heavenly music is constructed by wedding the divine sounds of Voice (musical setting) and Verse (text); the accidental texture is described at length in richly material terms:

> the bright Seraphim in burning row
> Their loud up-lifted Angel trumpets blow,
> And the Cherubick host in thousand quires
> Touch their immortal Harps of golden wires.[17]   (10–13)

And just as neutral sound in *Paradise Lost* is shaped into the form of either good or bad music, so, too, is sound in "At a Solemn Musick" wrought into either moral or immoral music: "Wed your divine sounds, and mixt power employ" (3), Milton's speaker pleads with the harmonious Sisters, Voice and Verse,

> That we on Earth with undiscording voice
> May rightly answer that melodious noise;
> As once we did, till disproportion'd sin
> Jarr'd against natures chime, and with harsh din
> Broke the fair musick that all creatures made
> To their great Lord, whose love their motion sway'd
> In perfect Diapason, whilst they stood
> In first obedience, and their state of good.   (17–24)

The "melodious noise" of heavenly music is contrasted with the "harsh din" produced by "disproportion'd sin." Marrying a good text to a proper musical setting shapes sound into "melodious noise," but the action of sin, by contrast, is "disproportion'd," or inharmonious, and its dissonant clash with "natures chime" results in a "harsh din." This bad music, in turn, has the further material effect of shattering the "fair musick" made by prelapsarian creatures.

This dichotomy of the ontology and agency of good and bad music seems fully to anticipate Milton's conception in *Paradise Lost*, but there is, once again, an important qualification. In "At a Solemn Musick," while the "melodious noise" of heavenly music is described as a literal acoustic phenomenon, the "harsh din" made by sin is not. By "literal acoustic phenomenon," I refer not to whether music is being given form and accident as a physical object but to whether music is heard within the poetic reality or simply used as a rhetorical figure of speech. When "disproportion'd sin" breaks the "fair musick" once made by obedient creatures, the reader is not being directed to imagine that the Fall was a musical event in which dissonance interrupted the prelapsarian symphony. Instead, the reader quickly grasps that Milton is speaking in a metaphoric register, in which dissonant music serves as a metaphor for disobedience to God. As Milton gives voice to a moral vision opposing heavenly obedience to God with fallen, sinful disobedience, music modulates in his poem from being represented as a real acoustic object to being represented as a metaphor.

In the 1634 entertainment he wrote to be performed at Ludlow Castle, however, Milton retains his conception of music as ethically charged — produced by and expressive of good or evil — while consistently and vividly evoking sound as a real, not metaphoric, acoustic phenomenon. The friendly guardian spirit, disguised as the shepherd Thyrsis, gives the brothers an account of two contrasting musical performances — first the "light fantastick round" of Comus (*A Mask*, 144), and then the song sung by their sister, the Lady. Here is Comus' music:

> The wonted roar was up amidst the Woods,
> And fill'd the Air with barbarous dissonance,
> At which I ceas't, and listen'd them a while,
> Till an unusuall stop of sudden silence
> Gave respit to the drowsie frighted steeds.

And here is the Lady's:

> At last a soft and solemn breathing sound
> Rose like a steam of rich distill'd Perfumes,
> And stole upon the Air, that even Silence
> Was took e're she was ware, and wish't she might
> Deny her nature, and be never more
> Still to be so displac't. I was all eare,
> And took in strains that might create a soul
> Under the ribs of Death. (*A Mask*, 549–53, 555–62)

The spirit's account of the contrasting music of Comus and the Lady recapitulates the musical properties delineated in the earlier lyric poems while fully rendering music as a material acoustic phenomenon. Comus and his band of followers shape sound into the form of "barbarous dissonance" with the accident of a "wonted roar." But this immoral music is also a real acoustic object that literalizes the figurative "harsh din" of "At a Solemn Musick" as a "barbarous dissonance" that (note the physical verb) *"fill'd* the Air" (emphasis added). This dissonance, in turn, is demonstrated to have powerful agency on the "frighted steeds."

The rich description of the Lady's song is even more evocative in laying out the material ontology of music and its resulting agency. Here, Milton does not so much rely on the conceptual framework of form and accident to imply a physical body, but instead directly describes the sound of music in physical, even animate, terms. The Lady's act of singing is an act of "breathing sound" so that it is "soft and solemn." So transcendent is the Lady's creative art that the acoustic phenomenon of music seems almost to take on life itself, to breathe. Once that "breathing sound" emerges into its environment, Milton describes it as a physical object, rising through the air "like a steam of rich distill'd Perfumes." Unlike the hackneyed synesthetic modifier "silver" in the Nativity ode, here the synesthetic description of sound dispersing like aroma is to my knowledge original, and, what is more, viscerally evocative of music as highly refined, ethereal matter.

In continuing the Spirit's account of the Lady's song as it disperses through its environment, Milton adopts an allegorical mode of description that might, at first, seem to retreat from the world of materiality. The Lady's "soft and solemn breathing sound" surprises the personified allegorical figure of Silence, and is presumably so pleasing to this allegorical entity that she longs to deny her own nature as a lack of sound. The allegorical mode here is, in fact, counterintuitively, a rhetorical move employed by the Spirit more vividly to evoke the material effect of the Lady's song as it disperses through its physical environment. By personifying the abstract concept of Silence, Milton translates an absence into a physical presence that can then interact with the materiality of the Lady's music: Silence "wish't she might... be never more / Still *to be so displac't*" (emphasis added). With Silence as a displaceable physical entity, Milton can emphasize the physical presence of sound.[18]

The poet continues to avail himself of the allegorical mode as the Spirit says he "took in strains that might create a soul / Under the ribs of Death." This claim confronts us with what seems like incontrovertible evidence of a dualist philosophy: the soul is imagined as an entity distinct from the personified body of Death. But with the Spirit's claim that the Lady's good music potentially has the material agency to endow Death with a soul, Milton is thinking in monist terms in at least two respects. The first is the power of music to animate inanimate entities. Death is, of course, the absence of life; to create a soul in Death is the ultimate affirmation of the power of music (we recall from "At a Solemn Musick") to pierce dead things with "inbreath'd sense." The second element of monist thinking is a more profound anticipation of Milton's representational strategy in *Paradise Lost*. Death, of course, appears as a character in Milton's epic, and he stands with his mother, Sin, as the only fully realized allegorical entities in the poem. While allegorical characters, who are composed of abstract concepts rather than matter, would seem to deny the animist materialism underpinning Milton's universe, Stephen Fallon argues that Milton's use of Death and Sin actually confirms the poet's overarching materialist ontology.[19] Because pure evil itself is, according to

Augustine, the "privation of entity," Milton intentionally represents Death and Sin as allegories so as faithfully to register their lack of material substance.[20] Allegories have no matter, and hence have no soul. But if that is true, then Milton precisely anticipates his materialist concept of soulless allegory in the 1634 *Mask:* without the operation of the Lady's song, there is no soul under the ribs of Death. Once again, the imaginative task of trying to represent music and its effects encourages Milton to think in terms that he would later formalize as a rigorous philosophical system. These poetic traces of Milton's intellectual development even suggest that thinking about music, as much as thinking about divorce or the nature of Creation, fueled the evolution of Milton's philosophy from dualist to monist.

"The Whole Man Is the Soul": The Musical Analogy for Monism

I have thus far been exploring how Milton's poetic depictions of music explicitly drive his patterns of thought toward monism and the larger system of animist materialism. There is, however, a governing feature of Milton's treatment of music that forms not an explicit but an implicit relation with his monism. Recall that in "At a Solemn Musick," Milton initially evokes music as a real acoustic object but then shifts into metaphoric representation: the literal "melodious noise" of the sphere-born sisters becomes the figurative "harsh din" of the Fall. The shift into metaphor, however, is not permanent in the poem. At the close of the lyric, Milton merges the acoustic and metaphoric dimensions of music in a vision of humanity's redemption. First, as we have seen, music has a metaphoric sense:

>   disproportion'd sin
> Jarr'd against natures chime, and with harsh din
> Broke the fair musick that all creatures made
> To their great Lord, whose love their motion sway'd
> In perfect Diapason, whilst they stood
> In first obedience, and their state of good.

But then the terms change:

> O may we soon again renew that Song,
> And keep in tune with Heav'n, till God ere long
> To his celestial consort us unite,
> To live with him, and sing in endles morn of light.
>   ("At a Solemn Musick," 19–28)

In the hortatory hope that fallen human beings will renew their prelapsarian song, Milton seems to be invoking music metaphorically: the song figures a relationship of proper submission to God — a swaying of motion in "perfect Diapason" while standing in obedience. This is surely the case. But in the final vision of the poem, music once again becomes a real acoustic event: humanity joins the celestial consort to participate in the literal music making so richly described earlier in the poem. To live with God in heaven is quite literally to sing God's praises in "endles morn of light." Milton thus realizes a model of music in which sound is *simultaneously* an acoustic phenomenon and a metaphor for a creature's relationship with God. This strikingly original model of simultaneous identity, achieved at the close of "At a Solemn Musick," consistently governs Milton's subsequent depictions of music throughout his career, from *A Mask* (1634) until *Paradise Regained* (1671).[21]

In its distinctive elision of the traditional division between the sensory phenomenon of sound and the intellectual phenomenon of meaning, this model presents an analogy with the mature Milton's monist model, which elides the traditional division between body and soul. "The whole man is the soul, and the soul the man," declares Milton in *De doctrina Christiana*.[22] Music is at once soul — a metaphoric valence — and body, a sonorous acoustic presence. The two components are not, ultimately, separable. This relation is, of course, only analogous; I am not suggesting that Milton considered music a living being with a body and a soul. But I am suggesting that thinking about music as existing simultaneously in two dimensions that are somehow both distinct and overlapping provided Milton with an intellectual structure conducive to reasoning about the resistant concept of a human ontology inhering in two dimensions that are somehow both separate and unified. As Fallon sympathetically says of *De doctrina Christiana*, "Milton struggles...to articulate monism with a vocabulary tempered by centuries of dualism."[23] To this I would add the mental difficulty of *thinking* about monism within an inherited philosophical discourse that systematically schematized body and soul as separate concepts. Music provided, for Milton, a surrogate discourse in which he could reason about the unity of seemingly separate things without the conceptual baggage of inherited Christian theology. Whether Milton ever recognized the analogy between his model of music and his model of human ontology is not, ultimately, important. Probably he did not. What is important, however, is that in addition to the explicit ways explored above in which representing music in poetry influenced Milton's development of monism and animist materialism, it is also apparent that thinking about music afforded the poet the opportunity, perhaps available nowhere else in his intellectual life, to come to rational terms with one of the central paradoxes of his mature theology.

PART TWO

HUMAN EMBODIMENT

CHAPTER 3

Milton on the Move
Walking and Self-Knowledge in Paradise Lost

RYAN HACKENBRACHT

In book 11 of *Paradise Lost*, after the Son has judged the sinful couple, Eve turns to Adam and, in an attempt to ease the blow of their sentence, beckons him to work the garden with her:

> let us forth,
> I never from thy side henceforth to stray,
> Wherere our days work lies, though now enjoind
> Laborious, till day droop; while here we dwell,
> What can be toilsom in these pleasant Walkes?
> Here let us live, though in a fall'n state, content.[1]

Eve's speech suggests that she understands places in Eden — as well as her own identity — in terms of where she has walked. Her sense of self, we might say, operates within a peripatetic framework. Her speech also raises the possibility that walking may mitigate their current distress, and she searches for a remedy for the Fall in an activity central to their prelapsarian routine. Eve's comment raises a number of questions about the experience of walking in Milton's epic. Does walking allow Adam and Eve a certain measure of control over their new depravity? Does peripatetic motion indeed possess the psycho- and physiotherapeutic qualities Eve ascribes to it?[2] How do Adam and Eve's strolls in the garden compare with Satan's striding on the battlefield, and what can the seemingly pedestrian activity of walking reveal about a character?

As a religious and philosophical metaphor, walking occupies an important place in the Western literary imagination. From Ovid's characterization of the human as *ad sidera vultus*, upright and thus capable of deep contemplation, to John Bunyan's adaptation of *christianus peregrinans*, the Christian pilgrim, walking is a powerful mechanism for self-expression in both Greco-Roman and Judeo-Christian traditions.[3] With regard to the early modern period, scholars note the close relationship between the human body and subjectivity. Michael Schoenfeldt shows how Milton and others sought to "express the material self as a site of inwardness," and Mary Floyd-Wilson and Garrett Sullivan demonstrate that inwardness relied upon an outward interaction with the natural world.[4] David Quint identifies the act of falling in *Paradise Lost* as a Miltonic topos of engagement with Lucretius, for whom motion was integral to atomistic philosophy.[5] Mandy Green notes Milton's indebtedness to Ovid in scenes like Eve's flight from Adam, and Jonathan Post points out that *Paradise Lost* traffics in the expulsion tradition of Masaccio and other artists, for whom "the representation of motion begged larger questions involving human freedom."[6] In her essay in the current collection, Lara Dodds shows how Milton reconfigures the Homeric gestures of furrowing one's brow and blushing, which in *Paradise Lost* evince Milton's artful method of epic revisionism. As Dodds and others observe, *Paradise Lost* furthers a classical interest in how human vitality is mediated through the body.[7]

However, scholars have not recognized that walking is a major motif within epic, nor that Milton's transformation of that motif has profound implications for the self, embodiment, and materiality in *Paradise Lost*.[8] Milton's concern for the physicality of the self derives from the Old Testament, as scholars have shown, but it also has classical origins.[9] Homer was an important source of Milton's materialism, and much of the Renaissance poet's fascination with heroic bodies is inherited from Greek epic. The current essay thus recovers the neglected place of walking within the epic tradition while emphasizing the Homeric quality of Milton's thinking about the self, physical matter, and objects in motion.

In *Paradise Lost*, Milton reinvents walking as a physical register for the growth or decline of a character's self-knowledge. Milton uses types of peripatetic motion — walking, striding, stumbling, migrating, and tracing — to thematize internal conflicts of free will and obedience to God. In the garden of Eden, walking teaches Adam and Eve about their God-given roles. After the Fall, walking is the means by which they learn about their new, fallen state. While walking brings Adam and Eve self-knowledge, for Satan, Sin, and Death, a sinful style of walking perpetuates their habits of self-deception. By performing forbidden motions, the unholy trinity distance themselves from God and bury truths they would just as soon forget.

By imbuing walking with spiritual value, Milton participates in a longstanding generic inquiry into the relationship between ambulation and cogitation. How and when feet move, and where they do and do not go, is a fresh lens through which to view Milton's relationship to classical epicists. As C. S. Lewis discerns, epic is concerned with the "enlargement" of its subject, and as Quint observes, the genre is "committed to imitating and attempting to 'overgo' its earlier versions."[10] I suggest that bodily motion is a valuable tool for marking how generic enlargement occurs in Milton's epics, as he reinvents epic matter for Protestant readers. With a muscle memory spanning centuries, some feet in *Paradise Lost* walk in the manner and gait of Achilles before them, and they too fall into ruts of self-deception and pride. However, other feet diverge from the classical track. By trailblazing new paths, their owners discover valuable Protestant truths about faith, the self, and obedience to God.

From Ilium to England: Walking in Literary and Historical Contexts

As Milton and other early modern epicists were aware, walking was a crucial image of ancient epic poetry, and it was closely allied to a hero's personality and fate.[11] In the *Iliad*, vitality is represented not through the body but, more specifically, through bodily motion.[12] Vitality is construed as μένος, which is a warrior's "might" or "force" manifested in quick motion on the battlefield.[13] Bodily postures are often used to designate a warrior's social status, and μακροβάμων (a man taking long strides), is a keyword signifying a great military leader.[14] During the duel between Paris and Menelaus, Paris ἐρχόμενον...μακρὰ βιβάντα (approaches...with long strides), in a false show of confidence.[15] Telamonian Ajax terrifies the Trojans by advancing upon them with μακρὰ βιβάς (long strides), and he later advances μακρὰ βιβάσθων (with long striding), when challenging Hector.[16] Similarly, when enraged at the death of Sarpedon, Glaucus rallies the Trojans for an assault upon the Greeks by μετὰ Τρῶας κίε μακρὰ βιβάσθων (coming amid the Trojans with long striding).[17] Throughout the *Iliad*, striding is an indication of a hero's martial valor, and it reinforces the Homeric notion that the self is constituted in the physical body.[18]

In the *Odyssey*, striding assumes new meaning, and Homer's later epic speaks to his first when revising this motif. Rather than broadcasting a hero's valor, the stride of a great man signals the heights from which he has fallen. In the underworld scene in the *Odyssey*, the ghost of Achilles tells Odysseus, βουλοίμην κ' ἐπάρουρος ἐὼν θητευέμεν ἄλλῳ, / ἀνδρὶ παρ' ἀκλήρῳ, ᾧ μὴ βίοτος πολὺς εἴη, / ἢ πᾶσιν νεκύεσσι καταφθιμένοισιν ἀνάσσειν (I would rather be upon the earth as a servant to another man — some tenant farmer with barely enough to survive — than be lord over all the wasted dead).[19] Achilles then departs μακρὰ βιβᾶσα κατ' ἀσφοδελὸν λειμῶνα (with long striding through the asphodel meadow).[20] Striding is now an ironic activity, since it marks Achilles's fall from a great warrior to an underworld shade. The *Odyssey* thus engages and deflates the significance attached to striding in the *Iliad*, and Achilles's sad steps in the second epic mock his heroic bounds in the first.

While Homer permits only the greatest heroes to stride on the battlefield, Virgil is even more restrictive, and Aeneas and Turnus are the sole striders in the *Aeneid*. Virgil reserves striding for their epic conflict. In book 12, Turnus moves "rapido cursu" (with rapid running), and he advances upon the Trojans "ac veluti montis saxum de vertice praeceps / cum ruit avulsum vento" (as when a boulder, wrenched free by the wind, falls headlong from a mountain summit).[21] Turnus and Aeneas engage in single combat "ac velut ingenti Sila summove Taburno / cum duo conversis inimica in proelia tauri / frontibus incurrunt" (as when on great Sila or highest Taburno, two bulls charge with foreheads bent down in hostile conflict).[22] When Turnus turns and flees, he is not alone: "Aeneas, quamquam tardata sagitta / interdum genua impediunt cursumque recusant, / insequitur trepidique pedem pede fervidus urget" (fiery Aeneas — although his knees, slowed by the arrow's wound, occasionally hamper him and refuse their course — pursues stride for stride and presses hard after the anxious one).[23] Aeneas's virtue as an epic hero is conveyed in his ability to race after his opponent, though gravely injured.

Virgil's improvement upon Homer complicates an existing moral dilemma in the unjust slaughter of Hector. By picturing Aeneas as wounded and striding, Virgil revisits the moment when Achilles chased Hector around the walls of Troy. Aeneas, Virgil suggests, channels both heroes. Like Hector, Aeneas suffers for his people, but like Achilles, he will succumb to "furiis accensus et ira / terribilis" when he plunges his sword into Turnus's heart.[24]

In addition to its literary importance, walking in Milton's own day was lauded as a salubrious pastime associated with gardening.[25] For instance, Stephen Blake, author of *The Compleat Gardeners Practice* (1664), praised the "pleasant walking" that might be had in a well-constructed garden. Drawing an analogy between physical and spiritual motion, he suggested that walking possessed soteriological value and could help a person "walketh in the way of peace."[26] Similarly, in his translation of Jean de la Quintinie's *The Compleat Gard'ner* (1693), John Evelyn wrote, "certainly nothing affords more Delight, first, than to have a *Garden* well seated, of a reasonable largeness, and fine Figure." Of primary importance is that the garden be "Neat, for Walking," which is beneficial for "the preservation of Health." Throughout the manual, Evelyn's foremost principle for organizing trees, bushes, and flowers is "the Beauty and Pleasure of the Walk."[27]

For those who could afford such luxury, walking in one's garden was a cherished pastime and an increasingly popular subject of discussion in Milton's England.

Early accounts of Milton's life record that walking was a major part of his daily routine. His eighteenth century biographer, John Richardson, noted that Milton's habit of walking went back to his youth, when the Lady of Christ's roamed the city streets and "Sometimes saw a Play, and visited Publick Walks."[28] The antiquarian John Aubrey, drawing on information from the poet's nephew, Edward Phillips, observed that Milton's "exercise was chiefly walking." "After dinner," Aubrey wrote, "he used to walke 3 or four houres at a time (he alwayes had a garden where he lived); [and then] went to bed about 9."[29] Milton also walked in less enjoyable ways, such as when being led by the hand of his nephew on the arduous trek to Whitehall, which Barbara Lewalski suggests was a humiliating affair for this "proud man."[30]

Several instances in *Paradise Lost* evoke the author's personal experience with walking and horticulture. For example, when Satan arrives in Eden and sees "goodliest Trees loaden with fairest Fruit" and feels the garden's "purer aire" and "gentle gales" (*PL* 4.147, 153, 156) on his face, we might imagine the blind Milton walking around his own garden, perhaps with daughter Deborah on his arm, touching the trees and enjoying the cool breeze. This personal and cultural context, as well as the epic tradition, supplied Milton with many reasons to ponder walking in relation to the self, as well as to consider the allegorical significance of its manifold forms. The literary tradition and the historical context offer us fresh routes into *Paradise Lost*, as we examine how Milton reinvents the epic motif of walking by aligning it with the Protestant virtues of obedience, humility, and trust.

"By steps we may ascend": Peripatetic Virtue in the Prelapsarian World

In *Paradise Lost*, the act of walking is central to prelapsarian activities and the acquisition of self-knowledge. Selves in Milton's epic are malleable, and Adam in particular is subjected to outward and inward sculpting by God, which Adam acknowledges when asking, "Did I request thee, Maker, from my Clay / To mould me Man[?]" (*PL* 10.743–44).[31] In book 5, Raphael tells him that if he and Eve are obedient, "Your bodies may at last turn all to Spirit, / Improv'd by tract of time, and wingd ascend / Ethereal, as wee" (5.497–99). Adam reiterates that information and states, "In contemplation of created things / By steps we may ascend to God" (5.511–12). Since he was "For contemplation...formd" (4.297), Adam's thoughts turn to the metaphorical steps of intellectual rigor necessary for his progression into a higher being.

However, Adam's claim that "By steps" he and Eve might advance is also a literal statement. Raphael has been careful to point out that Adam and Eve must first prove obedient by working the garden. Already keen to exercise his intellect, Adam puns on "steps." He signals his understanding that to be obedient, he and Eve must continue their walks around the garden as they tend to its flora and fauna. The "created things" they will contemplate refer dually to abstract consideration of God's creation and to the plants and animals they observe on their daily walks. Adam plans to obey by fulfilling the two tasks assigned to him: using his intellect and walking the garden with Eve.

Furthermore, Milton's animist materialism imbues walking in *Paradise Lost* with far greater significance than mere obedience. Denying the Cartesian division of the self, Milton envisions body and soul as two points along the same spectrum of matter existing *ex Deo*, as an emanation of God. Accordingly, as Raphael explains in *Paradise Lost*, "body [will] up to spirit work" and Adam and Eve's bodies "may at last turn all to Spirit...and wingd ascend" (5.478) like the angels. For Milton, knowledge of the body was also knowledge of the soul. For Adam and Eve, knowledge of how to exercise their muscles is also knowledge about themselves. Since Adam and (by extension) Eve came from their "Native Soile" (11.270), they bear an intimate connection with the earth as their progenitor. That connection is established through their feet and maintained in their routine of walking the paths of Eden.

Adam's knowledge of what we might call peripatetic virtue comes from Raphael, but Eve's arrives through a much more sinister source. Satan, "Squat like a Toad, close at the eare of *Eve*" (4.800), fills her mind with a fantasy of flying—a glorious vision of corporeal and intellectual ascension.[32] In book 5, Eve explains her dream to Adam, wherein a divine creature exhorts her to taste the fruit, forsake walking, and fly:

> Taste this, and be henceforth among the Gods
> Thy self a Goddess, not to Earth confind,
> But sometimes in the Air, as wee, sometimes
> Ascend to Heav'n, by merit thine, and see
> What life the Gods live there, and such live thou.
> ⋯⋯⋯
> Forthwith up to the Clouds
> With him I flew, and underneath beheld
> The Earth outstretcht immense, a prospect wide
> And various: wondring at my flight and change
> To this high exaltation.   (*PL* 5.77–81, 86–90)

Eve faces the temptation that, as the queen of creation, she should fly rather than walk, when in fact walking is essential to her identity as a gardener.[33] By discriminating between these types of bodily motion, Eve learns a crucial truth about herself. She now knows that she is capable of altering her state; she can reinvent herself, if she chooses. Just as she now knows that there is an alternative to walking—flying—so too does Eve learn the difference between actuality and potentiality, the self as it is and the self as it might be.

Eve's satanically inspired knowledge of bodily motion invites a new interpretation of her need for separation preceding the Fall. In book 9, Eve proposes to Adam that they "divide [their] labours" (*PL* 9.214) and work apart. Recognizing that walking should be a social activity and that "by steps *we* may ascend to God" (emphasis mine), Adam desires to work the garden with Eve. "These paths & Bowers," he tells her, "doubt not but our joynt hands / Will keep from Wilderness with ease, as wide / As we need walk" (9.244–46). However, Eve is not content with Adam's assurance that Eden's paths will stay as wide as need be. Mindful of her dream and the guilt she felt when flying, she would make the paths of Eden wider and wider. As if fearful of leaving those paths and anxious to cement her connection with her "Native Soile," she wants to "Lop...or prune, or prop, or bind" all the "wanton growth" (9.210, 211) that impedes the movement of her legs and feet. Intent on improving her walks, Eve unknowingly sets herself up for the temptation she wanted to avoid: that she can improve herself apart from God, and that she can fly and not walk.

Later in book 9, Eve shares this sin with Adam, who likewise imagines himself capable of a bodily motion superior to walking. When Adam and Eve eat the fruit, they "fansie that they feel / Divinitie within them breeding wings / Wherewith to scorne the Earth" (9.1009–11). Adam's original understanding of the self in motion came from Raphael and centered on obedience. After eating the fruit, however, his knowledge of himself changes. Imagining himself with the wings of an angel, he begins to share Eve's satanically inspired understanding of the self as being able to improve its status apart from God.

Holy Trailblazing: The Expulsion as Migration

Walking also plays a primary role in the discovery of self-knowledge in the Fall's aftermath, when Adam and Eve consider how their daily activity of roaming the garden will change. In response to Adam's deep thoughts of judgment and death, Eve beckons him to work the field with her and resume their "pleasant Walkes." Hopeful that the consequences of the Fall can be mitigated, Eve encourages Adam to resume where they left off. Eve bears a more intimate connection with the geography of Eden than her spouse, and she assumes that walking the garden will continue to be enjoyable and free of the Fall's effects.[34] In a moment of wishful (or desperate) optimism, she imagines that peripatetic motion will serve as a bridge back to the prelapsarian world and self. But before Adam and Eve have a chance to test this theory, Michael descends to deliver the final sentence of expulsion from the garden.

Adam and Eve express their understanding of the Expulsion as a loss of bodily movement, as well as of place.[35] They are now denied the ability to walk where and when they did before. Eve laments the "unexpected stroke, worse then of Death!" wherein she must leave "these happie Walks and Shades" (*PL* 11.268, 270), now that she can no longer walk on her native soil. Adam, too, is concerned with how exile will change the way he walks. Contemplating this new concept of expulsion, he asks Michael,

> In yonder nether World where shall I seek
> His bright appearances, or footstep trace?
> For though I fled him angrie, yet recall'd
> To life prolongd and promisd Race, I now
> Gladly behold though but his utmost skirts
> Of glory, and farr off his steps adore.   (11.328–33)

The passage indicates that Adam understands walking differently from Eve, and that before the Fall he performed a special type of walking reserved for him alone.[36] For Adam, walking was sequence and *sequor*—a literal following in the "track Divine" (11.354) of his Maker. In the sense Milton uses here, tracing signifies the activity of "follow[ing] the footprints" of another, as the *Oxford English Dictionary* (*OED*) notes.[37] Tracing the tracks of where the Father "walk[ed] in the Garden" (*PL* 10.98), Adam literally roamed the paths of divinity. This physical activity was an intimate affair between himself and his creator, and it mirrored his inward devotion to God.

Adam defines his relationship to God through walking, and after the Fall he learns the meaning of fallenness through restrictions upon his feet. As he listens to Michael, Adam comes to realize that just as he can no longer walk in the Father's track, so he is no longer in the Father's presence but somewhere outside of it. In Milton's epic, access to knowledge about the self depends in an Augustinian manner upon one's proximity to God and, consequently, one's knowledge of God.[38] At Michael's declaration of expulsion, this knowledge is conveyed through geographic limitations imposed upon peripatetic motion. Adam now knows the distance between himself and God through his corresponding distance from the paths of God.

Walking allows Adam to understand his new proximity to God, and it also allows Eve to learn about her new proximity to Adam. "Thou to mee," she says at the Expulsion, "Art all things under Heav'n, all places thou" (*PL* 12.617–18). She exhorts Adam to "lead on," and she claims that "In mee is no delay; with thee to goe, / Is to stay here" (12.614–16). Before the Fall, Eve was keen to go her own way, but now she understands that walking is a social activity. She learns that her rightful place is by Adam's side and that she can obey God by walking with Adam and following in his track.

The sentence of expulsion is softened by Michael's account of sacred history, which introduces Adam and Eve to a new kind of social walking: migration. Books 11 and 12 of *Paradise Lost* present a series of relocation narratives, as godly individuals obey the Holy Spirit, uproot their homes, and settle in new lands. Michael identifies three purposes of migration, and the knowledge of those purposes allows Adam to understand his own predicament. The first narrative celebrates Noah's righteousness as a man who — like Adam — will forsake all he knows and voyage into a treacherous world. Through the story of the ark, Adam comes to see migration as salvific. Migration is a divine device for bypassing apocalypse and preserving those whom God loves. In addition, Michael tells Adam that Noah's story is "To teach thee that God attributes to place / No sanctitie" (11.836–37). Adam learns that Eden was special not because of any intrinsic value but because God walked with him there — and if there, then anywhere.

Additionally, Michael's narrative of Abraham shows that migration is essential to godly nation-building. Michael explains that Abraham will leave "his Gods, his Friends, and native Soile / Ur of Chaldæa...trusting all his wealth / With God, who call'd him, in a land unknown" (*PL* 12.129–30, 133–34). The phrase "native Soile" would have resonated with Adam since it suggests a parallel between Abraham's abandonment of Ur and Adam's departure from Eden. Michael is careful to emphasize that in his migration, Abraham will not wander aimlessly but will be "call[ed] by Vision...into a Land / Which [God] will shew him" (12.121–23). Abraham's obedience to God in relocating will engender Israel, and the chosen nation will demonstrate its obedience through peripatetic motion.

In Michael's narrative of the Israelite exodus from Egypt, Adam learns that migration is the means by which God tests the faithful. Moses and Aaron, Michael discloses, will be selected by God "to claim / His people from enthralment" and bring them into Canaan (12.170–71). Guided by a column of cloud by day and a pillar of fire at night, the Hebrews will move out of an alien country and into "the Land / Promisd to *Abraham* and his Seed" (12.259–60). By means of this third narrative, Adam now knows that migration is God's instrument for testing the faithful throughout the generations.

As a result of Michael's narratives, Adam interprets the Expulsion not as an exile but as a holy migration that will prepare the way for subsequent holy migrations. Additionally, Adam discerns that though they are forbidden to walk in Eden, he and Eve can continue to walk in a godly manner, both literally and metaphorically. Their expulsion need not be a wayward wandering, as Cain's will be. Adam declares that he and Eve can "love with feare the onely God, [and] walk / As in his presence" (12.562–63). Though the physical paths of God have become taboo, they can obey by walking *as if* in those paths.

Consequently, expulsion is a punishment Adam and Eve must endure, but submission to this new restriction upon their feet is their first step toward redemption. After the Fall, as before, their obedience assumes a peripatetic form, and Adam and Eve "hand in hand with wandring steps and slow, / Through *Eden* took thir solitarie way" (12.648–49). Their first act of obedience was to walk the garden and tend to its plants and animals, and their last act of obedience is also to walk as God commands. Though they have lost the place where God walked with them in the cool of the day, they have not lost their peripatetic relationship with God. As a result, Adam and Eve walk out of Eden confident that their expulsion is a holy migration and that they can still follow the divine track, even though they can no longer see it.

"These our motions vain": Satan's Epic Strides and Infernal Stumbles

Eden affords Milton an opportunity to theorize what obedience looks like when it takes on flesh, and heaven and hell serve as sites for investigating walking in relation to the sin of pride. In a creative revision of the classical motif, the greatest heroes in *Paradise Lost* do not stride. The Son, Michael, Abdiel, and Adam and Eve are only ever stepping, walking, or tracing — but never striding. Milton is careful to point out that, by contrast, Satan strides after he is inwardly fallen, and that Death moves with "horrid strides" (*PL* 2.676) when challenging his father at hell's gates. In *Paradise Lost*, Milton transforms battlefield striding into an activity reserved for sinful creatures.[39] This has major implications for our understanding of one of the most memorable conflicts in the epic, when Abdiel halts Satan's stride and — like David subduing Goliath — drives the archangel to his knees.

At the beginning of the war in heaven, Satan appears on the battlefield with the equipage and gait of a Homeric hero, and his arrogant swagger infuriates Abdiel. At the vanguard of his army, prissed up like an "Idol of Majesty Divine" (6.101), Satan approaches the celestial city:

> *Satan* with vast and haughtie strides advanc't,
> Came towring, armd in Adamant and Gold;
> *Abdiel* that sight endur'd not, where he stood
> Among the mightiest, bent on highest deeds,
> And thus his own undaunted heart explores.
>   O Heav'n! that such resemblance of the Highest
> Should yet remain, where faith and realtie
> Remain not; wherefore should not strength and might
> There fail where Vertue fails, or weakest prove
> Where boldest; though to sight unconquerable?
> His puissance, trusting in th' Almightie's aid,
> I mean to try.   (6.109–20)

In this moment of epic revision, Milton engages Homer and repurposes peripatetic motion to reflect Protestant values. Satan strides with all the pride and vigor of Achilles, but Abdiel humbly "step[s]"

(6.128) from amid the heavenly ranks. Addressing Satan, "Proud, art thou met?" (6.131), Abdiel delivers a stroke on the archangel's helm that forces Satan to his knees and curbs his prideful progress: "ten paces huge / He back recoild; the tenth on bended knee / His massie Spear upstaid" (6.193–95). Abdiel is mindful of a truth the archangel has forgotten: any strength they have is not their "own but giv'n" (4.1007), as Gabriel will later remind Satan.

The difference between Abdiel's steps and Satan's strides is the difference between obedience and disobedience. Lauded in classical epic, striding in Milton's Protestant epic is an outward and visible sign of an inward corruption. Satan does not learn from his encounter with Abdiel but continues to adopt diabolic motions that perpetuate his desperate attempts at grandeur. When Satan is apprehended in Eden, Gabriel recognizes him by his proud "gate" (4.870), reminiscent of the "vast and haughtie strides" he saw on the heavenly battlefield. Though he is fallen physically and inwardly, Satan persists in a type of movement that he believes befits his high station. In actuality, Satan's strides render him all the more ridiculous. Like Achilles's strides through the asphodel fields of the underworld, Satan's strides in hell magnify the great heights from which he has fallen.

When Satan falls to hell, Milton sustains the connection between peripatetic motion and a character's capacity for self-knowledge. Repulsed at his prostrate position on the burning lake, Satan's first action is to pull himself upright and exchange the turbid surface of the waves for what he hopes will be rest on solid ground. As a celestial being who has only known heaven's fields and streets, Satan is surprised to find that hell's terrain causes him discomfort. Breaking his chains and fanning his wings, he rises from the lake

> till on dry Land
> He lights, if it were Land that ever burn'd
> With solid, as the Lake with liquid fire;
> And such appear'd in hue, as when the force
> Of subterranean wind transports a Hill
> Torn from *Pelorus*, or the shatter'd side
> Of thund'ring *Ætna*, whose combustible

> And fewel'd entrals thence conceiving Fire,
> Sublim'd with Mineral fury, aid the Winds,
> And leave a singed bottom all involv'd
> With stench and smoak: Such resting found the sole
> Of unblest feet. (1.227–38)

Satan discovers that unlike his pleasant walks in heaven, walks in hell are injurious. Shortly thereafter, he declares, "long is the way / And hard, that out of Hell leads up to light" (2.432–33). Metaphorically, their way out of hell is paved with difficulties, but Satan also acknowledges that, quite literally, the ground of hell is hard on the angels' feet. Satan's encounter with hell's terrain is the first moment in *Paradise Lost* when self-knowledge might be attained. Treading on the sulphurous ground, Satan has an opportunity to realize the extent of his fall. However, his pride gets in the way, and he glories instead in having defied divine mandate. By rising and walking, he commits an upright motion — now prohibited — reminiscent of his celestial motions in heaven. Though the terrain of this new abode is rough, he reasons that only beings still divine in nature would experience such discomfort in hell.

Similar to Adam and Eve in the garden, the fallen angels learn about their new lodgings through their feet. Having alighted on the hard ground of hell, Satan asks, "Is this the Region, this the Soil, the Clime…that we must change for Heav'n[?]" (*PL* 1.242, 244). The same massive spear that once threatened Michael now serves as a cane to "support uneasie steps / Over the burning Marle, not like those steps / On Heavens Azure" (1.295–97). When Satan summons his troops, the fallen angels move with "painful steps o're the burnt soyle" (1.562). By imitating Satan's own motions when he scrambled across the hellish landscape, the angels perpetuate the lie that though physically fallen, they are unfallen mentally.

Belial, in particular, exemplifies the angels' refusal to learn from their limbs and see themselves for the fallen creatures they are. During the diabolic congress of book 2, he disputes Moloch's claim that the angels can only continue to rise, since ascent is the fit motion for divine beings. "In our proper motion we ascend / Up to our native seat," Moloch says, "descent and fall / To us is adverse," to which Belial responds, "[God] from heav'ns highth / All these our motions vain, sees and derides" (2.75–77, 190–91). Ever the clever one, Belial puns on "motions." He suggests that God sees both their motions of revenge as well as their illegal motions in rising from the lake. The progress of their bodies — like the progress of their plans — is vain in the sense that it is "idle" and an indulgence in "personal vanity," as the *OED* notes.[40] When refuting Moloch's plan of ascension, Belial explains that the angels have already adopted a new type of forbidden movement. By breaking their chains, walking, and gathering in illegal convocation, the angels have assumed diabolic motions that will undoubtedly attract God's attention.

Belial's recognition that the angels' *transgressus* is also their transgression leads to further self-deception. Nervous about the diabolic motions they have performed, Belial's plan is for the angels to cease moving altogether. Rather than ascending, as Moloch proposes, they should continue "sitting" (*PL* 2.164) in hell and do nothing. By refusing to move, they can wait out God's fury and hope that the Father will in time forget about them. Belial's greatest fear is annihilation, which he describes as being "swallowd up and lost / In the wide womb of uncreated night, / Devoid of sense and motion" (2.149–51). Rather than risk vitality any further, Belial would cease all movements, diabolical or otherwise, with the hope that the angels might find salvation in stasis. But sitting does not help Belial any more than striding helps Satan, and both postures serve only to perpetuate the angels' illusion that they can recover from their fall and move as they once did in heaven.

Bestial Motion and Self-Deception in Eden

The relationship between walking and self-knowledge is also central to Satan's arrival in Eden and his activities there before the Fall. After Satan passes through the cosmos, it is with "willing feet / On the bare outside of this World" (*PL* 3.73–74) that he first contaminates the earth, much like a Spanish conquistador stepping foot on the

New World.[41] His first act is exploration, and upon arriving in Eden, he exclaims, "But first with narrow search I must walk round / This Garden, and no corner leave unspi'd" (4.528–29). Satan seeks to learn about Eden by perambulating it, and he assumes that the paths Adam and Eve walk can lead him to knowledge, as well. In book 9, Satan views Eden through the serpent's eyes and exclaims,

> O Earth, how like to Heav'n, if not preferr'd
> More justly, Seat worthier of Gods, as built
> With second thoughts, reforming what was old!
> For what God after better worse would build?
> ....
> With what delight could I have walkt thee round,
> If I could joy in aught, sweet interchange
> Of Hill, and Vallie, Rivers, Woods and Plaines,
> Now Land, now Sea, and Shores with Forrest crownd,
> Rocks, Dens, and Caves; but I in none of these
> Find place or refuge.   (PL 9.99–102, 114–19)

Satan imagines his experience in the garden as a delightful promenade, wherein he interacts with this new world by means of walking. However, as Satan is painfully aware, he is unable to walk. Having committed himself to a "foul descent" (9.163) into the serpent, he has forsaken the upright motion proper to angels and humans and condescended to the gait of an animal. Satan moves "on his reare, / Circular base of rising foulds, that tour'd / Fould above fould a surging Maze" (9.497–99). As he "rowl[s] / In tangles" (9.631–32), his bodily contortions mirror his mental convolutions. Refusing to walk, and choosing instead to roll, Satan cuts himself off from self-knowledge and experiences "a failure of the intellect to comprehend its situation," as Anthony Low puts it.[42] Satan deceives himself by believing that he has been "constraind" (9.164) to enter the snake, but in truth he has chosen to adopt a bestial motion.

While peripatetic motion grants Adam and Eve increased self-knowledge, bestial motion perpetuates Satan's personal illusions. It furthers his self-induced victimization and reinforces the lie that he is not responsible for his actions. "With what delight could I have walkt thee round," Satan tells the earth, had he not been constrained to animal motion; "with what delight," he whines, had not God elevated the Son to bring about Lucifer's fall. Bestial motion feeds Satan's insatiable sense of self-pity. As he bemoans his foul incarnation and inability to walk, bestial motion shields Satan from the uncomfortable truth that he alone is responsible for his fallen condition.

When Satan tempts Eve, his strategy is to offer her an opportunity to walk as she has never done before. As we have seen, the practice of tracing God's paths is an activity reserved for Adam. Only Adam — not Eve — traces God's footsteps and the track divine. Yet when Satan leads Eve to the tree, he lies and claims that its fruit enabled him to "trace the wayes / Of highest Agents" (9.682–83) — that is, of celestial creatures. Suddenly, Eve is given an opportunity to trace the footsteps of a higher being, as Adam does.

Satan's temptation also suggests that tracing celestial beings might reveal those beings to Eve. Throughout Milton's epic, theophany — like tracing — is a gendered and unequal experience. Raphael is commanded to "Converse with *Adam*"; the Son descends and asks, "Where art thou *Adam* ... I miss thee here"?; and Michael is instructed to "reveale / To *Adam* what shall come in future dayes" (*PL* 5.230, 10.103–04, 11.113–14). Theophany is reserved for Adam and imparts knowledge to him specifically. Satan has already planted a desire for theophany within Eve, when she dreams that "one shap'd and wing'd like one of those from Heav'n" (5.55) appears to her, and not to Adam. Here in book 9, Eve is tempted to believe that the dream has come true. A special messenger — a brute capable of elocution — has at long last appeared to her rather than to Adam. Disappointingly, it is a reptile instead of an archangel. Nonetheless, it offers her a unique chance to do something only Adam can do: trace divine footsteps and thereby imitate the celestial motions of the gods.

The temptation of tracing is part of why Eve reaches for the forbidden fruit, and she disobeys God by performing an illegal motion. The serpent suggests that in order to commune with celestial beings, Eve must continue to move her body in ways that are against God's law. Tracing divine steps is not permitted to Eve, but rumination on this unlawful type of walking encourages her to go one step further, so to speak, and spawns a chain reaction of illegal motions. One sinful motion leads to another, and in quick succession, Eve reaches for the fruit, plucks it, and eats it (*PL* 11.781). In *Paradise Lost*, sin engenders sin, and bodily motion registers Eve's progression into worsening states of fallenness.

Satan's Track and the False Conquest of Sin and Death

Tracing is fundamental to the way Adam relates to God and Eve to Adam, and it is also integral to the relationship between Satan, Sin, and Death. After Satan passes through hell's gates, Sin and Death manufacture a bridge to Earth:

> *Sin* and *Death* amain
> Following his track, such was the will of Heav'n,
> Pav'd after him a broad and beat'n way
> Over the dark Abyss, whose boiling Gulf
> Tamely endur'd a Bridge of wondrous length
> From Hell continu'd reaching th' utmost Orbe
> Of this frail World.   (*PL* 2.1024–30)

The bridge they construct is a parody of the scriptural "narrow gate" and "straight way" that lead to life.[43] Only the faithful traverse the narrow gate and straight way, but the bridge created by Sin and Death is broad enough to carry all manner of people into wickedness. In book 10, it is described as "a passage broad, / Smooth, easie, inoffensive down to Hell" and a means to "easie thorough-fare" across the cosmic abyss (10.304–05, 393). In contrast with Adam's singular activity of tracing God, diabolic motion is an activity undertaken by many. The ramifications of that motion are no less than a bright world consumed by sin, a steady flow of souls to hell, and Satan's reign until Christ's victory on the cross.

In a parody of Adam tracing God's footsteps, Sin and Death follow in the track of their own father and deity, Satan. Their bridge from hell to earth is "a path / Over this Maine from Hell" that follows in the "track / Of *Satan*" (10.256–57, 314–15). When Satan returns from earth and greets his daughter, he is delighted at what they have constructed. Sin tells him, "Hell could no longer hold us in her bounds, / Nor this unvoyageable Gulf obscure / Detain from following thy illustrious track" (10.365–67). The bridge pleases Satan because it reinforces his delusion of divinity, since like the Father he now has followers of his own to trace his tracks.

In a diabolic imitation of the Great Commission, Satan commends Sin and Death to dwell and reign on earth. Sin and Death will indeed rule, but their ease in crossing this causeway deceives them into thinking that their reign will be unending. But Sin and Death are only temporary conquerors. They are ignorant of a truth Michael will soon share with Adam, which is that Christ will one day defeat them.[44] Unlike the migration of Adam and Eve out of Eden, which leads to Christ and thus to humanity's salvation, the "transmigration" (10.261) of Sin and Death is a journey toward their demise. Unbeknownst to them, a second Adam will one day reverse the effects of their diabolic motion. At the harrowing of hell, Christ will reclaim the causeway and liberate the captives who follow in his track.

When Satan returns to hell, he spreads his delight in diabolic motion to the other fallen angels. He brags, "By *Sin* and *Death* a broad way now is pav'd / To expedite your glorious march" (10.473–74), and his pride is evident even at the etymological level. The word "expedite" derives from the Latin *expedio, -ire*, meaning "to free the feet" as if from a snare.[45] Satan gloats that, in fact, two great things have been accomplished: a bridge has been built that will free the fallen angels, and the way has been cleared for their feet in anticipation of that infernal exodus. His hope is that like Sin and Death, the angels will engage in illegal tracing and follow his track to earth.

Satan's surprise at the angels' subsequent transformation into serpents is a result of the self-deceptions generated by diabolic motion. At the end of his proud speech, Satan is caught off guard by the hissing that greets him, at which he "wonderd, but not long / Had leasure, wondring at himself now more" (10.509–10). The angels "thick swarm[ed]" as vermin, "rould in heaps," and fell "down" (10.522,

558, 542). Satan realizes that instead of mobilizing the fallen, he has wrought their humiliating immobilization. When he adopted the animal movements of the snake in the garden, Satan assumed it was only a temporary sacrifice. Now, he realizes that bestial motion never left him; rather, it has spread to others. In his attempt to move in ways of his own devising, Satan has inadvertently cut himself off from celestial motions and ensured the continued debasement of himself and his followers.

Conclusion: Motion and Epic Revisionism

In conclusion, I would like to propose that bodily motion is a valuable guide for navigating Milton's epic revisionism, as we trace the signs of his engagement with his classical predecessors. Like Homer and Virgil, Milton participates in a generic inquiry into the physicality of heroic virtue and how the self is found in muscle, sinew, and bone. When Priam comes before Achilles, he demonstrates his vast love for Hector not through pleading but through the unthinkable gesture of genuflection. Similarly, Aeneas proves the extraordinary lengths of his devotion by pursuing Turnus stride for stride — despite his shaky legs — until the threat to Rome's future is extinguished. In Milton's epic, Adam and Eve practice obedience through the simple and humble act of walking. Their muscles are a source of self-knowledge, and Adam and Eve learn about themselves before and after the Fall by moving their bodies in ways that are pleasing to God.

For Milton and the epic tradition, it is bodily motions that matter, and not simply the body alone. In this regard, this essay offers us a new method for examining early modern notions of the body through the perspective of motion. Miltonic heroes move and thereby have their being, and in *Paradise Lost*, motion is fundamental to the operations and articulations of the self. The Old Testament was one source for Milton's fascination with physicality, but Homer was another, and pre-Socratic Greek literature provided Milton with an important conceptual framework for exploring the physical embeddedness of the self. The Homeric epics conceive of death as the absence of bodily animation, and the ghost of Achilles significantly describes the dead to Odysseus as νεκύεσσι, or "corpses," because for him a body without motion is not a self—it is nothing. Rather, the self is the body in motion. Thus it is better to slave one's life away toiling at the earth with sweating and aching limbs than to lie motionless within it.

However, Milton deviates from classical epic by putting the generic conversation on motion into dialogue with the Reformation and Protestant values. In *Paradise Lost*, Milton reinvents the classical formula that casts walking as a reflection of masculine virtue. In classical epic, the stride of Achilles, Ajax, Aeneas, and Turnus is that person's glory and a sign of his martial prowess. By contrast, in Milton's epic, the only two characters who stride are Satan and Death. Significantly, their striding—and *all* striding in the poem—is sinful and vainglorious. In his re-creation of this epic motif, Milton relocates peripatetic virtue in the humble and quiet walking of Adam and Eve, as they tend the flowers and talk with God in the cool of the day. For the epic heroes of *Paradise Lost*, walking is a God-given tool for demonstrating humility, obedience, and trust. It is the means by which Adam and Eve gain knowledge about themselves before the Fall and afterward, as they walk together, apart from one another, and in God's presence and out of it.

Walking in Milton's epic thus encourages us to interpret the Expulsion from Eden as a triumph, not a defeat. Adam and Eve now know through hard trial that it is better to submit to divine will than to oppose it. Walking, they learn, can bring a certain measure of joy to fallen people in a fallen world. As Michael explains, their obedient departure from Eden marks the beginning of a series of holy migrations to come. The faithful few in subsequent generations—Noah, Abraham, and Moses—will hearken to the guidance of the Holy Spirit and relocate to places of God's choosing. In doing so, they will anticipate the singular virtue of the messiah, the "second *Adam*" (*PL* 11.383), and pave the way for the most important walk in history: the slow march of Christ through Golgotha to the hill of his crucifixion.

CHAPTER 4

Radical Relations

The Genealogical Imaginary and Queer Kinship in Milton's Paradise Regained

ERIN MURPHY

The year that Charles II was born, William Slatyer published a new royal genealogy. The 1630 *Genethliacon* traced Charles's lineage back through Christ to Adam and Eve to God, describing Adam as a monarch, "in his time the great Lord and King of the world."[1] Slatyer's dedicatory poem to King Charles follows another to King James, indicating that the author had begun working on the genealogy before 1625.[2] The decision to publish it in 1630, however, suggests Slatyer's attempt to mark the birth of the new heir by celebrating his divine lineage.[3] Slatyer, who had served as chaplin to Anne of Denmark, would have known James's subtle work to connect Christic genealogy with royal lineage. His publication of a text explicitly synthesizing the two endorsed and exalted the divinity of Stuart genealogy, reinforcing the monarchic authority of their line just as Charles I became the father of Charles II.

Or so it seems. Despite the text's endorsement of the lineal right of Charles and his offspring, Slatyer's dedicatory epistle belies the power of his biblical genealogy to distinguish royalty since all people are descended from "one and the same our first parent," concluding that his text may be used by those well beyond the Stuarts to "find and shew themselves" in the same chain as Adam and Christ.[4] Slatyer's text represents the paradoxical nature of genealogy as particularizing and universalizing, hierarchicalizing and leveling, and stabilizing and destabilizing that played out across the seventeenth century. This essay reads Milton's *Paradise Regained* as participating in this seventeenth century politics of biblical genealogy, and argues that the poem's radical representation of kinship continues to resonate with debates about the embodied politics of the genealogical imagination today.

The paradoxes of Slatyer's project help us to place Milton's work in a longer story. As Elizabeth Povinelli explains, "The genealogical imaginary did not die when the sovereign's head tumbled. Nor was it replaced by intimacy as a new form of association and attachment. Something more — and less — interesting is happening."[5] Povinelli describes the democratizing of genealogy but cautions that this shift does not reduce the normative influence of reproductive thinking: "Polity no longer unfolded...from the point of view of the sovereign family. But now everyone could have a little heritage of his or her own — diagrammed as a personal tree — a stake in some plot that tracked generationally. And, remember, though a petite cosmology, the genealogical grid now organizes democratic state dispensations like inheritance, marriage, child welfare, and capital gains."[6] Here, the dark side of Slatyer's happy promise that all English people can share in the fruits of his genealogical labor because they come from "one and the same our first parent," a claim echoed in Satan's insistence in *Paradise Regained* that "all men are Sons of God," begins to surface. A democratizing of genealogy can challenge monarchic claims of authority, but it also opens up additional avenues for scrutiny enabling new modes of state power.

Just months before Slatyer's genealogy appeared, as the nation anxiously awaited the birth of an heir, Milton wrote "On the Morning of Christ's Nativity," a poem full of anticipation that famously refuses the sense of Christ's birth as a moment of fulfillment: "But wisest fate says no / This must not yet be so."[7] Of course, unlike Slatyer, the poem makes no explicit connection between the birth of Christ and the birth of royal heirs. By representing the attempt to properly understand the meaning of Christ's birth as a struggle to establish temporal perspective, however, the poem already contains a critique of the reproductive futurity that underwrites the Stuart project, a critique Milton develops in his antimonarchic tracts. If even the birth of Christ cannot be understood as divine fulfillment, attempts like Slatyer's to infuse the royal birth with divinity begin to lose their force.[8]

At the end of Milton's career, as Prince Charles now sat on the throne as Charles II, his *Paradise Regained* offers yet another representation of the coming of the Son of God, sounding its own "not yet" (3.397) as it unsettles any sense that such an event can be represented or comprehended fully. As Jonathan Goldberg writes, both the Nativity ode and *Paradise Regained* "witness a beginning, an opening they do not seek to close, an opening that cannot be closed. The temporality in these poems — "not yet" — renders singular identification impossible."[9] Though many critics have argued the political stakes of *Paradise Regained* involve a critique of Charles II, the epistemological challenge posed by the poem still calls for a fuller understanding of its engagement with the Stuart ideology of hereditary monarchy.[10] In other words, the poem is not only an exploration of the meaning of kingship or sonship but an examination of the intersection of the two. Though the poem's narrative draws most heavily on Matthew and Luke, it strikingly omits a key element of these Gospels' exploration of the Son — the Christic genealogies. While some seventeenth century commentators struggled to "harmonize" the seemingly disparate genealogies, *Paradise Regained* brings the two Gospels together by consistently erasing or at least downplaying these genealogical ties.

Genealogical thinking provides a key epistemological lens for the ways in which identity and temporality grounded monarchic authority in the period. Here, I reconsider how *Paradise Regained*'s engagement with *the* Son challenges both the Stuart genealogical project and, implicitly, the reproductive futurism of the postdynastic state that would replace it. The poem's exploration of the instability of identity and temporality contests the logic of hereditary monarchy.[11]

The opaque return to the mother at the end of the poem leaves open the question of how this radical reimagining of family will inform the politics to come, a question connected to the way in which this text explores shifting ideas about reproduction and political power. Thus, *Paradise Regained* revisits issues of birth and temporality explored in the Nativity ode but now focuses on kinship as a structure of knowledge capable of anchoring political authority. By exploring how the poem wrests the meaning of Christ's kinship explicitly from Satan and implicitly from the Stuarts, I hope to begin showing how its vision of family relations not only establishes the humanity of Jesus but also in turn helps define a conception of the human that undergirds the postdynastic contractual citizen.[12] Continually resisting Satan's claim that "relation stands," the poem's representation of the Son's family connections resonates with Judith Butler's call for a transformative understanding of kinship as "a kind of doing…an enacted practice" rather than a "hypostatized structure of relations."[13] As such, Milton's depiction of Jesus's kinship might be understood as not just antimonarchic but potentially queer. I choose the anachronistic term "queer" to register the poem's radical representation of kinship because I believe it helps us to see a kind of antinormative possibility in this inchoate moment in the history of the genealogical imaginary. In *Paradise Regained*, Milton's resistance to the reproductive structures underlying lineal monarchy lead him to refuse not just hereditary kingship but, at least temporarily, the normative demands of a kinship that must always speak its name.

Biblical Genealogy and the Stuart Project

If one of the central questions of *Paradise Regained* is what the meaning of "son" is, it was a question that had echoed across the political landscape of Milton's entire life.[14] James I famously put questions of what a son was and should be at the center of Stuart ideology with *Basilicon doron*, written for his presumed heir, Prince Henry.[15] It was his later tract dedicated to the eventual Charles I, however, that explicitly connected monarchic lineage to that of Christ himself. James's 1620 *A Meditation upon the 27.28.29 Verses of the XXVII. Chapter of Saint Matthew*, his advice book for Prince Charles, deploys the typology of kingship by describing Christ's "inauguration" as "*a good paterne to put inheritors to kingdomes in minde of their calling, by the forme of their inauguration.*"[16] James describes the coronation of Jesus as "King of the Jews" at the Crucifixion as doubly ironic, hence literal, arguing that the mocking declaration of Christ's kingship reveals divine intent despite its speakers' intent. Though James does not describe the Stuarts as direct heirs of Christ, he draws a parallel between his own relationship to Prince Charles and God's relationship to Jesus, infusing hereditary monarchy with divinity: "*And as to the subiect, whom can a paterne for a Kings Inauguration so well fit as a Kings sonne and heire, beeing written by the King his Father, and the paterne taken from the King of all Kings?*"[17] James both emphasizes the lineal connection between his son and himself, and insists that Christ's descent demonstrates God's support of monarchy. While *Basilicon doron* had previously urged Prince Henry to ignore "foolish curiosities upon genealogies," this text takes a much more reverential view, noting that the title "King of the Jewes" is "so carefully set doune in the genealogie of Christ, written by two Evangelists."[18] Using the case of Christ to define the proper ascent of kings, he argues, "it was necessary that *Christ* in the time of his passion should approue himselfe to bee lineally descended from *Dauid*, yea euen next heire to the croune of the *Iewes*."[19]

Eminently savvy, James tries to avoid the dangers of genealogy, even as he invokes its importance in the Gospels to bolster the dynastic claims of his son. First, characteristically wary of genetic claims, James does not go as far as Slatyer, who will detail the Stuarts' descent from Adam through David and Jesus.[20] In this, he recognizes that, despite its authorizing force, genealogy also opens up the king's legitimacy to scrutiny. Second, he attempts to ward off the perils of the forward thrust of lineal inheritance, warning Prince Charles not to follow the example of Henry V, who tried to seize his father's crown before confirming the king's death. Though the succession of an heir promised political stability, that promise could transform into a disruptive threat if it directed too much attention to the future.

One of James's strategies for mobilizing the benefits of hereditary authority without being trapped by its more inconvenient vicissitudes was to support the genealogical writings of others. By granting John Speed the license to produce the biblical genealogies for the Authorized Version of the Bible in 1610, the King endorsed an author whose genealogical texts strove to verify both theological and political authority, strengthening James's attempts to intertwine the two. Unlike Slatyer's *Genethliacon*, Speed's elaborate biblical arbors tracing Christ's descent from Adam and Eve did not continue through to James I. The political stakes of Speed's genealogical work are clear, however, in his 1611 *The History of Britain*, which details the story of the kings of England and specifically defends James I's lineal right to rule against claims by the Jesuit Robert Parsons.[21] James rewarded and perpetuated Speed's support for the Stuarts by renewing his license for the biblical genealogies in 1620, the same year that the king published his meditation on Matthew emphasizing Christ's Davidic lineage.

Speed began his genealogical work in the 1580s, assisting Hugh Broughton in the compilation of *These Genealogies Recorded in the Sacred Scriptures (1592)*.[22] Broughton lauded the genealogies of Jesus in Matthew and Luke, distinguishing them from "those prophane ones, which S. Paul condemneth."[23] In addition to the arbors he produced for the King James Bible, Speed provided several other contextualizing publications, including the 1616 *Jesus of Nazareth, King of the Jews*, which sought "to proue that Jesus the Sonn of the virgin both from Joseph and Marie was the only heire of Dauids terrestiall Kingdom of Canaan. And in that respect and right is ever called King of the Iewes."[24] By insisting that Jesus is not just any son of David but the only true heir, Speed pursues the kind of genealogical investigation that *Paradise Regained*'s Satan undertakes when he attempts to determine "in what degree or meaning" Jesus is the "Son of God," rather than just one of the "Sons of God" (4.516, 517, 520) The importance of the Davidic Messiah to both James and Speed demonstrates how the Gospels offered a resource not just for a typology of kingship but also for hereditary monarchy in particular. Though the New Testament genealogies (which appear only in Matthew and Luke) promise to provide knowledge of Christ, their divergence simultaneously produces questions about his identity. In Matthew, the genealogy frames the entire Gospel, appearing immediately after the heading "The book of the generation of Jesus Christ, the son of David, the son of Abraham" (Matt. 1:1) and tracing 14 generations from Abraham to David, then another 14 generations from David to Jesus. Marshall D. Johnson argues that they thus serve as a midrash on the titles of "Son of David" and "Son of Abraham," emphasizing the Davidic Messiah.[25] By fully unfolding the Davidic descent and narrating the Annunciation to Joseph instead of Mary *before* turning to the birth of Christ (Matt. 1:18–25), Matthew focuses on Jesus's monarchic and patrilineal claims.

In contrast, Luke proceeds from the Annuciation to Mary through the birth and the baptism before finally detailing the genealogy of Christ. Once Luke arrives at the genealogy, however, he provides a much more extensive lineage than Matthew does, beginning with Christ and working backward to trace his origins to Adam and God. By historicizing the title "Son of God," Luke insists on the continuity of lineage, "avoiding metaphysical and adoptionistic connotations" regarding the divine filial relation.[26] The resemblance of Luke's genealogy to "Graeco-Roman pedigrees" seems to make it an even better model for hereditary monarchy than Matthew.[27] As Johnson explains, however, such resemblance is only formal, since the content of Luke's genealogy surprisingly turns away from earthly monarchy, rejecting the royal line of Judah: "Rather than enumerating the royal succession from David to the exile, as does Matthew, Luke proceeds from David to his third son born in Jerusalem, Nathan...and from him through a series of unknown names up to Shealtiel and Zerubabel and thence, again through a series of unknown names, to Joseph."[28] With its emphasis on the importance of lineage to Christ, Luke's comprehensive genealogy has the potential to bolster royal claims based on inheritance. Such claims are potentially undercut, however, not only by the genealogy's partial displacement of royal descent but also by its more expansive and inclusive history.[29] Thus, the paradoxes of genealogy extend beyond the differences between Matthew and Luke, as Luke's genealogy itself reveals the tensions within its historical project.

In their efforts to harmonize the differences between the two Gospels, Speed and other seventeenth century biblical genealogists described Matthew as providing the "monarchic" or legal line through Joseph, and Luke as tracing the "natural" genealogy through Mary. This categorization illuminates James I's choice of Matthew as a text conducive to the project of fusing divine and monarchic lineage. Matthew's representation of Christ's genealogy as starting with David rather than God or Adam, might even be seen as a model for the ways in which James often eschewed origins when he discussed lineal right, instead emphasizing the power of hereditary monarchy to stabilize the reigns that *followed* William the Conqueror or Henry IV.[30] As James anticipates and tries to control the passage of his kingship to his son, he fittingly chose to meditate upon Matthew, the text with the more compact, more monarchic genealogy.

By bringing together the promise of hereditary monarchy with the fulfillment of Christ's promise at the Crucifixion, James I unites two different versions of genealogical authority, exalting the Stuarts' lineal right and historicizing Christ's kingship as the Davidic messiah. By choosing to argue for the divine nature of political inheritance through a text focused on the Crucifixion rather than one representing the Annunciation, the Nativity, or the baptism of Christ, he describes the inheritance of the English throne as its own moment of fulfillment. This is exactly the kind of temporal collapse that *Paradise Regained* so famously resists as the Son refuses Satan's calls to seize the moment.

Of course, James's connection of his son to Christ grew more powerful in a way that that he never intended through the execution and subsequent martyrdom of Charles I in 1649. When Charles II ascended the throne after his time in exile, he and his supporters embraced the typology of kingship, aligning his rule with both that of David and Christ.[31] As David Quint argues, *Paradise Regained* "reverses and rejects Charles' inaugural typology" through its alternative narrative of Christ. Quint points out that the poem sounds a particular echo of Restoration propaganda describing the monarch as wearing a crown of "bryars and thornes" in order to contest the Christic nature of kingship.[32] Though the poem steers clear of representing the Crucifixion, its ironic redeployment of the image of a king's "wreath of thorns" shows the centrality of temporal reorientation to its redefinition of kingship when the Son refuses Satan's offering of a crown:

> What if with like aversion I reject
> Riches and Realms; yet not for that a Crown,
> Golden in shew, is but a wreath of thorns,
> Brings dangers, troubles, cares, and sleepless nights
> To him who wears the Regal Diadem,
> When on his shoulders each mans burden lies;
> For therein stands the office of a King,
> His Honour, Vertue, Merit and chief Praise,
> That for the Publick all this weight he bears.
> Yet he who reigns within himself, and rules
> Passions, Desires, and Fears, is more a King.   (PR 2.457–67)

When James I warns Prince Charles that Christ's "crowne of thornes" provides a "perfect description of the cares and crosses" of kingship, he looks back to the Crucifixion as a historical event that positions Stuart monarchy as divine fulfillment.[33] When the Son in *Paradise Regained* uses this language *before* the Crucifixion, the poem challenges earthly monarchy in two ways. First, as Quint argues, it refuses the identification of earthly monarchs with Christ as fellow martyrs. Second, it also removes the imagery of Christ's suffering from a reading of history in a way that rejects the political temporality that equates lineal succession with divine fulfillment. This jarring moment of anachronism thus performs what Goldberg calls the "not yet" of the poem, challenging not only the typology of kingship but also the claims of fulfillment underlying hereditary monarchy.[34] Unlike the biblical genealogists who had used Christ's descent to shore up Stuart rule, Milton's poem again and again denies the stabilizing power of lineage and, as we will see, offers a vision of Jesus's kinship as performative rather than ontological, a kind of doing rather than a state of being.

Redefining Sonship

The publication date of *Paradise Regained* places it in a relative lull in the succession crises that marked most of the seventeenth century. The Stuarts were back in power and the Exclusion Crisis was still a decade away. But the proclamation that placed Charles II on the throne had placed anxious emphasis on "inherent birth-right," "next heir," "blood royal" and lineal descent in order to secure the monarchy by grounding it in a biologically reproduced chain of bodies rather than in the mortal body of any one king.[35] And though worries about the possible ascent of James II had not yet erupted, the infertility of the marriage of Charles and his queen was already known. On the eve of the Restoration, Milton's *The Readie and Easy Way* had countered the reproductive promise of hereditary succession by contrasting the disruptive nature of monarchic mortality to the "eternal" and "immortal" quality of a senate.[36] After the Restoration, *Paradise Regained* again represents the limits of earthly genealogy, refusing to let "relation stand" in any transparent way.

With the connection between Christ's genealogies and Stuart propaganda more firmly in mind, we can now reconsider John Rogers's crucial point that *Paradise Regained* never describes "the Son's sonship as an absolute, as a position to which he is entitled by virtue of an unequivocal, primogenitive bloodtie to the Father."[37] Instead, the poem places the language of primogeniture in the mouth of Satan, "His first-begot we know" (PR 1.89), as he so desperately tries and fails to place the Son in a narrative that will make him comprehensible. In the poem's most direct articulation of the question of sonship, Satan sounds like a frustrated genealogist as he queries the tension between a particular and a universal sense of lineage that marks the biblical genealogies of Christ, especially that of Luke:

> Thenceforth I thought thee worth my nearer view
> And narrower scrutiny, that I might learn
> In what degree or meaning thou art called
> The Son of God, which bears no single sense.
> The Son of God I also am, or was;
> And, if I was, I am; relation stands:
> All men are Sons of God; yet thee I thought
> In some respect far higher so declared. (4.514–21)

When Satan admits that the title "Son of God" "bears no single sense," he seems to express the paradox we started with in Slatyer's *Genethliacon*: though historicizing Christ's lineage has the potential to strengthen his claim of divine kinship, this genealogical appeal to Adam as ancestor simultaneously dilutes his unique familial status. Satan's query also reflects the gap between the two Gospel genealogies that we have already seen, as it registers that Luke provides a narrative in which "all men are sons of God" through their descent from Adam, and only the more specific Davidic lineage offered by Matthew marks him as a different kind of Son. Like a biblical genealogist, Satan calls upon Jesus to harmonize the two different ideas of divine sonship. Rather than providing a better synthesis of the two texts, however, the Son refuses the question and *Paradise Regained* emphasizes the insufficiencies of genealogy and offers an alternative vision of divine kinship.

Though the poem follows Mark by opening with the baptism and draws heavily on Matthew, scholars have long seen its greatest debt as lying with Luke, the Gospel with the most extensive genealogy of Jesus, extending back to Adam and God, and the strongest association with Mary.[38] So the poem's most important biblical source is both the most genealogical and the most maternal. Though *Paradise Regained* invokes and then omits Luke's genealogy, it offers a prominent representation of Mary. Thus, the poem's engagement with Luke brings into relief its exploration of both filial and maternal relations, and helps us to register its antigenealogical exploration of kinship.

As we have seen, Luke follows the baptism with the genealogy of Jesus, historicizing the divine declaration "by tracing the sonship of Jesus through a succession of figures from the Old Testament and

Judaism back to God, emphasizing at once the Lukan concern for the continuity of the history of salvation and also the culmination of that history in the new beginning in Jesus."[39] As he begins his story, the narrator of *Paradise Regained* echoes the opening verse of Luke's genealogy, "being (as was supposed) the son of Joseph" (Luke 3:23), with the line "From Nazareth the Son of Joseph deem'd" (PR 1.23). Instead of introducing Jesus's genealogy, however, this line introduces the baptism. By citing this particular line about Joseph's own dubious fatherhood, the narrator follows Luke in ironizing earthly paternity. By removing the line from its original context in the biblical genealogy, he draws attention to the poem's erasure of genealogy as a mode for knowing "sonship." Thus, as in other places in Milton's oeuvre, the poem draws on a genealogical text for antigenealogical purposes.[40] With the word "deem'd," *Paradise Regained* highlights the instability that biblical genealogists like Speed worked so hard to erase.

The poem's antigenealogical engagement can be seen from the start in its well-recognized interweaving of the four Gospels. Though the narrator starts by invoking Luke's genealogy, he follows Mark (and to some extent John) by actually beginning his story with the baptism. By starting with the baptism, not the Nativity, the poem deemphasizes Christ's birth and replaces it with a more mediated moment of familial recognition. In this way, *Paradise Regained* follows *Paradise Lost*'s introduction of the Son through his elevation rather than his begetting. When God describes Jesus in *Paradise Regained* by saying, "I have chose / This perfect Man, by merit call'd my Son" (PR 164–65), he echoes his proclamation in book 3 of *Paradise Lost* that the Son is "By Merit more then Birthright Son of God" (PL 3.309), but he actually goes a step further. The human incarnation is not the Son of God by merit more than birthright, but just by merit. As Gordon Teskey argues, the poem "is here promoting an idea of the Son as a human being without any metaphysical ground in the Father."[41] Rogers contends that Jesus's sonship has become provisional and is hence only defined by the performance of the title.[42] Although Satan is obsessed with Jesus's lineage, God's description of Jesus as the man "call'd" rather than born his son suggests he takes a different view.

If beginning with the baptism emphasizes the performative nature of kinship, the way in which this event is refracted through multiple voices, including those of the narrator, Satan, Jesus, and Mary, underscores this understanding of divine kinship. Some multiplicity already marks the contrasting accounts of the Gospels: in Luke 3:22 and Mark 1:11, the voice addresses Jesus directly, declaring, "Thou art my beloved son." Here, the declaration serves as a direct interaction between God and the "beloved Son," seemingly informing both Jesus and the assembled crowd. In Matthew 3:17, however, the voice addresses the crowd with "This is my beloved son," suggesting either that Jesus already knows this information or that he receives it indirectly. If Matthew's narration suggests that Jesus already understands himself as "the beloved Son," the difference between this account and those of Luke and Mark might be understood as the difference between expressive and performative speech. In this view, "This is my beloved son" merely reveals an already existing relation, while "Thou art my beloved son" calls the filial relation into being by interpellating Jesus as the Son. Such a distinction, however, obscures the performative nature of even the former version. The presence of witnesses in both versions emphasizes the extent to which the declaration of paternity makes kinship a relation that takes on different meanings in different contexts, rather than one fixed by birth.

Paradise Regained never directly quotes the Gospel accounts of the voice and does not resolve the issue of address. Instead, the poem seems to exacerbate this issue, emphasizing the reader's distance from the event and refusing to comment on whether or not Jesus himself already has, needs, or wants God's verification of his lineage. The first account of the baptism comes to us through the narrator: "the Fathers voice / From Heav'n pronounc'd him his beloved Son" (*PR* 1.31–32). The narrator departs from all three Gospel accounts by explicitly describing the voice as paternal, while simultaneously not specifying the addressee. As the poem unfolds, both Jesus ("my Father's voice, / Audibly heard from Heav'n, pronounc'd me his, / Me his beloved Son, in whom alone / He was well pleas'd" [1.283–86]) and Mary ("Son own'd from Heaven by his Father's voice" [2.85]) repeat the paternal description of the voice and the opaqueness of address.

By constantly blurring the addressee, Milton's poem does more than keep open questions of what Jesus knows. Though the declaration by the voice should serve as a clarifying moment, the poem refuses any stable sense of what was said. By leaving the content of the proclamation opaque, the poem focuses on its power as a speech act that establishes new relations among the characters rather than merely revealing a preexisting kinship. Since the relation of speaker to auditor remains unclear, however, it also remains unclear exactly what relations are being created. According to genealogical logic, the declaration of a filial relation should provide clarity and stability, but the absence of a specific auditor for the declaration undermines such promise and calls attention to the mobility and instability of kinship.

The poem's rewriting of the Gospels to omit a specific recipient of the voice's message also aligns with the way in which the singing angels cut short verse 1:15 from John, which reads, "As the Father knoweth me, even so know I the Father: and I lay down my life for the sheep." The angels instead sing, "The Father knows the Son; therefore secure / Ventures his filial Vertue, though untri'd" (*PR* 1.176–77). By reporting the Father's knowledge of the Son from the first half of the formulation ("As the Father knoweth me") without the Son's parallel knowledge of the Father from the second half ("even so know I the Father"), the angels offer no verification of what the Son knows, leaving us to wonder about the extent of the epistemological gap between God and Jesus. By reassigning Jesus's words to the angels, the poem recasts paternal knowledge, making it a subject for a community of witnesses rather than the stable bond of a reciprocal relation between father and son.

The sole speaker in the poem to specify the addressee of the proclamation is Satan, whose general unreliability is exacerbated by the fact that he offers three different versions of the baptismal pronouncement. When reporting to his followers, he offers the poem's only direct quotation of the voice, "And out of Heav'n the Sov'raign voice I heard, / This is my Son belov'd, in him am pleas'd" (*PR* 1.84–85).

Through this close echo of Matthew 3:17 ("This is my beloved son, in whom I am well pleased"), Satan denies the direct proclamation to the Son himself found in Luke and Mark. When he speaks to Jesus, however, Satan revises his initial report to remove the paternal divine voice entirely: "Our new baptizing Prophet at the Ford / Of Jordan honour'd so, and call'd thee Son / of God" (1.328–30). Here, he implicitly cites John 1:32–34, in which the only voice to name Jesus is John's, once again avoiding the more intimate connection between God and Jesus depicted in Luke and Mark. By drawing on John to refuse the heavenly nature of the declaration, Satan seems either to try to trouble Jesus's memory of the event, as made visible by the enjambment between "Son" and "Of God," or to draw him into providing a fuller account of himself.

By the end of the poem, however, the frustrated Satan reveals the duplicity of his second account of the baptismal declaration by admitting to Jesus that he was witness to a voice other than John's: "by voice from Heav'n / Heard thee pronounc'd the Son of God belov'd" (PR 4.512–13). Satan's description of this pivotal speech act now conforms to the same opaque formulation as that of the narrator, the Son, and Mary. He even suddenly uses the same verb, "pronounc'd," as the narrator and the Son do. Still, Satan continues to resist divine paternity by failing to describe the voice as the "Father's" and juxtaposing earthly and heavenly lineage: "Then hear, O Son of David, Virgin-born; / For Son of God to me is yet in doubt" (4.500–01). Here, Satan separates Davidic and divine lineage in order to emphasize the mortal nature of his opponent but, as we will see, the poem shows us how this disentangling can be used to very different ends.

Though it begins with a direct representation of the baptism, *Paradise Regained* goes on to depict recollections of the Annunciation, choosing Luke's account of Gabriel's announcement to Mary rather than Matthew's story of the angelic visit to Joseph. Formally, the poem revises Luke's version by offering only retrospective and mediated accounts of the Annunciation, but its rewriting of the content illuminates its antigenealogical stakes most clearly. In Luke 1:32, Gabriel explicitly links Jesus's reign to his earthly lineage, telling

Mary, "the Lord God shall give unto him the throne of his father David." In *Paradise Regained*, however, the only speaker to describe David as Jesus's father is Satan, including his reference to Jesus's hereditary right to earthly rule: "But to a Kingdom thou art born, ordain'd / To sit upon thy Father David's Throne" (*PR* 3.152–53).⁴³ Mary, whom one might expect to directly echo the terms of the Annunciation, instead separates the familial title from the monarchic promise, telling her son that "Thy Father is the Eternal King" before informing him that he has been prophesied to "sit on David's Throne" (1.240). God also echoes Luke's story of the Annunciation but he makes an even more extreme revision than Milton's Mary. Describing "that solemn message late, / On which I sent thee to the Virgin pure / In Galilee, that she should bear a Son / Great in Renown, and call'd the Son of God" (1.133–36), God omits all references to David, as well as all references to an earthly monarchy.

The Son refers to David directly and indirectly, but never uses the term "father." He does once seem to refer to himself as David's "true heir" but it is in the context of rejecting Satan's call for him to take action: "My brethren as thou call'st them; those Ten Tribes / I must deliver, if I mean to raign / David's true heir" (*PR* 4.403–05). In this same breath, the Son also distances himself from the genealogical connection Satan makes between him and the ten tribes with the sarcastic phrase "as thou call'st them." In other words, he only echoes Satan's genealogical language in order to refuse it.

The Son also seems implicitly to refuse the supposed force of the elaborate family trees Speed had produced for the King James Bible, informing Satan that "when my season comes to sit / On David's Throne, it shall be like a tree / Spreading and over-shadowing all the Earth" (*PR* 4.147–48). As Elizabeth Sauer has points out, when Jesus describes his "season," he says it shall be "like" a tree, not actually a tree.⁴⁴ And in case Satan or anyone else had missed the sense that Jesus is not talking about a reign grounded in earthly understandings of lineage, Jesus follows this first prophecy with the threat that his ascent will be as "a stone that shall to pieces dash / All Monarchies besides throughout the world" (4.150). Having refused to submit to the demands of earthly lineage, Jesus instead leaves behind these questions of his paternity to go "unobserv'd / Home to his Mothers house private" (4.638–39), returning to a mother who has modeled for him a process of seeing oneself in terms beyond earthly genealogy.

Denaturalizing the "Natural": Milton's Mary

Though Satan focuses his energies on the question of the meaning of the "Son of God," the poem also takes up the question of what it means to be the "mother" of the "Son of God," extending its contemplation of kinship to the maternal. As we have seen, seventeenth century theologians trying to harmonize Christ's genealogies generally began by declaring that Matthew was tracing his "legal" lineage through Joseph, while Luke was following his "natural" descent through Mary. Reading *Paradise Regained* as implicitly countering the genealogists's emphasis on the transparency and stability of the "natural" maternal line, I want to join Rachel Trubowitz in arguing that that the poem's "unconventional" representation of Mary's very peculiar motherhood continues its decentering of birth as the defining element of kinship, hence implicitly undermining the blood claims of hereditary monarchy.[45] This genealogical context also lends new support to Mary Beth Rose's crucial analysis of the prominence of Mary in the poem as related to broader political questions about maternity and authority. Unlike Rose, however, I contend that Milton's parallel depictions of the Son and Mary do not rest on an ontological sense of kinship (as Rose puts it, the poem "exalts the Son as a hero not for what he does, but because of what he is: a son") but, rather, work to imagine the filial and maternal as performative relations.[46]

At the end of *Paradise Lost*, Michael's lesson reorients Adam's understanding of the "promise of the seed" away from the ideas of reproductive fulfillment and lineal stability, which would later form the cornerstone of hereditary monarchy.[47] By contrast, Eve's exposure to the promise remains mysterious; since we have no access to her dreams, we do not know exactly what she knows when she reports, "By mee the Promis'd Seed shall all restore" (*PL* 12.622). Through its representation of Mary, however, *Paradise Regained* offers a maternal version of Adam's paternal reorientation. Her lament in book 2 emphasizes the way that she struggles to understand her maternity:

> But I to wait with patience am inur'd;
> My heart hath been a store-house long of things
> And sayings laid up, portending strange events.
> Thus Mary pondering oft, and oft to mind
> Recalling what remarkably had pass'd
> Since first her Salutation heard, with thoughts
> Meekly compos'd awaited the fulfilling.   (PR 2.103–09)

As we have seen, Milton follows Luke's account of the Annunciation to Mary, and here the poem emphasizes her ongoing attempts to understand this initial proclamation about her special maternity. By describing her affective state as one of patience, she refuses the temporal prematurity of reproductive promise while simultaneously resisting a clear sense of an ending by waiting not for a fulfillment but a "fulfilling" (2.109).[48] In this way, she is a key participant in the poem's temporality of the "not yet."

Dayton Haskin demonstrates how Milton's Mary, as a "bearer of the Word" who "exercises the authorly roles of preserving, interpreting, and combining diverse texts into a unique personal synthesis," serves as a model for the Son's own attempt to understand himself.[49] Trubowitz points out that although the mother and child are represented in the poem as physically distant, the resemblance of Mary's pondering and the Son's meditations represents a spiritual unity. Thus, the bond between mother and son is not one of nature but one of spirit, as Mary epitomizes Milton's redefinition of ideal maternity: "Rather than naturally transmit pure English identity and a reformed national ethos through her pure breast-milk, Milton's new mother affectively nourishes the unity of spirit that consolidates the reformed post-dynastic nation."[50] Trubowitz's analysis shows how the poem establishes a crucial but crucially denaturalized vision of motherhood through Mary. Hence, the poem's simultaneous omission of Luke's genealogy and expanded depiction of Mary brings us to the heart of political issues of lineage.

By following Luke's account of the Annunciation to Mary, the poem focuses attention not just on the Son's maternal lineage but also on the issue of maternal knowledge of lineage. Thus, though I come to a different conclusion than Rose, I agree with her that Thomas Hobbes's discussion of maternal power "provides a close and revealing parallel to Milton's deployment of the Virgin in *Paradise Regain'd*."[51] Famously, Hobbes argues that "in the state of nature, it cannot be known who is a *child's father* except by the *mother's* pointing him out; hence he belongs to the *mother* ... the offspring goes with the womb."[52] This maternal certainty for Hobbes begins with the mother's sense of herself: "in the state of nature, every woman who gives birth becomes a *mother* and a *Mistress*."[53] Rose argues that Mary exercises just such maternal authority in *Paradise Regained*, since it is "the Virgin's presence that confirms the Son's origins and provides knowledge of his birth."[54]

But Mary is a very unusual mother, and her knowledge here is delivered to us in a mediated form. Unlike the presence of the baby with his mother at the end of the Nativity ode, the Son's connection to Mary in *Paradise Regained* is cast in retrospective terms, both by his reflection on her words (*PR* 1.227–58), and her own reflection on her experiences of motherhood (2.66–109). Though the narrator, Satan, and the Son name Mary as the Son's mother, she never calls herself a mother, even as she directly meditates on her relation to her son. In this she follows the biblical script: in Luke 1:38, the title Mary articulates in response to Gabriel's pronouncement is "handmaid of the Lord." Neither Gabriel in Luke, nor God in *Paradise Regained* ever utters the title of mother. By choosing Luke's account of the Annunciation, the poem focuses on Mary's knowledge. By representing the Annunciation as a moment in the past that Mary ponders, the poem emphasizes the reflective and constructed nature of her parental role. Though the act of birth and the actions of her son may be beyond her control, the poem represents her performance of motherhood as active and ongoing. For Mary, one might say that the "storehouse" replaces the womb as the defining site of her motherhood. So though the act of birth may make the

Hobbesean mother transparent to herself and others, Milton's Mary requires more.

Of course, the seemingly straightforward declaration "the offspring goes with the womb" does not do justice to the complexity of Hobbes's vision of mothers.[55] Hobbes draws attention to maternal dominion in order to denaturalize paternal right, but he doesn't stop there. Though Hobbes insists that the mother initially has the right of dominion over the child, he also denies that the right to a child is grounded in generation, "For the life which the *mother* gave him (not by *generation* but by *looking after* him) she takes away by *abandoning* him; hence the obligation which arose by the gift of life is cancelled by the *abandonment*."[56] So though the mother has dominion over the child "by right of nature," her relation to her child is governed by will and mutual obligation (she protects the child "on the condition that he will not be her enemy"), not a maternal bond.[57] In other words, Hobbes works to move as quickly as he can away from birth to contract, radically redefining motherhood as a state of mutual obligation, one that is chosen by both parties, is artificial and constructed, and can be alienated.[58] Thus, the oft-cited "the child follows the womb" belies how thoroughly Hobbes strives to denaturalize motherhood. In their radical representations of maternity, both *De cive* and *Paradise Regained* emphasize the role of knowledge and agency in motherhood. If *Paradise Lost*'s Sin figures a perverse version of Mary, part of the horror she represents is her inability to convert the contingencies of maternity into the choices of motherhood. To put this more directly, Sin's rape and continual violation by her own children signal maternity's recalcitrant status as a state devoid of choice, making it a key site for Milton's revision of kinship. As Hobbes and Milton struggle to imagine a different kind of motherhood, *De cive* makes the mother-child relation a generic one of self-interest and self-defense, while *Paradise Regained* offers the relationship between Mary and her son as one of affective and textual reflection.

These representations of motherhood sit in stark contrast to the "natural" ones depicted by biblical genealogists striving to authenticate Jesus as the Son of God and the Son of David. When Speed provides yet another text defending and explaining the genealogies in

1616, one of the issues he takes up is Mary's maternity. In his genealogy in the Authorized Version, Speed tries to clear up the confusion caused by the presence of the three different "Maries" who sit in the generation preceding Jesus: "three Maries recorded as the mothers unto Christ and unto his Apostles: which were Marie the Virgine, Marie surnamed Salome, and Marie Cleopas." He goes on to explain why Mary the Virgin, not either of her two sisters, is the only mother of Christ in order to argue that Jesus "was the only heire of Dauids terrestiall Kingdom," "knowne and reputed to be the onlie son of them both by the double right, and most iust title, is stiled and called King of the Iewes."[59] Speed's use of the language of knowledge and reputation demonstrates the tension within the genealogical project. Though Speed's intent is to use lineage to authenticate Christ's identity, the problem of the three "Maries" and his need to write so many pages augmenting his arbors underscore the inadequacy of reproduction alone in providing legitimation and continuity. In a way, the very work of genealogy underscores kinship as a kind of "doing," rather than a relation that stands.

THE GENEALOGICAL IMAGINARY AND MILTON'S QUEER KINSHIP

Though *Paradise Regained* includes the fullest depiction of the Son and Mary in Milton's oeuvre, the divorce tracts twice invoke the Holy Family in ways that also undermine genealogical understandings of Christ. In *The Judgement of Martin Bucer*, Milton emphasizes the difference between human reproduction and the promise of the seed embodied in the birth of Christ: "Now the proper and ultimate end of mariage is not copulation, or children, for then there was not true matrimony between Joseph and Mary the mother of Christ, nor between many holy persons more; but the full and proper and main end of mariage, is the communicating of all duties, both divine and humane, each to other, with utmost benevolence and affection" (YP 2:465). In *Tetrachordon*, Milton invokes Mary and Joseph as he rejects reading Genesis 2:24 as defining the end of marriage as reproduction: "Else many aged and holy Matrimonies, and more eminently that of *Joseph* and *Mary*, would be no true Marriage. And that maxim generally receiv'd, would be false, that *consent alone, tho' copulation never follow, makes the Marriage*" (YP 2:610). Thus, rather than providing a model of lineal inheritance for hereditary monarchs like the Stuarts, Christ's family offers a model of kinship grounded in consent, not reproduction.

The significance of Milton's separation of the marital and the reproductive relations of the Holy Family becomes clearer when we turn to Speed's 1616 "To the Christian Reader." The epistle explains the iconography uniting Joseph, Mary, and Jesus at the end of his biblical genealogy: "The lineage of our blessed Saviour (which is our principall scope) is knowne by a Chaine-like traile, continued from Adam to Sem... And lastly to our Saviours parents, linked together (as other marriages here are) by the sculpture of an hand in hand." For Speed, Mary and Joseph provide the historical continuity that authenticates Christ's divinity, crucially represented by a genealogical "chain." When Milton depicts the Holy Family in the divorce tracts, he emphasizes the lateral relation between Mary and Joseph, deliberately distinguishing it from Mary's relation as "mother of Christ." The temporal promise of the domestic in these tracts still looms large, but it is one of a typology of couples who mirror relations of intimacy and consent from Adam and Eve to Mary and Joseph to the seventeenth century husband and wife, as "fit and matchable conversation... shall restore the much wrong'd and over-sorrow'd state of matrimony, not only to those mercifull and life-giving remedies of Moses, but, as much as may be, to the serene and blissfull condition it was in at the beginning" (YP 2:239–40). When he imagines Mary and Joseph as an ideal couple, Milton represents their marriage not as a site of divinely infused reproduction but instead as a model of choice and affection. Again and again, Milton refuses genealogy, still using the image of the couple "hand in hand" (*PL* 12.648) from the genealogies, but breaking them free from Speed's "chain-like traile."

Through its continual refusal of either ontological or natural conceptions of sonship and maternity, however, *Paradise Regained* does something more than simply replacing the vertical relations of genealogy with the horizontal ones of marital contract, swapping lines of inheritance for alliances of marriage. Through its reorientation of even vertical kinship relations, the poem simultaneously opens them up for transformation and subjects them to constant inspection. This is exactly the kind of double bind that Butler warns about when she points out that the state recognition that promises to legitimate non-heterosexual configurations of kinship may paradoxically "result in the intensification of normalization."[60] The democratizing of genealogy that served to challenge monarchic claims of authority has the potential to open up additional avenues for scrutiny, enabling new modes of state control.

Paradise Regained registers this paradox by contrasting the parallel struggles of Mary and the Son to make meaning of their kinship to Satan's desperate attempts to discover a fixed meaning of Jesus's filial relation. The difference between the two can be understood as reflecting changes in what D. R. Woolf describes as the genealogical imagination. Rather than representing a search for unbroken lineage, the process of inquiry upon which the Son embarks seems much like the work of those in the seventeenth century still committed to genealogy as a mode of historical knowledge but only when it is understood in relation to corroborating texts in the context of a broader historical picture. Mary's parallel process fits with the crucial role women played in this particular mode of history making. At the moment that Woolf argues that genealogies were becoming "much less a pseudo-biblical series of begats emphasizing continuity, and much more a bridge connecting the political present to a famous person in the historical past whose deeds had a significance beyond the family," Milton's poem radically imagines the biblical narrative itself as much less a pseudo-genealogical series of begats, and much more as a story of the ongoing textual construction of a self.[61]

Povinelli's warning about the tenacity of genealogy participates in a broader conversation within queer studies about political temporality, a conversation that helps us to understand more fully the stakes of Milton's representation of Christ's kinship. The shift in the genealogical imaginary creates what Michael Warner describes as "an acute contradiction":

> Modernity has been marked, at least since Locke, by the ebb of kinship and biological reproduction from the organization of social life. Yet in other ways reproductive sex has become an even more pervasive measure of value in modernity. Patrilineal succession may have ceased to be a self-evident gloss on the social order or its continuity from past to future, but the result is that everyone now has generational consciousness.... The forms of reproductive narrative have proliferated under this pressure.... Whether we bear children or not, our lives converge on a future that continues to be imagined not as the activity of other adults like ourselves, but as the inheritance of children.[62]

This diffusion of reproductive promise from lineal monarch or aristocrat to citizen subject deals a blow to the hereditary foundations of kingship, but simultaneously produces a heteronormative political temporality. Lee Edelman describes this political temporality grounding the emergence of "secular theology" as "reproductive futurism," which we might understand as the real heir to the Stuart genealogical promise.[63] When James I parallels Jesus's inheritance from David with Prince Charles's inheritance of his own kingship, he makes the royal heir the earthly embodiment of the reproductive futurity offered by the infant Jesus. In the modern secular politics described by Edelman, the promise of the infant Christ is transferred to the more general figure of "the Child" (not to be confused with any actual child or children), who becomes "the living promise of a natural transcendence of the limits of nature itself."[64] Edelman rails against the ways in which this more generalized promise of reproduction brings with it a crippling orientation to the future at the cost of the present. With their concerns about the obsession with progeny, these critiques echo James I's fears about anxious heirs, showing that modernity's reproductive futurism remakes but also reenacts the temporal paradox of hereditary monarchy.

To the extent that Milton's nonreproductive Mary and Joseph have a child without sexual reproduction, they may be understood as epitomizing what Edelman calls "the specifically heterosexual alibi of reproductive necessity," through which the promise of progeny relieves the heterogenital act of the "despiritualized burden of its status as sexual function."[65] But such an interpretation would not do justice to the effort Milton's depiction of the Holy Family in *The Judgement of Martin Bucer* makes to distinguish human procreation and the promise of Christ, as it inherently pushes against the Stuart conflation of divine and human inheritance. It would also fail to register how the "not yet" of the Nativity ode and *Paradise Regained* refuse the imagining of the infant Christ as a figure of fulfillment, at least frustrating attempts to conceptualize the future through the figure of the Child. In connecting the divorce tracts and these two very different poems, I do not intend to describe Milton's work as cohering into a seamless ideological statement about the politics of reproductive futurity. What I want to suggest is that his depictions of Christ's familial relations sit amid a tangle of changing ideas about the political promise of reproductive futurity.

When Satan demands that Jesus account for his divine lineage, the "perfect man" refuses. By emphasizing the constructed, textual, and provisional nature of kinship, Milton's poem both destabilizes political claims based upon lineage and opens up new avenues for political power through surveillance. Through its focus on the Son's resistance to Satan's invasive questioning, *Paradise Regained* seems to imagine and combat the emerging threats of such surveillance. Drawing attention to the political stakes of this dynamic of monitoring and resistance, Quint argues that the poem offers not just a specific attack on the Stuarts, but also a more general assault on "monarchy as part of the larger configuration of the modern nation-state, the sponsor, whether in royalist or republican guise, of a new statistical science and instrumental rationality."[66] This equation of Stuart power with that of the modern nation-state, however, occludes the shift in genealogical thinking crucial to new forms of political power. In other words, the poem's antimonarchic representation of kinship helps create the power Quint sees Milton trying to resist. Refusing to let "relation stand," *Paradise Regained* contests the ontological understanding of familial relations upon which hereditary monarchy staked its claim. But the meaning-making kinship practices modeled by Mary and the Son in *Paradise Regained* make the familial available for surveillance and constant questioning, enabling the new mode of power Quint ascribes to Satan: "The Prince of this world seeks ever more detailed information on those he would make his subjects and his field of knowledge would include the inner realm of identity itself."[67] By showing the "perfect man" walking away from the prying eyes of the satanic genealogist, *Paradise Regained* begins to contest this new power.

Thus, the poem offers a potentially radical representation of kinship. Rather than defying the political power of inheritance by emphasizing the importance of the couple, as Milton does elsewhere, it represents even filial and maternal relations as performative. Though this refusal of the ontological status of kinship could subject familial relations to normative forms of intimacy, the poem seems to resist such heteronormative pressure in three ways. First, a denaturalized mother-son dyad replaces the couple as the center of the domestic. Second, the promise of reproductive futurity is replaced with the temporality of "not yet," which paradoxically refocuses attention on the present. Finally, though both the Son and Mary develop accounts of their familial relations in ways that seem to expose them to more questioning and surveillance, the opacity of the baptismal pronouncement and the Son's resistance to any definition of his relations seem to delegitimize this alternative power. This resistance is not, as Quint's argument might suggest, generic antistatism but a resistance of a form of familial power different from that anchoring hereditary monarchy — a form of power that may be embodied in the state but need not be.

As the promise of the future is redistributed from one heir to all Englishmen, so is the danger of such a temporal orientation. By ending his last poetic representation of Christ not with the babe in the manger but with the adult son returning home to live with his mother, Milton depicts the first true "millennial" as defying any simple idea of individual or narrative development, presenting a disruptive imagining of kinship and temporality. It is in this poetic exploration of theology, more than in the Son's rejection of the "homosexual temptation," that *Paradise Regained* seems most potentially queer, as it displaces the heterosexual couple of *Paradise Lost* with a radically redefined mother-son dyad.[68] In the divorce tracts, Joseph, Mary, and Jesus are invoked in order to deny the centrality of reproduction to marriage, offering an alternative vision of the intimate couple form as defining the domestic, and imagining a nongenealogical link to Edenic origins through the normative, typological relations among couples. *Paradise Regained* confounds such normativity, defining the Holy Family not through the married couple but by a mother and child who defy reproductive futurity.

The radical nature of that final opaque image of son-mother intimacy is so different from that of Milton's normative imaginings of marriage that one recent critic has argued that the poem imagines the Son "as solitary," and hence "not human."[69] Though the Son may reject the offers of sexual and conversational coupling offered by Satan, however, the poem imagines him not "as solitary" at all but as returning to his mother. I want to suggest that, rather than making the Son "not human," this final gesture toward a kinship that evades representation constitutes a radical moment in Milton's writing that resists the tyrannous demands of defining humanity through the intimacy of the couple. Through a kind of feedback loop, the Son's much discussed humanity helps redefine the category of the human itself.[70]

This image of mother and son has the potential to lead us to the secular theology of the Child lamented by Edelman. In Milton's depictions of the Holy Family, however, such a path is not yet set in stone. *Paradise Regained*'s commitment to epistemological uncertainty and temporal deferral resists the promise of birth, whether in the form of a lineal monarch or the premature promise of the Son's Nativity or baptism. The poem appears in a moment in which the political role of family is a matter of explicit struggle. As Povinelli says, the struggle does not end with the beheading of the monarch. But the battle over monarchy puts these struggles into relief in explicitly political, theological, and epistemological ways in the century in which Milton writes.

PART THREE

ANGELIC EMBODIMENT

CHAPTER 5

Milton's Strange Angels

REBECCA BUCKHAM

> As the crickets' soft autumn hum
> is to us,
> so are we to the trees
> as are they
> to the rocks and the hills.
> — Gary Snyder, from "Little Songs for Gaia"

Having just described and defended his "passion" for Eve, Adam becomes interested in angelic affection. Given his own recent experience of "Transported touch," Adam wants to know how angels touch each other: "Love not the heav'nly Spirits, and how thir Love / Express they, by looks onely, or do they mix / Irradiance, virtual or immediate touch?"[1] Regardless of details, what Adam really wants to know is whether angels experience with each other the same pleasure he does with Eve. Adam gets his answer right away, as soon as the angel "with a smile that glow'd / Celestial rosie red, Loves proper hue, / Answer'd" (PL 8.618–20). Raphael blushes, and while the blush may simply be accessory to Raphael's answer, merely a segue to speech, it is possible to read the blush *as* the answer itself, disclosing as much to Adam in its involuntary response as the articulated account of angel sex that

Raphael proceeds to offer. A blush is a response Adam must recognize: he has just described his first night with Eve, how "To the Nuptial Bowre" he "led her blushing like the Morn" (510–11). Raphael's blush opens up a sympathetic space wherein Adam finds his own human experience of "commotion strange" confirmed in the angel's expressive countenance.

Learning that Milton's angels make love meets some deep need we have to be affirmed in our own embodiment.[2] But what Raphael describes is some strange sex:

> Whatever pure thou in the body enjoy'st
> (And pure thou wert created) we enjoy
> In eminence, and obstacle find none
> Of membrane, joynt, or limb, exclusive barrs:
> Easier then Air with Air, if Spirits embrace,
> Total they mix, Union of Pure with Pure
> Desiring; nor restrain'd conveyance need
> As Flesh to mix with Flesh, or Soul with Soul.   (8.622–29)

Despite the fact that Raphael shows up in Eden as a familiarly embodied being — complete with anthropomorphic loins and thighs (*PL* 5.282) — *actual* angel bodies, we learn, are not held together by membranes and joints, and are not composed of limbs. Furthermore, Raphael's language causes us to critically reflect on our own sexual experience. *Are* limbs obstacles? *Do* membranes function as "exclusive barrs?" Do we experience the paradox of "restrain'd conveyance" and if so, does such activity inhibit pleasure, as Raphael intimates, or perhaps heighten it?[3] What kind of mixing happens in human sex, if it is not "total"? Does the human mode of embodiment categorically change the experience of sexual pleasure?

While the involuntary disclosure that is Raphael's blush invites recognition, the account it precedes produces a more critical scrutiny that reads back skeptically on the preverbal moment — to what extent *is* the signification of Raphael's blush available to Adam, or to us? The reader's encounter with Milton's blushing angel gives rise to the sort of relation Drew Daniel describes in his work on early modern melancholy: "some sort of loose perceptual community...a tenuous, infra-thin state of fellow feeling" that remains "indeterminate" when affective response gives rise to critical reflection that doubts the accessibility of another's experience; the connection is "an affective bond-which-is-also-a-gap."[4] I am interested in bonds that are also gaps between Milton's readers and his angels, in how the poem makes it possible for readers to respond to an affective state like angel pleasure as one we recognize, yet insists on preserving as a qualifier of response a skeptical space for experiential disparity. Raphael exits rather expediently upon the close of what has become, in this unexpected divergence, a somewhat awkward conversation, and so does not give Adam much of a chance to further explore the bonds and gaps between his experience of pleasure and the angel's. I would like do just that.

Raphael's claim that angels enjoy a more refined version of the pleasure proffered by Eden's bower establishes continuity between his and Adam's experiences, which reiterates the general point of the book 5 discourse on matter. The poem's most explicit statement of Milton's monist materialist commitments, Raphael's "one first matter all" speech is delivered to appease Adam's concern over whether the Edenic food he and Eve offer their guest will sit well with his divine digestive tract (*PL* 5.401–02). In the passage, Raphael describes a continuum of substance on which "all things" are arrayed by degree of rarefaction, such that the "more refin'd, more spiritous, and pure" something is, the "neerer to [God] plac't or neerer tending" (472–79). Having imaged the "gradual scale" by which everything will eventually "return" to God—the source of material being—by describing how plants convert physical nutriment into increasingly "sublim'd" forms of matter, Raphael posits that angelic and human intellection are developmentally sequential and so ought to be understood as "differing but in degree, of kind the same" (490). By the same logic, Jonathan Goldberg posits that "the sexual intercourse of the first couple is on a continuum with what Raphael describes, much as human and angelic appetite are, much as human and angelic embodiment are as well."⁵ Human sex and Raphael's "Union of Pure with Pure / Desiring" thus differ only in degree, not kind.

Part of this essay's aim is to challenge the evaluative tone of Raphael's statements about the angelic and the human. In its emphasis on continuity, Raphael's model merely shifts into a monist cosmos the hierarchical thrust of the more traditionally dualist models that Milton resists. In articulating the differences between things as incremental and positional—"more refin'd, more spiritous, and pure"—rather than substantial, the poem uses the comparative, which is by default also evaluative. Raphael's implication that angel sex is unilaterally superior to "whatever" Adam "in the body enjoy'st" echoes Raphael's earlier distinction between angels, "purest spirits," and humans, "in part / Spiritual" (*PL* 5.405–06): angels are purely spiritual while humans are (only) partly so. Raphael sells angelic sex as the harder drug: if it is *like* human sex in its most essential qualities it is also *better* than any sex that Adam has had.

While the comparative flags likeness, it also reveals Raphael's claim to kin(d)ship with Adam to be something of an ontological Pandora's box. How much "more spiritous" are Milton's angels than his humans? At some point on the continuum of substance Raphael describes, does angelic rarefaction present itself as more different than can be accounted for by Raphael's assertion of material continuity? Raphael's sweeping gesture—"*whatever* pure thou in the body enjoy'st" (my emphasis)—suggests the angel's inability to fully understand Adam's passion for Eve. It appears that we, too, may not be able to fully identify "whatever" angel sex is. In presenting difference that cannot be accounted for as easily as Raphael's reductive claim to kin(d)ship suggests, the poem pulls away from its general commitment to a continuum of substance, and so also resists its own evaluative thrust. If angel sex is just different, how can it be better?

Within the discourses informed by evolutionary science, an emphasis on continuity brings with it the risk of what Jesús Rivas and Gordon M. Burghardt term "anthropomorphism by omission," which is generally "the failure to consider that other animals have a different world from ours." Scientists who "do not deliberately acknowledge that different species have different perspectives and priorities than we do...may draw anthropomorphic conclusions that are erroneous."[6] For example, the tendency to see human language as a more evolved form of comparatively rudimentary systems in animals risks obscuring how those animal systems exceed any account that could be given by the comparison to human language.[7] In their study of Milton's angels, critics have sometimes operated by a similar failure. Robert West argues that Milton's representation of angels is really in the greater service of his ideas about humans: "Milton's purpose...is to emphasize his picture of man's nature by its parallel in angel's nature....Milton seems to have shaped his doctrine of angels less by its own intrinsic requirements than by the related and more important requirements of his anthropology."[8] Such an approach omits how Milton's representation exceeds whatever preconceived "doctrine of angels" may be at work in the poem.

West assumes that whatever ideas about humans are conveyed in *Paradise Lost* can be consolidated into a "picture of man's nature." Obviously, Milton held some very definite notions about what it is to be human — most clearly articulated in the emphasis throughout *Paradise Lost* on humans as the divine image. However, while Milton's representation of hungry, passionate angels does do important work to elevate Adam in his own human situation, its effect goes beyond the merely illustrative function that West articulates. The poem also explores the "whatever" that is the experience of being human. While studies of animal biology and behavior reveal the boundary of human and nonhuman to be increasingly elusive, the problem of human identity is not a new one. For early modern people, the supranatural was often the site of such inquiry, as Walter Stephens shows in his study of witchcraft theory, which evidenced a persistent preoccupation with accounts of sexual congress between human and demonic beings.[9] In dismissing as superstitious the period's obsession with demonic sex, we fail to recognize how our own investigations are motivated by shared interests and anxieties. For us, animals — not angels — provide one key site wherein to locate our pursuit of what it is to be human. Early modern accounts of sex with demons exhibit a similar fascination with and uncertainty about the difference between human and nonhuman as accounts of chimpanzees who are observed to masturbate while looking at a copy of *Playboy*, or of an illegally captured female orangutan who was shaved, chained to a couch, and turned into a sex slave.[10] Milton's attention to angels does more than simply affirm our human condition; it draws that condition into question and so participates in an ongoing tradition of inquiry into what it means to be human — inquiry that is perhaps itself the heart of the answers it seeks.

Scholars have often stressed the theological or philosophical implications of the continuity between angels and humans drawn by Raphael's claim. Milton's depiction of angels who can eat, drink, and be merry at the earthly table of Adam and Eve does indeed help convey Milton's unorthodox views on matter. However, like his account of heavenly sex, Raphael's description of how angels eat and eliminate raises more questions about embodiment than answers — questions that are explicitly about the angelic, but also have implications for the human experience of what it is to be an embodied being. Does "ambrosial" and "mellifluous" food have taste? Does such food really require digestive processes, or does it simply dissolve on angel tongues the way it "transpires...with ease" out the other end? Does Raphael even have an anus? In generating more speculation about the morphology of heavenly bodies than it cares to or can address, *Paradise Lost* extends an invitation not only to think or to believe something about angels but also to encounter them.

We might consider how Milton's angels present one face of what ecological thinker Timothy Morton calls "the strange stranger."[11] Understanding ecology to be much more than a science — it involves "all the ways we imagine how we live together" — Morton describes an interconnectedness that is not holistic or totalitarian but rather quite vexed in the ambiguity of its material relations. Interested in how having more of one kind of knowledge often means having less of another, Morton describes the epistemological situation he terms "the mesh":

> The more we analyze, the more ambiguous things become. We can't really know who is at the junctions of the mesh before we meet them.

Even when we meet them, they are liable to change before our eyes, and our view of them is labile.... This stranger isn't just strange. She, or he, or it — can we tell? how? — is strangely strange. Their strangeness itself is strange. We can never absolutely figure them out. If we could, then all we would have is a ready-made box to put them in, and we would just be looking at the box, not at the strange strangers. They are intrinsically strange.[12]

If Milton's angels are familiar, they are strangely so. Having knowledge of what Milton *thought* or *believed* about angels and humans is like having knowledge that humans and their great ape cousins — primate "kin" and so in evolutionary terms "of kind the same" — share all but a small fraction of their DNA. Significant in its own right, such knowledge does not account for the provocatively vexed relations involved in cross-species encounters. The strangeness of the orangutan or angelic other exceeds whatever knowledge an evolutionary study of primate relation can offer, or whatever claims to familiarity are made by the divine messenger to Milton's Eden.

Such strangeness is quite possible — and perhaps most provocative — within relations of similarity, as the evolutionary analogy suggests. Thus, we might approach the angel-human relation in *Paradise Lost* in the terms of a morally neutral version of Milton's "knowing good and evil, that is to say of knowing good by evil" — knowing difference by knowing similarity — as Milton demonstrates in *Areopagitica*.[13] This backlighting is part of what Milton's monist materialism makes possible: far from settling the question of human-angel relation, Raphael's claim further focuses critical scrutiny on these beings that seem at times to be so human. What is really important about Milton's position on matter is not so much the *fact* of it, but what it *facilitates*. Milton's representation of angels relocates the epistemological grounds on which to gauge what is familiar and unfamiliar, from the abstract terrain of the philosophical and theological to the embodied bounds within which we live, move, and have our being, shifting attention to a fresh and exciting inquiry about sameness and difference. Within the terms of this inquiry, the question "what are angels?" initiates a whole new mode of investigation, one that breaks free from belabored efforts to define ethereal substance or explain incorporeal bodies. Adam's question about angelic sex performs such a shift: his initial statement is more declarative than inquisitive, insisting that the experience of pleasure must be a shared one—"Love not the heav'nly Spirits"—while his continuation acknowledges the possibility that angel bodies look (or rather, feel) quite different from his and Eve's: "how thir Love / Express they, by looks onely, or do they mix / Irradiance, virtual or immediate touch?" In its attention to strange angel bodies—bodies that are both familiar and unfamiliar—the poem revises our understanding of what it is to be a bodied being, flagging other modes of embodiment while also directing more self-conscious attention to our own. The declaration that Adam and Raphael "[differ] but in degree, not kind" may hold true of the material stuff angelic and human bodies are made of; however, the poem is also interested in a different kind of difference than a focus on substance can address.

Milton's angels present only one face of what Morton terms the strange stranger. In a cultural moment increasingly aware of the needs of other organisms, yet less able to foster ethical response to those others, the task of theorizing cross-species encounter becomes more pressing. I do not expect to welcome an angel to my table, but I do find myself in close contact with many nonhuman others, some of whom are guests within my home but many of whom are hosts to me in theirs. It matters how I perceive and represent these others. This essay thus addresses the risk of anthropocentrism in the fields of animal studies and cognitive ethology. In probing the nature of kin(d)ship via the reader's encounter with Milton's angels, I hope to gesture toward a strange kind of kinship, a kinship that does not require Raphael's kindship, and so preserves a space for nonevaluative difference.

Adam's own cross-species encounter generates anxiety about different modes of embodiment. Having invited his angelic guest to join him and Eve for dinner, Adam urges Raphael to taste the garden's bounty, yet not without some qualification that the meal may be "unsavourie food perhaps / To spiritual Natures" (PL 5.401–02). While "unsavourie" suggests mere preference—Raphael might not like earthly food, despite Eve's culinary efforts "not to mix / Tastes, not well joined, inelegant, but bring / Taste after taste upheld with kindliest change" (lines 334–36)—Adam's emphasis on Raphael's angelic "nature" raises significant concern about the distinction between human and angel. Regardless of whether Raphael might not *like* Adam's food, Raphael may not *need* food at all. Raphael takes this latter concern to be the source of Adam's anxiety, for his response establishes angel bodies *as bodies*:

> Therefore what he gives
> (Whose praise be ever sung) to man in part
> Spiritual, may of purest Spirits be found
> No ingrateful food: and food alike those pure
> Intelligential substances require
> As doth your Rational; and both contain
> Within them every lower facultie
> Of sense, whereby they hear, see, smell, touch, taste,
> Tasting concoct, digest, assimilate,
> And corporeal to incorporeal turn. (5.404–13)

With respect to food, that angels and humans "*both* contain / Within them every lower facultie / Of sense" (my emphasis) by which they assimilate corporeal nutrition troubles the poem's desire to make the difference between Adam and Raphael merely one of degree. Given the implication that heavenly food must still be subject, for angels, to the nutritional processes by which "corporeal to incorporeal turn," we must consider that the nectars and dews of heaven are just as corporeal or gross to the angels as are the plants and gourds of Eden to Adam and Eve. According to Joad Raymond, the passage resists a symbolic or spiritual reading, "instead emphasizing the virtue of pure pleasure, and finding it in material food and drink."[14] Fully granting the corporeality of angel sense, on which Raphael insists, sets up an experientially analogous relation between human and angel that requires an emphasis on the contingency of material experience. Such contingency is at the heart of Raphael's opening discourse on digestion, which proceeds to construct material relations in just such an analogous manner.

Raphael's bid for angelic embodiment is an ecological one, identifying angels as fellow creatures and identifying Adam as one among the many life forms dependent on God for sustenance. Raphael extends his discussion of angels and humans to consider how the same process by which bodies take in and transform food from the corporeal to the incorporeal governs all things:

> For know, whatever was created, needs
> To be sustained and fed; of elements
> The grosser feeds the purer, earth the sea,
> Earth and the sea feed air, the air those fires
> Ethereal, and as lowest first the moon;
> Whence in her visage round those spots, unpurged
> Vapors not yet into her substance turned.
> Nor doth the moon no nourishment exhale
> From her moist continent to higher orbs.
> The Sun that light imparts to all, receives
> From all his alimental recompense
> In humid exhalations, and at even
> Sups with the ocean. (PL 5.414–26)

The moon image, in particular, emphasizes universal materiality. It closely mirrors the opening description of bodies that "concoct, digest, assimilate": as the "lowest" of "those fires / Ethereal" — the celestial body closest to earth — the moon nutritionally assimilates the air, purging its "Vapors" of whatever cannot be used and turning what is left "into her substance." This nutritional process not only links the moon to the digesting angel body that opens the passage but also to the eliminating angel body that follows it in the narrator's discreet suggestion that heavenly beings also rid their bodies of waste (5.438–39). If establishing the materiality of angels likens them to humans, it also likens them to everything else that exists. In Raymond's analysis, by giving Raphael an appetite Milton builds his argument for the "continuity of matter across all of Creation."[15]

By expanding his discussion of the digestive process to consider how all things — "whatever was created" — assimilate food and purge waste, Raphael establishes analogous relations between the bodies that are the immediate focus of the passage — angel, human — and the various material entities he goes on to list. Rather straightforward, these relations are determined by one-to-one correspondences: the angel body, or the human body, is equally analogous to each of the other bodies under consideration, such that [angel:earth::angel:sea:: angel:moon] and so on. The same goes for the human, which is also like all of these. Since each entity in this string of analogies is interchangeable with any other, any entity could be the primary analogue to which all the others are compared, such that [moon:angel::moon :human::moon:sea] and so on. Any way the entities are paired, the result is the same: all things need food, and so are equally dependent on God's provision.

However, Raphael's attempt to align angels with all other material entities pulls away from its emphasis on individual bodies. In setting up the analogies between various bodies, including Adam's own, the passage articulates the joints and sinews of a greater, cosmic body whose frame is composed by all other lesser bodies — angel, human, elemental, and celestial alike. Drawing on the popular notion of the body as a microcosm, the passage folds the individual elements — earth, sea, moon, and so on — into the organism that supplants them as the primary analogue to angel and human, the cosmos itself, such that the entities become its diverse "parts," analogous *not* to the angel or human body as a whole, but to "every lower facultie / Of sense" within a body. As in individual bodies, corporeal food moves through this great, global body, becoming more incorporeal with each digestive phase.

This feeding action links the composing parts of the cosmic body in a clearly hierarchical manner, which is consistent with early modern understandings of the human body as well as the metaphorical, often politically inflected uses to which the body-as-microcosm was put.[16] Indeed, Adam's response to Eve's dream suggests just such a hierarchical approach to the body (*PL* 5.100–09). Just as reason occupies a privileged position within the individual body, the sun in Raphael's description rules over the lesser celestial bodies, the air, sea, the earth itself, and everything else. Of course, the most accessible models for Milton's readers of such organizational schemas were classical ladders of ascent and the great chain of being, both of which assign positions of ontological privilege to those elements or entities higher up in a grand cosmic scale.

Posing a subtextual challenge to hierarchy, however, is the contingent nature of the analogies on which the framework of this cosmic body depends. While the passage is driven by Milton's beliefs about matter and so overtly interested in identifying the similar needs of things that share substance, the relations invoked by the analogies that compose the cosmic body register an alternative mode more elusive in its ontological play. Explicating how "grosser" forms of materiality feed "purer" ones, Raphael networks entities together in more complex analogies than those setting up the one-to-one correspondences, such that [earth:sea::sea:air::air:moon::moon:sun]. While the simpler analogies generalize in order to make the basic point about shared substance, these analogies require conceptual fluidity: to the sea, earth is corporeal; to the air, the sea; to ethereal fire, the air. In their availability as raw food matter, earth and sea (and all the elements) are equally corporeal, equally gross; likewise, they are equally pure when the relations are inverted. Focused not on the entities themselves but on their relations with other entities, these analogies erect an alternative ontological framework that puts the terms of embodiment in constant flux.[17] Corporeality and incorporeality, gross and pure — these emerge as perceptual constructs that cannot be so straightforwardly mapped onto a universally descriptive ontological axis.

Yet this alternative ontology depends to some extent on isolating entities from one another, which troubles my interest in relations. To array the relations of the moon — with earth, sea, sun, and so on — is to merely produce a specifically lunar ladder of ascent. However, this is a *specifically lunar* one. More accurately, then, rather than eliminating hierarchy, this alternative ontology multiplies it in a way that is at least to some extent self-canceling. Instead of erecting just one continuum of substance on which all things are conceptually located, the passage explodes like a poetic big bang, giving rise to infinite ladders of ascent, as many as there are things that exist. In fact, Raphael's "one first matter all" speech includes both these conceptual schemes. Similarly setting up both intra- and interspecies relations, the passage erects a dominant ladder by which "all things" are arrayed, as well as all the many ladders of all those many things, determined by the limits of bounds, proportions, and kinds. Milton's interest in digestion playfully blurs the categories of "body" and "spirit" in such a way as to set up more prolific distinctions in the wake of the poem's overt dismantling of dualistic understandings, and so challenges the kind of easy statement Raphael makes about angel-human continuity.

In its representation of heavenly and earthly interaction, the poem itself generates the conflict between spiritual and corporeal forms, which are only distinguished as such when they bump up against each other. When Gabriel suggests to Uriel how difficult it would be to keep Satan out of Eden if in fact he were there — "hard thou knowst it to exclude / Spiritual substance with corporeal bar" (*PL* 4.584–85) — his positioning of spiritual and corporeal collapses the complexity of Miltonic substance by exclusively associating angelic substance with spirit and earthly matter with body.[18] It creates a binary that relegates the heavenly and earthly to opposite ends of a universal conceptual continuum that only works by alignment, and so does not account for how the spiritual includes the corporeal, or how the corporeal gives rise to the spiritual. Such interplay between spiritual and corporeal is the very point of Raphael's discourse on digestion, whereby the plant possesses states of corporeality and incorporeality unique to its botanical form. Given that Raphael's experience of heavenly matter is just as material as Adam's experience of earthly matter, the comparative valuation "more spiritous, more pure" only makes sense when Raphael tries to speak of heaven's materiality within the bounds of its earthly equivalent. It is only in comparison to Adam and Eve's experience of food that angelic nourishment is pure or incorporeal. The poem's hierarchical impulse may therefore be as much a product of poetic and narrative demands as of Milton's own commitments.

Like Gabriel's alignment of "spiritual substance" and "corporeal bar," accommodation collapses the complexity of material relations in *Paradise Lost*. Raphael frames his narrative as a figurative descent into the realm of body, marked by a further corporealizing of otherwise "pure" matter. Asked to explain heaven, Raphael admits the difficulty of his representational task:

> what surmounts the reach
> Of human sense, I shall delineate so,
> By lik'ning spiritual to corporal forms,
> As may express them best. (PL 5.564–67)

Raphael's opening statement establishes the figurative potential of the concept of embodiment. His suggestion that he will "liken" heavenly to earthly forms follows paradoxically on his use of the verb "delineate," which suggests a rather two-dimensional narrative method. Indeed, the poem's imaginative embodiment of angels is hardly a matter of such mechanical computing, and belies Raphael's caveat as too reductive to properly describe the work of accommodation. Accommodation is not simply a rhetorical strategy that Raphael adopts from the end of book 5 through book 8. As such, it is not simply a way to dumb down heavenly events for the sake of Adam's limited earthly imagination, although Raphael certainly presents it so. Accommodation is a more fundamental mode of encounter.

The metaphorical possibilities of embodiment made it a particularly rich concept in early modern theological debate over the sacrament of communion. Indeed, the question at stake was one of embodiment: are the bread and wine literally or metaphorically the body and blood of Christ? Finding in the conflict over the doctrine of transubstantiation evidence of a larger cultural shift in understandings of reality,

Robert Watson addresses the semiotic implications of the theological crisis: "The difference between identifying things with an absolute material essence, or else believing them to achieve their identity only within the experiential scope of each individual, correlates with the difference between doctrines of Real Presence (as articulated by the Fourth Lateran Council in 1215) and doctrines (notably Protestant ones) that place the transformative miracle within the subjectivity of the recipient, however unworthy — a kind of host-reception theory articulated in various ways by leading Renaissance theologians."[19] William Madsen similarly approaches the transubstantiation debate — so imbricated with other discourses in the period — for how it crystalized more general concerns about the nature of reality and representation. Contesting claims that Milton understood accommodation to participate in a mythic or sacral project, Madsen considers what Milton's "sacramental theory" reveals about the poet's approach to figuration. Quoting from *De doctrina Christiana*, Madsen stresses that for Milton the elements "are analogies or similitudes which represent rather than present a spiritual reality," and extends this theological cleaving of sign and signified to Milton's view of metaphor.[20] In articulating divergent positions on how the bread and wine ought to be understood to embody Christ — do they literally "present" or metaphorically "represent" divine presence — Madsen further crystalizes the stakes, for a poet like Milton, of what was the period's central theological debate.

The sacramental debate parallels what has been the critical debate regarding Milton's angels in interesting ways. Does Milton "present" angels or "represent" them? Ever since Samuel Johnson's complaint that Milton "unhappily perplexed his poetry with his philosophy," scholars have attempted to account for the poem's inconsistent delineation of angels.[21] The sorts of things that happen to angel bodies during the war in heaven have been the source of much critical frustration. While their "liquid texture" allows them to "Limb themselves, and colour, shape or size / Assume, as likes them best, condense or rare" (*PL* 6.348–53), angels on the battlefield are trapped by their own armor, which causes them physical distress (6.656–57). C. S. Lewis contests that the war in heaven is not so "poetically grotesque" as Johnson laments but, rather, a genuine attempt to depict angels as the "aerial spirits" that Ficino popularized in the period — *not* immaterial yet characterized by "incredible swiftness and almost unlimited powers of transformation, contraction, and dilation."[22] For Lewis, the real source of inconsistency is not in any of the poem's descriptions but in Raphael's qualification, which in its exclusive association of angels with the spiritual and of humans with the corporeal diverges from the poem's dominant representative "scheme," in which angels *are* corporeal, if in a rather atypical (spiritual) manner. To make sense of Raphael's anomalous qualification, Lewis suggests, "I am not at all sure that *corporal* here means more than '*grossly* corporal,' 'having bodies like ours.' The adaptation which Raphael promises may consist not in describing pure spirits as material, but in describing the material, though strictly unimaginable, bodies of angels as if they were fully human."[23] Lewis's response to Johnson shares something with the Reformation attempt to preserve the spiritual meaning of the body and blood while rejecting mystical claims to Real Presence: some significant change happens, but its significance has to do with experience rather than substance. Most important is not whether accommodation *presents* angels, but how accommodation *represents* them. In describing accommodation as an adaptation of one kind of body — the "bodies of angels" — into the terms of another — "as if they were fully human" — Lewis directs attention away from metaphor itself as the site of meaning and toward the particularity of the experiential context at work for its audience. Thus, the debate over the nature of metaphorical discourse resonates with my interest in how Milton's monist materialism does not simply make *something* available in its insistence on shared substance; more significantly, it makes *some* particular *thing* available in its probing of boundaries between things. In the terms of the "host-reception theory" Watson describes as the Protestant stance on Communion, the miracle of metaphor happens "only within the experiential scope of each individual."

Ultimately, however, Lewis defends the book 6 account as a literal attempt to depict angels as the aerial bodies Ficino described, and so merely replicates Johnson's desire for narrative consistency, missing the more provocative potential of metaphorical representation. But metaphor need not deny immateriality to Milton's angels or belie Milton's narrative strategy as anything less than sincere. In what follows, I offer an account of metaphor as truly representational in its attempt to embody angel bodies in the terms of human ones. This account embraces narrative inconsistency as part of its productive metaphorical work, which functions to keep the poem's representation of angels strange. To further develop an account of metaphor's provocative representational potential, I would like to consider the primary definition of metaphor that Madsen invokes, articulated by W. B. Stanford: "the process and result of using a term (X) normally signifying an object or concept (A) in such a context that it must refer to another object or concept (B) which is distinct enough in characteristics from A to ensure that in the composite idea formed by the synthesis of the concepts A and B and now symbolized in the word X, the factors A and B retain their conceptual independence even while they merge in the unity symbolized by X."[24] Like other standard accounts of metaphor, Stanford's emphasizes conceptual unity. An approach to metaphor informed by the sort of strangeness Morton describes, however, admits metaphors whose success resides not only in their ability to produce synthesis but also a fair amount of dissonance. Furthermore, while the language of merging suggests the relations of metaphor are neutral and mutual, as if two parties take the same number of steps to meet in the middle, this is not necessarily the case. In fact, Stanford's definition is confused on this point, since he also identifies the metaphorical term X as "normally signifying an object or concept (A)," and so locates metaphorical origins within a particular experiential domain. Thus, metaphor involves a primary participant A, the experiential context of which drives the metaphor, and a secondary participant B. This inequality registers the anthropomorphic implications of metaphorical discourse, especially when we talk about animals. Finally, I would like to place a stronger emphasis on the "conceptual independence" Stanford does nevertheless maintain, and so better resist metaphor as unification.

This final section has two aims: I would like to test out Stanford's definition in a reading of one of the most critically problematic moments during the war in heaven, angels in armor; in doing so, I will extend this notion of metaphor to better account for the experiential aspect of accommodation. I will then use this reading to show how metaphorical representation dislocates embodiment from any particular experiential field. To set up the relational — and so ecological and ethical — stakes of the reader's encounter with warring angels, however, I first show how Satan's wound, like Raphael's blush, both invites and impedes recognition.

Explicitly cued by Raphael as a narrative accommodated for a human audience, book 6 has generated much critical debate over whether and in what way the account of the war in heaven ought to be considered metaphorical. Given Raphael's attention to an experience that, with its "Engins and...Balls / Of missive ruin" (*PL* 6.518–19), cannot have much meaning for unfallen Adam, the poem's descriptive energies are directed as much at engaging an audience outside its narrative as within it. Satan's wounding by the archangel Michael exemplifies the narrative's attempt to elicit more embodied reader response than that offered by the unfallen Adam, for whom pain and death remain merely conceptual entities. After exchanging verbal assaults, the two celestial beings engage their weapons, of which Michael's proves the more formidable:

> the sword
> Of *Michael* from the Armorie of God
> Was giv'n him temperd so, that neither keen
> Nor solid might resist that edge: it met
> The sword of *Satan* with steep force to smite
> Descending, and in half cut sheere, nor staid,
> But with swift wheele reverse, deep entring shar'd

> All his right side; then *Satan* first knew pain,
> And writh'd him to and fro convolv'd; so sore
> The griding sword with discontinuous wound
> Pass'd through him. (6.320–30)

Satan's wounding by Michael provokes a visceral moment of engagement across textual bounds.[25] In its parabolic syntax, the passage actually inscribes the jagged cut onto the page, driving deep and discontinuous in lines 323–27, each clause after the introductory colon extending its tortuous path to the experiential heart of the descriptive moment — "then *Satan* first knew pain" — before turning with its own "swift wheele reverse" to reinforce the wound in lines 328–30, which throb with the sympathetic resonances of "sore...sword... wound."[26] The central clause is set off from the convoluted lines on either side of it by the hard caesura in line 327, and its minimalist diction pauses for a moment not unlike the way the brain freezes just before registering pain. Reducing the distance between reading and being-read bodies, the passage invites *us* to grimace as Michael's smiting sword entangles *our* entrails. Readerly guts writhe with Satan's.

But Satan doesn't have guts, technically, of which we are reminded as soon as we experience this vicarious disembowelment. Indeed, almost as quickly as it extends the invitation to feel Satan's wound, the passage revokes it: "but th' Ethereal substance clos'd / Not long divisible" (6.330–31). In just half a line, injured angel flesh magically heals itself, the article elision having performatively seamed the actual ethereal stuff of Satan's body into one metric beat to fit the iambic pentameter. The only evidence of the wound is the "stream of Nectarous humor" that "issuing flow'd / Sanguin, such as Celestial Spirits may bleed" and Satan's "Armour staind" (6.332–34). Hardly does this nectarous fluid qualify as blood that any reader would recognize. The blood's descriptor reveals itself to be ambiguously adjectival: *how* is this "Sanguin" fluid like blood — in its color? in the way it leaks out and stains Satan's armor?[27] Furthermore, in recalling Satan's sweet sobriquet for his fallen fellows — "the Flowr of Heav'n" (*PL* 1.316) — the line casts doubt on the figurative nature of flowers in *that* moment even while it invites skepticism about the literality of blood in this one. The qualified clause reads back retrospectively on the whole incident, revealing to the reader the metaphorical context for what she has just experienced: like the "tears such as angels weep" from book 1, Satan's wound is a wound such as angels may receive; his pain is pain such as angels may feel. *Is* this a wound we can identify with, and *is* this pain like the pain we've just virtually felt? The poem checks itself, and in so doing adjusts our response.

Sonorously bleeding, as it were, from one term into the next, the trio of "sore...sword...wound" in the description of Satan's smiting by the archangel Michael marks out key participants — wounds, armor, pain — in the metaphorical representation that is the book 6 account. Angel wounds, armor, and pain together form what may be thought of as an assemblage functioning as a nonliteral means of signaling the nonetheless materially significant concept of war in heaven. I want to explore this battle assemblage in one of those moments that Johnson writes off as distastefully polluting Milton's poetry with his philosophy. Despite their innovative technology, things start to look dire for Satan and his followers when Michael's army begins ripping up the heavenly landscape:

> Their armor help'd thir harm, crush't in and bruis'd
> Into their substance pent, which wrought them pain
> Implacable, and many a dolorous groan,
> Long strugling underneath, ere they could wind
> Out of such prison, though Spirits of purest light,
> Purest at first, now gross by sinning grown. (PL 6.656–61)

The poem's attention to armor as an impediment to angel bodies is one place where the traditional trope of descent as corporealization seems to be at work, thus reinforcing Raphael's hierarchical model of continuous matter. Playing with ontological associations, the passage appears to set up a causal relation between sin and corporeality, such that the explanation for why the rebel angels are trapped in their own crushed armor looks to be a change in their substance, from ethereal bodies — Ficino's aerial spirits — to something more dense and compact, like earthly materiality.[28] Yet, this does not make sense given that the unfallen angels are similarly encumbered by *their* armor, as Raphael relates the effect of cannon fire on Michael's troops:

> which on the Victor Host
> Level'd, with such impetuous furie smote,
> That whom they hit, none on thir feet might stand,
> Though standing else as Rocks, but down they fell
> By thousands, Angel on Arch-Angel rowl'd;
> The sooner for thir Arms, unarm'd they might
> Have easily as Spirits evaded swift
> By quick contraction or remove.   (6.590–97)

Since whatever change the rebel angels' bodies manifest as a result of sinning is presumably not one the "Victor Host" has undergone, and since the unfallen army is as much impeded by its armor as Satan's, the change cued by "gross" in line 661 must *not* be the corporealization of angel form. These descriptions occur too closely together for them to suggest mere oversight on the part of an author caught up in the grandiosity of poetic vision. Milton is obviously interested in thinking about angels who are vulnerable and can feel pain in both innocent and sinful states.

The passage about the fallen angels does include another possibility for what "gross" might indicate, if not corporeality. The contrast is between "Spirits of purest light, / Purest at first" and those which are "now gross by sinning grown." Here, the passage suggests grossness as not denser but more shadowy matter, the antithesis of light as the property not of weightlessness but of brightness. If brightness is the primary physical attribute that angels lose when they sin, then the description of angel armor — and so perhaps the whole war narrative — must be metaphorical, since it would be absurd to claim that fallen angels are crushed by their armor because they have lost their heavenly brightness. Of course, the historical argument would remind us that brightness and obscurity are often associated causally in the period with dilated and compacted states of matter — that Ficino's aerial spirits were light in both senses of the adjective, both bright in appearance and lightweight because their airy molecules were spaced farther apart. And, in Milton's thinking, brightness-thinness-purity often form an associative chain. However, the unfallen angels' similar predicament drives a wedge between light indices, pulling apart the conceptual adhesive that binds a spectrum of brightness and one of density; Michael's army, though presumably still quite bright, is also hampered by its armor. In resisting an easy assimilation of readily available notions of corporeality and incorporeality, Milton's representation insists on preserving a space for the strangeness of angel bodies.

Returning to a formal consideration of metaphor, the signification of this martial assemblage may be parsed in the following terms: the human experience of warfare (A) — derived in this case mostly from epic tradition — provides the metaphorical representation (X) that attempts to communicate whatever it is (Y) that is responsible for the psychosomatic experience of impeded, pained angels (B). As the source of X, the human dimension drives this metaphorical representation. I have added a factor Y to account for what is missing in Stanford's definition, that other term that would help to preserve the autonomy of B in its encounter with A. From the perspective of ecological ethics, it is crucial that Y has a place in metaphorical relation, and that it remains undefined and undefinable: Y is what makes B a strange stranger, the unfamiliar that qualifies and challenges claims about the familiar. Notice that the complex analogies I described early in the chapter are at work here, such that A:B::X:Y. The human experience of warfare is to the angel experience of cosmic struggle as the assemblage of battle — wounds, armor, and pain — is to whatever is the source of angelic vulnerability. Or, to highlight the experiential heart of the metaphorical episode, what is being compared is the analogous relations A:X::B:Y. As my reading of Raphael's speech on cosmic digestion stressed, complex analogies like these do not directly compare entities themselves but, rather, their relations to other entities, and so are less instrumental than generative. While traditional approaches understand metaphor to connect two terms that are already known independently of each other, Milton's metaphorical war attempts to describe something that is otherwise unknown in the terms of what is known.

In undertaking several projects simultaneously, the war in heaven does present problems for Milton. He wants to convey a material war in heaven fought by material beings. While God must obviously win this battle, Milton wants to represent it as genuinely epic in its stakes, which requires on the part of both armies strenuous effort and significant risk. Milton also wants to animate a doctrine of ethereal substance, which means that angels must be depicted as material but with unique properties that make them not fully available to the epic project. But I hope that my reading has helped make sense of some key moments of incoherence in a more attentive way than do approaches that either find the poem's inconsistency aesthetically distasteful or explain it away as a product of misinformed reading. Critics have sometimes had trouble synthesizing Raphael's caveat that his narrative will be accommodated — implying that angelic experience is not like human experience — with his qualification of that qualification: "though what if Earth / Be but the shadow of Heav'n, and things therein / Each to other like more than on Earth is thought" (PL 5.574–76). My argument finds no conflict in Raphael's statements; heaven and earth can be compared, but contingently. They are like and unlike each other; this is the representational mode of the familiar/unfamiliar. Yet accommodation is not simply a matter of "like, but not like" — it is a matter of *how* like and *how* not like. My reading allows the poem's inconsistency on angelic morphology to stand. By refusing to solve the question of substance, this inconsistency actually helps to preserve the angelic other as other. The poem's interest in angel armor reveals its resistance to closure on the question of angel substance: it wants to ask the question "what are angel bodies like?" but does not want to fully answer it.

Since readers of *Paradise Lost* are also readers of the world outside its textual bounds — what the period often called the "Book of Nature" — Milton's representation of angels has ecological and ethical implications for our own encounters. The problem of metaphorical discourse is also more fundamentally the problem of perception, which plagues ethological study: we cannot study or talk about animals in order to understand them without conceptually extending our own bodies. When I peer at an octopus through the aquarium glass and fix my gaze on its features that are most homologous to my own eyes, I fail to consider how the octopus might actually perceive me through photoreceptors in those eight suctioned arms rather than what appear to me to be its organs of perception.[29] Thus, octopus "eyes" are really not eyes at all, and octopus "arms" might be more like eyes; to speak of octopus eyes and arms is to speak metaphorically.

The limits of language need not inhibit efforts to learn about nonhumans, however. Modeling their stance of "critical anthropomorphism" on the philosophical position that negotiates between "naïve" realism and extreme skepticism in the study of perception, Rivas and Burghardt recognize the inescapability of human subjectivity in the study of animals: "Perhaps anthropomorphism is only harmful in science when it is unacknowledged, unrecognized, or used as the basis for accepting conclusions by circumventing the need to actually test them."[30] Furthermore, they argue that a self-conscious anthropomorphism can be a useful tool in inquiry, and applaud studies that encourage creativity in facilitating human experience of the animal's *Umwelt*.[31] Their emphasis on creativity serves as an invitation to bridge scientific and other avenues of knowledge about the nonhuman, such as the literary. Acknowledging and embracing the role of the imagination in our attempts to account for the nonhuman are especially crucial if we wish ethology to have ethical import, if we want the study of difference to give rise to modes of response to difference.

Milton's representation of angels in *Paradise Lost* can help facilitate this sort of self-conscious anthropomorphism. In closing, I want to return to my opening reading and briefly consider the ecological and ethical import of my emphasis on modes of embodiment as it pertains to Adam's encounter with an angelic other. If Milton's book 6 representation of armored angels prefers to play with — rather than define — the concept of angelic embodiment, Raphael's description of angel sex outright resists talking about angel bodies in the terms of embodiment. Indeed, the contrast between Adam's "body" in line 622 and Raphael's own angelic "eminence" in line 624 suggests how nonsensical it is to speak of angels as having bodies at all. Their incorporeal mixing is after the manner of particulate matter, molecules of "ductile and homogenous" angel substance that, as Lewis imagines, "mix like wine and water, or rather like two wines."[32] Of course, we *do* speak of both water and wine as bodied things — a body of water, or a full-bodied red wine. How might we understand the bodies of Milton's angels as similarly metaphorical? If some critics of the poem have been overly eager to claim the bodies of Milton's angels in the service of projects that are really about humans, others have resisted any discussion of Milton's angels in the terms of embodiment. Yet Milton's angels are neither disembodied beings nor beings that have bodies like ours. Speaking anthropomorphically of angel bodies is not necessarily problematic. What is problematic is doing so without qualification. When speaking of the bodies not of wine or water — or perhaps even of Milton's angels — but of living beings, doing so without qualification is an ethical failure.

Asserting that Milton's angels are "creatures, not merely instruments of narrative," Joad Raymond better accounts for the angels of *Paradise Lost* than scholars who treat them as extensions of Milton's philosophical or theological commitments. According to Raymond, "*Paradise Lost* repeatedly focuses on the similarities and dissimilarities between human and angelic experience."[33] As Raymond's additional comment intimates — that the poem performs this attention "with an extraordinary tact" — there is an ethical posture to be taken with respect to how we approach and articulate relations across difference.[34] Evidence of this ethical attention can be found in Adam's question to Raphael, which preserves the integrity of angels as genuine others: "Bear with me then, if lawful what I ask; / Love not the heav'nly Spirits, and how thir love / Express they, by looks onely, or do they mix / Irradiance, virtual or immediate touch?" (*PL* 8.614–17). Adam's sensitivity to Raphael's angelic otherness is emphasized by his repeated plural pronouns: "how *thir* love / Express *they*...do *they* mix" (my emphasis). While Adam's reference to "love" carries the risk of anthropocentric assumption, the pronoun he attaches to it maintains an important space for difference. Adam uses the only word he can, yet qualifies it. Adam's qualification introduces the sort of ontological Möbius strip that troubles fields of study, the perils — which might also be possibilities — of anthropomorphic discourse. It acknowledges that angels probably have a different way of expressing love and, therefore, that whatever angels express is their own form of love and so may not be what he experiences as love at all. Adam does not simply ask *whether* angels express love; he asks *how* they express it. His question calls into further question the ways in which angels and humans are like and unlike each other, suggesting a more nuanced attention to modes of embodiment than has generally been extended to Milton's angels. Raphael is, after all, a "Heav'nly *stranger*" (PL 5.316; my emphasis).

CHAPTER 6

Dark Looks and Red Smiles
Homeric Gesture and the Problem of Milton's Angels

LARA DODDS

What makes an angel blush? This is the question that seems to be raised at the end of book 8 of *Paradise Lost*, where Adam, himself "half abash't," asks Raphael how angels express their love, "by looks only, or do they mix / Irradiance, virtual or immediate touch?"[1] When the angel replies, his countenance is transformed with a "smile that glow'd / Celestial rosy red, Love's proper hue" (8.618–19). Critical commentary on Raphael's red smile has been frequent, and it often focuses on what it is *not*: he "does not blush like a Victorian schoolgirl";[2] his color signals "fitting warmth" or "enthusiasm," rather than "shame." It is "tempting" but incorrect to see the blush as a "token of Raphael's embarrassment" or as "repressed adult society's embarrassment at childhood's innocent and unrestricted interest and delight in sexuality."[3] In another line of interpretation, Raphael's red color does not signify passion at all. Instead, it is a "simple case of color symbolism," merely an indication of Raphael's status as seraph, which means we are "mistaken" to interpret this reaction as a "blush of embarrassment" or Raphael's color as one of several "human metaphors for love."[4] Most commentators assume Raphael's coloring to be a blush but then chastise readers who attribute to Raphael the feelings usually associated with blushing. As James Grantham Turner explains, "There is no question of an archangel's being embarrassed, though Milton might trick us into thinking so at first."[5]

The interpretive anxiety arising from Raphael's rosy red smile is a remnant of the long-standing critical misunderstanding, discomfort, or even embarrassment caused by what Joad Raymond describes as the "creatureliness" of the Miltonic angel.[6] Samuel Johnson notoriously claimed that Milton had "unhappily perplexed his poetry with his philosophy" through "the description of what cannot be described, the agency of spirits," and scholars have struggled since to reconcile the apparent contradictions posed by the angelic characters, who are clearly not the beings of pure spirit described by Aquinas.[7] The questions posed by Johnson's critique have continued to be important for studies of Milton's angels: is their representation plausible, logical, decorous? In the first comprehensive treatment of the topic, Robert West argues that the problems of logic and decorum detected by Johnson are inherent in Milton's material, a result of the conflict between doctrinal definitions of the angel and the actions demanded by epic narrative.[8] West attempts to distinguish between those moments in the poem where the angels and their actions are doctrinally true and those where they are merely expedient or conventional. By contrast, Arnold Stein thought the angels were fully conventional. He answers Johnson's complaint by allegorizing the angels and their actions as "epic comedy" and a metaphor for the perfecting of the will.[9] More recently, however, the angels have been recognized as manifestations of the ontology of *Paradise Lost*. In most recent accounts the angels are science fictional extrapolations of Milton's theology and natural philosophy. As Stephen Fallon writes, "Milton places corporeal angels in his true poem because he believes in them."[10] If the angels of *Paradise Lost* eat or fight or have sex or blush it is because they, like humans, are part of the "one first matter all" of God's creation (PL 5.472).

The integration of the angels into a more thoroughly historicized account of Milton's theology and natural philosophy, however, makes the question of Raphael's rosy red smile only more pressing. If the angels are machines, then a blush may be metaphor or literary convention. If angels are pure spirit, then a blush is an error that must somehow be explained away. In the monist universe of current Milton criticism, however, the blush, if it is one, draws together many of the questions posed by the intertwining of materialism and theology in Milton's thought. The blush is a fulcrum for the questions debated by Raphael and Adam in book 8 of *Paradise Lost* because an individual's capacity (or incapacity) for blushing has implications not only for his or her psychological state but also for his or her status in the social hierarchy and relation to the larger community. In early modern psychology and physiology, the blush was understood as an involuntary expression of passion that demonstrates to others, somewhat paradoxically, the blusher's guilt and innocence simultaneously. To blush is to acknowledge shame and, in doing so, demonstrate one's capacity for moral probity. One early modern commentator explains that individuals blush because "nature, being afrayde, lest in the face the faults should be discovered, sendeth the purest blood to be a defence and succour, the which effect, commonly, is judged to proceed from a good and virtuous nature, because no man can but allowe, that it is good to be ashamed of a fault."[11] The blush is thus a highly significant social sign: by advertising an individual's acknowledgment of and regret for his or her fault, the blush signifies a submission to social norms and expectations.

The alternative is far more dangerous: to be incapable of blushing is to be shameless, which indicates a rejection of social expectations. The blush thus enacts a highly complicated self-consciousness that arises internally from an involuntary motion of the blood and externally from the observation of others; the blush brings about both an awareness of the blusher's own body and also the place of that body within a larger social collective. In the words of another early modern commentator, the blush signals humanity's divided nature, which "partaketh of the same general nature with the Angels" and thus "shameth to behold it selfe placed in a body which hath fellowship with brute beasts."[12] This understanding of the blush leads to the conclusion that an angel, by some definitions of an angel, cannot blush because angels are not divided in nature as human beings are. In fact, some neoclassical theorists of the epic concluded that angels could not serve decorously as the machines of Christian epic for the same reason that they cannot blush; such beings cannot have the motivations, emotions, or passions necessary for poetry that delights. John Dennis warns poets against "luxuriant" descriptions of angels, which John Milton's most certainly are, because "these are Beings, of which no Man can have clear and distinct Ideas, because they have nothing which is common to us, neither distinction of Sexes, nor variety of Passions, nor diversity of Inclinations."[13]

The natural philosophical, theological, and social connotations of the blush thus explain the many anxious assertions that Raphael's red smile is not one. Recent studies of the angels of *Paradise Lost* argue that Milton's unorthodoxies reduce the distance between the human and the angel. As Fallon argues, Milton's poetry "consistently minimizes the ontological distance between angels and men."[14] Raphael's blush has received extensive commentary because it represents the greatest test of this claim. In this essay I suggest that the problem of Raphael's rosy red smile may be clarified by, on the one hand, an examination of a broader discourse of coloring in *Paradise Lost* and, on the other, a more careful historicization of Raphael's smile within the conventions of gesture in the classical epic tradition. Milton reconciles an early modern understanding of facial coloring, particularly red and white, as markers of an individual's physical and psychological state with literary conventions of gesture drawn from the classical epic tradition. In his colloquy with Adam, Raphael's sudden coloring follows, and contrasts with, another distinctive facial gesture, the "contracted brow" that indicates his disapproval of Adam's uxorious love for Eve (*PL* 8.560). In *Paradise Lost*, more broadly, however, Raphael's smile contributes to a discourse of coloring in which the sudden appearance of a red, or in some cases pale, countenance serves as an external marker of the intertwining of passion and volition. In this essay I examine the intersection of new materialism with literary tradition and argue that Raphael's gestures are possible because he is, like the other fallen and unfallen angels, the descendant of the

Homeric heroes. The angelic blush—like other crucial moments of gesture in the poem—is an illustration of Milton's debt to his epic predecessors. In the classical epics, gesture establishes character and, more significantly, articulates social relationships. In this essay I focus on two different forms of gesture—dark looks (which are probably the most common of angelic gestures) and Raphael's blush (which is apparently unique as a gesture among the unfallen angels)—to reveal the literary antecedents of Milton's material angels. In the central books of *Paradise Lost* (5–8), Raphael is sent to teach Adam about the universe and his place in it; the complex genealogy of his rosy red smile, which is at once a physiological event, a social sign, and an instance of epic gesture, establishes the possibilities and the limits of shared understanding between humans and angels.

In his recent and comprehensive study, Joad Raymond insists that the Miltonic angel is not mere *machinery*, a "fictional narrative device, modeled on humanity." Rather, in a poem that could be said to be foundationally "about angels," these supernatural beings demonstrate the interdependence of doctrine and narrative, poetry and theology in Milton's epic.[15] Thus, Raymond insists, we must attend to the angels *as* angels. Raymond's book, building on earlier work by Stephen Fallon and John Rogers, effectively counters Johnson's critique by showing that there is no "perplexing" of matter and spirit.[16] Milton's angels are not those of Aquinas but are instead corporeal. This focus on the angels' ontology, however, tends to obscure the importance of their literary antecedents among the heroes of classical epic. The angels of *Paradise Lost* speak, boast, fight, and even weep like the heroes of the *Odyssey*, the *Aeneid* or, especially, the *Iliad*.[17]

These epic antecedents are perhaps most present in the language that Milton uses to define the angels' affect and gestures. Gesture is a significant and understudied element of the epic texture of *Paradise Lost*. Embedded in the brief but evocative introductions that precede or follow characters' speeches, descriptions of gesture help create the formal, elevated style required of epic, while also supplementing words and action with nonverbal communication that can express intention, belief, or affect.[18] While not formulaic in the same way as the speech introductions of Homer's epics, gesture in *Paradise Lost* nevertheless serves many of the same functions.[19] As Donald Lateiner argues in his study of gesture in the Homeric poems, gesture can supplement the narrative in two significant ways. First, and in most cases, gesture supports speech and action, reinforcing and creating character through repetition. Repeated rituals of greeting, for instance, define and reinforce differences in status. Second, and more rarely, gesture may function to conceal or reveal hidden motivations when it seems to conflict with a character's speech. In this case, nonverbal behaviors can "provide something that words cannot say, or they can undercut and render problematic both instrumental acts and words."[20] In Homer's epics, gesture is a particularly efficient technique of characterization, interpretation, judgment, and commentary. Lateiner uses the encounter between Achilles and Priam in *Iliad* 24 to demonstrate the narrative power that Homer derives from the seemingly insignificant details of facial expression, stance, and posture. In this episode, Priam approaches Achilles privately to negotiate for the return of Hector's body. Gesture, both facial expression and posture, allows for the two men to mediate their competing interests and break the stalemate caused by Achilles's retention of Hector's body. Priam and Achilles do speak, but the series of gestures they perform are equally communicative. Priam kneels and clutches Achilles's knees. This gesture of supplication indicates Priam's deference to Achilles, but also asserts authority and prepares for the expected exchange of goods. Priam's gestures also allow the two men to weep together, an "unexpected social reciprocity,"[21] which further enables their reconciliation by temporarily shifting the men's relationships to one another. Only after Achilles acknowledges his fellow-feeling with Priam does he reassert his superiority as warrior and victor, an identity signified by an "angry glance from beneath his brows," an instance of the dark looks formula I discuss below.[22] In Homer's epics, Lateiner concludes, "posture and gesture have a propriety, truthfulness, and creative expressiveness of their own that transcend words."[23]

Milton likewise uses concise descriptions of gesture to develop character and advance the narrative. In *Paradise Lost*, the condensed phrases that communicate gesture are significant in two ways: on the one hand, they economically and powerfully characterize; on the other, they subtly locate characters and their actions within a long tradition of heroic poetry. In book 1, for instance, Satan concludes his speech to Beelzebub with "Eyes / That sparkling blaz'd" and his "Head up-lift above the wave" (*PL* 1.193–94). These brief descriptions of Satan's countenance and his physical posture efficiently capture the complexities of Satan's circumstances at the beginning of the poem. He remains prone, yet the intensity of his "sparkling" eyes reinforces the power of his words and subtly anticipates his argument that the "mind is its own place" (1.254). Likewise, the "uplift" head signifies Satan's continued resistance to his foe in spite of his prior defeat. In fact, the editorializing commentary throughout the first two books of the poem — Satan is "Vaunting aloud, but rackt with deep despair" (1.125) — testifies to gesture's power. Satan's complex relationship to the classical heroic ideals means that his gestures simultaneously fulfill both of the functions Lateiner identifies in the Homeric epics. While gesture works in concert with speech to construct Satan as a defeated enemy who remains resolute in his principles, the commentary of the epic voice attempts to drive a wedge between speech and action by suggesting that Satan's gestures hide his true psychological state.

It is a commonplace to associate the fallen angels with the heroes of classical epic, but it is less frequently recognized that all of the angels, both fallen and unfallen, share this literary heritage of nonverbal gesture.[24] But, as Richard Strier argues, the political and deliberative framework of Milton's theodicy creates "continuity between Heaven and Hell."[25] Literary conventions of characterization that link the angelic characters while distinguishing them from the human characters offer more subtle evidence of this continuity. Though divided between heaven and hell, the fallen and unfallen angels share a habitus built from the gestures of the Homeric heroes. The most notable of these gestures, and one that is performed solely by the angelic characters, is the gesture described by the Homeric formula υποδρα ιδων (*hupodra idon*).[26] Variously translated as "looking darkly," "glower" or "glare," or "dark glance," this formula appears 26 times in the *Iliad* and the *Odyssey* and is used to express powerful feelings of anger, indignation, or resentment.[27] Among the early modern translators, George Chapman (*The Whole Works of Homer*, 1616) describes Ulysses "folding" his brows or Hector with "countenance bent,"[28] and Ogilby (*Iliad*, 1660; *Odyssey*, 1665) typically uses a simple "frowning."[29] Pope is less consistent in his rendering of the formula, but makes up for that inconsistency with his vivid diction: "anger flash'd" from Ulysses's "disdainful eyes" or he replies "sternly" with "Indignation sparkling in his eyes."[30] In the latter example Pope uses Milton's allusion to the Homeric formula in *Paradise Lost* as the inspiration for his translation, which suggests that Pope recognized Milton's diction as an example of Homeric allusion.

In their roles as warriors, both unfallen and fallen angels frequently deploy dark looks. As James Holoka shows in his study of the dark looks of the *Iliad* and *Odyssey*, a dark look is a way for a speaker to assert his superiority, to show by his "facial demeanor that an infraction of propriety has occurred." The dark look charges "the speeches it introduces with a decidedly minatory fervency and excitement."[31] Thus Satan confronts Sin and Death with a "disdainful look" (2.680), and the gesture highlights Satan's perceived superiority to Death. Satan emphasizes his difference from this "execrable shape" (2.681): "Retire, or taste thy folly, and learn by proof, / Hell-born, not to contend with Spirits of Heav'n" (2.686–87). Satan's dark look indicates that Death violates decorum and propriety by attempting to block his voyage. When Sin's narrative of her origin reveals that Death is Satan's son, however, he moderates his dark looks and addresses him with "milder" and "smooth" (2.816) words. In this case, dark looks are a way for individuals unknown to one another to assert authority and dominance, while the revelation of a prior social relationship defuses the possibility of conflict.

The importance of dark looks for expressing antagonism and conflict is further demonstrated in the encounter between Satan and the angelic guard at the end of book 4. Again the epic voice uses the formula to express scorn and indignation. Each convinced (though only one correctly) of his superiority and righteousness, Gabriel and Satan exchange boasts accompanied by gestures that are descendants of the "dark looks" of Achilles and Odysseus. Gabriel first confronts Satan with "stern regard" (*PL* 4.878) and chastises him for breaking the "bounds prescrib'd / To thy transgressions" (4.879–80); Satan's impropriety is physical (he is an improper place), social (he improperly confronts Gabriel as an equal, which he no longer is), and metaphysical (his corruption is improperly intruded into the perfection of Eden). Satan, however, replies scornfully and with the same gesture. He addresses Gabriel "with contemptuous brow" (4.885) and asserts a superiority of experience that, he claims, derives from knowledge the unfallen Gabriel lacks. The similar exchange of dark looks between Hector and Glaucos in *Iliad* 17, provides context for this episode. When Hector is unable to retrieve the body of Glaucos's countryman Sarpedon, Glaucos rebukes him with a dark look. In Ogilby's translation, the "wofull Glaucus" turns to Hector and, "his Browes contracting, roundly chides."[32] As Holoka explains, this exchange of dark looks is notable for the way that it temporarily upends status hierarchy.[33] Hector is the superior warrior, yet he has failed in his duty to his allies. Glaucos is thus justified in his dark looks, and though Hector replies with dark looks of his own ("Hector lookt passing sowre at this"),[34] the consequence is a renewal and intensification of martial effort so that Hector may regain status and save face. In this context it is notable that, while Satan, "frowning stern" (4.924), attempts to continue the status competition signified by the exchange of dark looks, the outcome is quite different from that of *Iliad* 17. Gabriel is not pushed into further conflict but instead exempts himself with yet another Homeric gesture. "Disdainfully half smiling" (4.903), Gabriel sidesteps Satan's attempted provocation.[35]

While gesture can be used to reinforce a character's acknowledged identity and status, it can also punctuate moments of transformation or particular emotional intensity. Lateiner suggests that Homeric narrative occasionally features "dramatic, momentary, emotional disequilibria, characteristically conveyed by mien, posture, demeanor, gaze, and gesture."[36] In *Paradise Lost* such moments are frequently accompanied by changes in color, in which the face or countenance suddenly becomes pale or red. Throughout *Paradise Lost* such "coloring," for both humans and angels, is associated with moments of significant action and particularly intense affect. Early modern commentators described coloring as spontaneous and involuntary. Blushing cannot be feigned.[37] Of the moments of prelapsarian coloring in *Paradise Lost*, Adam's blanching when he recognizes Eve's fall demonstrates these qualities. He is suddenly "speechless" and "pale" when he recognizes Eve's action, and he appears briefly to lose conscious control of his body: "horror chill / Ran through his veins, and all his joints relax'd; / From his slack hand the Garland wreath'd for Eve / Down drop'd" (9.894, 890–93). In this instance, Adam's coloring is a visible sign of a complex mental state, while it also punctuates a significant moment in the narrative. Adam's paleness is not under his control; yet, significantly, his blanching is followed by a soliloquy that leads Adam to choose an action that is contrary to the horror and aversion — signified by his "pale" countenance — of his spontaneous passion. In Adam there is a division between passion and action; somewhat paradoxically, given that he makes the wrong choice, his will overcomes the passion that would prompt him to shun Eve's action.[38]

As we shall see, angels also color in *Paradise Lost*, but it would be wrong to assume that their changes in color occur in the same way or for the same reasons that humans blush or blanch. In fact, Raphael makes this very point when he explains that angels can take on any color that they choose. The distinct ontology of the angels allows them to "Limb themselves, and color, shape or size, / Assume, as likes them best, condense or rare" (*PL* 6.352–53), which suggests that their "coloring" remains under conscious control. As with the gender identity of the angels, however, these creatures have a theoretical capacity for variety that is much greater than what the narrative represents. In his own "proper shape" Raphael is graced with wings of "downy Gold / And colors dipt in Heav'n" (5.276, 282–83); however, when angels color in a way that impacts narrative it is always through the sudden appearance of a pale or red countenance. The most spectacular example of this kind of coloring is the repeated color change that reveals Satan's disguise at the beginning of the book 4. When Satan begins to speak he is "first inflam'd with rage" (4.9); however, his soliloquy is accompanied by further changes in color that reveal his passions and his true identity: "each passion dimm'd his face, / Thrice chang'd with pale, ire, envy and despair, / Which marr'd his borrow'd visage" (4.114–16). Satan takes care to dissemble his passions as soon as he is aware of them: he "each perturbation smooth'd with outward calm" (4.120). In this case, his gestures or, more specifically, his coloring reveal what he would otherwise conceal.

Satan's apparently involuntary color changes in this episode have been attributed to his fallen nature — the epic voice indicates that "heav'nly minds" are free from "such distempers foul" (4.118) — but the unfallen angels do sometimes experience spontaneous passions that are registered by color in their countenances. These gestures, however, do not require dissimulation. For the most part, the gestures of the unfallen angels reinforce the unity of passion and volition, desire and action that is characteristic of angelic ontology in *Paradise Lost*. Michael's gestures in his single combat with Satan in book 5 illustrate this unity through a complex interplay of coloring and the Homeric dark look. Michael addresses Satan with a "hostile frown / And visage all inflam'd" (6.261–62). The "hostile frown" is another dark look and indicates Michael's justified disdain for Satan's presumption, but his "inflam'd" visage, like the "fiery red" appearance of the angelic squadron discussed below, illustrates the traditionally heroic desire to demonstrate faith and virtue through military achievement. Raphael tells us that Michael was "glad" to face Satan because he hoped to defeat him and "end / Intestine War in Heav'n" (6.258–59). The sudden red coloring added to a dark look suggests the intensification of Michael's affective state as he encounters a circumstance — violent dispute among the angels — never before known in heaven.

A more complicated instance of angelic coloring occurs during the confrontation between Satan and the angelic guard at the end of book 4. Following Satan and Gabriel's exchange of dark looks, the

"Angelic Squadron" confronts Satan with a color change. While Satan continues to boast and threaten,

> th' Angelic Squadron bright
> Turn'd fiery red, sharp'ning in mooned horns
> Thir Phalanx, and began to hem him round
> With Ported spears. (4.977–80)

Initially "bright," the squadron responds to Satan's threats with a change in color — they "turned fiery red" — and a threatening movement of their own: they "port" their spears in order to surround Satan. The diction here illustrates the difficulty of describing the nature of angelic coloring: is the angels' red color a part of their military formation — the "Phalanx" that separates into two points to surround Satan — or is it a somatic response prompted by anger and indignation? In other words, is their color change tactics or is it passion? It is impossible to tell because in this case, unlike the color changes that accompany Satan's soliloquy or Adam's blanching upon Eve's fall, the two possibilities are entirely aligned.

The doubleness of the angels' coloring here also casts light on the notorious plowman simile that follows immediately after:

> as thick as when a field
> Of Ceres ripe for harvest waving bends
> Her bearded Grove of ears, which way the wind
> Sways them; the careful Plowman doubting stands
> Lest on the threshing floor his hopeful sheaves
> Prove chaff. (4.980–85)

As "the most discussed simile" in *Paradise Lost*,[39] it is, in John Leonard's words, "impossible."[40] On the one hand, the inconsistency between the aggressive stance of the angels' spears and the "waving" field of wheat that is said to be like them threatens to undermine the unfallen angels' superiority. On the other, the plowman figure raises further questions: his physical position suggests a comparison to Satan, but the plowman's psychological state ("careful"; "doubting") has often been judged incompatible with Satan's fallen state, leading to the proposal of other candidates.[41]

Characteristically, Stanley Fish argues that the "indeterminateness" of this simile is the point: "Good intentions and a willingness to serve do not assure success, which comes only if God wills it. If the existence of Gabriel's patrol is to be justified only in terms of need and sufficiency, Empson is right; it is for show."[42] The comparison of the spears to the waving wheat, therefore, is an indication of the psychic complexity of this moment for the angelic squadron. The ambiguity of the simile is matched by the ambiguity of the angels' red coloring. The angels become red because of their justified anger at Satan's infraction and/or the angels become red as part of strategy to eject Satan from Eden.

This overview of angelic gesture in *Paradise Lost* reveals what Raphael's pair of gestures at the end of book 8 shares with those of the other angels and also how they are unique. Superficially, Raphael's "contracted brow" followed by a "rosy red smile" resembles Michael's expressions in book 6. In both cases, a frown of rebuke is followed by a red countenance that reveals an intense affective state. However, the context in which these gestures occur — Raphael and Adam are talking about love and sex — overrides these similarities. Raphael's contracted brow, which has not, to my knowledge, attracted extensive commentary, transparently communicates his disapproval, but his so-called blush, as we have seen, does not. The narrator asserts that red is "Love's proper hue" (8.619), but, as the commentary that I quoted above suggests, this explanation has rarely been sufficient and the reason for this insufficiency is easy to identify. Raphael's blush troubles readers because it signifies a lack of decorum on Milton's part and because it potentially creates a feminizing association between Raphael and Eve, who is led "blushing like the Morn" (8.511) to the marital bed. In this context, C. S. Lewis's complaint is relevant: Milton's Eve "exhibits modesty too exclusively in sexual contexts, and his Adam does not exhibit it at all." Lewis does not believe that Eve's innocence is incompatible with sexuality, but he does think that the sexuality of the poem should not resemble modern sociosexual mores. It's "offensive," he suggests, for "female bodily shame" to be an "incentive to male desire."[43] If a woman's blush causes this much discomfort, how much more so an angel's? Therefore, commentary on Raphael's red smile—whether acknowledged as a blush or not—is almost always accompanied by gatekeeping language.[44] The significance of Raphael's red smile is various and multiple: shame, embarrassment, happiness, and pleasure are present, at the very least, in the frequent assertion of their absence. Here readers ask, as they don't with Michael, whether Raphael's gesture reveals more than he intends.

Perhaps this question occurs so insistently because Raphael's rosy red smile is the one instance of coloring that must signify across the species line. In fact, the narrator is quite explicit that when Raphael greets Eve she does not blush: "no thought infirm / Alter'd her cheek" (*PL* 5.384–85). Furthermore, the other cases of angelic coloring might feasibly be dismissed as a consequence of accommodation: perhaps Milton and his narrator Raphael simply describe the passions of the angels in the terms most accessible to human understanding.[45] Yet in this case, if Raphael and Adam are to understand one another, the nonverbal gestures of the "half abash'd" Adam and Raphael's "celestial red smile" must each be communicative of the speaker's inner state in a way that is legible to the other. Susan James observes that the passions are "transgressive" because they "cross two boundaries—that between soul and body, and that between the body and the physical space around it."[46] As we have already seen, angelic ontology means that the first of these transgressions likely does not signify for the unfallen angels. The soul-body divide does not have the same urgency for creatures that are "all Heart," "all Head, all Eye, all Ear/ All Intellect, all Sense" (6.350–51), as it did for seventeenth century philosophers writing about the passions. The second boundary however, is pertinent to the angels of *Paradise Lost* and particularly so at the end of book 8. James explains that the passions can create a "kind of involuntary thinking that goes on in and between the bodies of individuals."[47] Gestures, and the blush in particular, signify, as we have seen, socially: does Raphael's red smile therefore acknowledge—or even create—community that encompasses both humans and angels? This question is given special urgency by the placement of this exchange as the culmination of the central episode of *Paradise Lost*, books 5–8, in which Raphael fulfills his function as divine messenger. As such, we should recognize this exchange as the last of several efforts by the epic voice and the characters to articulate principles of similarity and difference with respect to materiality, species, and gender. To summarize briefly: Adam wonders whether angels can really eat, and is told that Raphael's true need for (and enjoyment of) the food Eve serves them is a demonstration of the "one first matter" that links all of creation through differences in degree rather than kind. Likewise, Adam's request that Raphael narrate the war in heaven prompts speculation about the relation between heaven and earth; Raphael says he will explain events in terms that humans can understand — "by lik'ning spiritual to corporal forms" (5.573) but also wonders whether heaven and earth are "Each to other like more than on Earth is thought" (5.576). When Adam takes over the narrative in book 8, his description of his creation, the creation of Eve, and their subsequent marriage raises similar questions within the earthly realm. Adam's initial observations of the pairing of animals and his colloquy with the Father interrogate the similarities and differences between humans and beasts, men and women. The question that I asked at the beginning of the essay — "what makes an angel blush?" — is thus another version of the primary concern of these central books of *Paradise Lost*: how are humans and, more precisely, Adam himself, to negotiate participation in the "one first matter" of a monistic universe with the distinctive subjectivity allowed by one's form, species, or gender?

Raphael's "contracted brow" is, of course, another version of the Homeric "dark looks." In my survey of the early modern translations of Homer, I found at least two instances in which the formula υποδρα ιδων (*hupodra idon*) was translated as contracted brow. In addition to the passage from Ogilby already quoted, Chapman describes Zeus speaking to Mars with a "contracted brow."[48] As in the examples I cited earlier, Raphael here uses this gesture to assert his superiority and chastise Adam for a failure of decorum or propriety. Adam has just confided that his love for Eve has led him to recognize her as an autonomous being, "in herself complete" (8.548), a fulfillment perhaps of the egalitarian impulses of the desire that he originally expressed to God. Raphael's frown, however, seems designed to silence Adam and serves as a means for Raphael to reacquire the discursive authority ceded when Adam offers to tell "My Story" (8.205). As we have seen, the dark look allows a character to assert superiority. In this case, Raphael's frown might be expected to bring an end to the conversation through the angel's correction of Adam's passion. That it does not—Adam does not frown back as Satan does, nor is he silenced—prepares for the complex function of the red smile that follows. While Eve's lack of blush in book 5 demonstrates that she does not fully share in Raphael's sociability, Adam's "half-abasht" response to his dark looks indicates that he does.

Like dark looks, a smile may be a gesture of superiority. And certainly there is some superiority in the speech that accompanies Raphael's rosy red smile. He assures Adam that

> Whatever pure thou in the body enjoy'st
> (And pure thou wert created) we enjoy
> *In eminence*, and obstacle find none
> Of membrane, joint, or limb.   (8.622–25; my emphasis)

Daniel Levine argues that a Homeric smile is always a sign of justified superiority, but Raphael's red smile is more complex.[49] Unlike Gabriel's smile in book 4, Raphael's is accompanied by a change of color. Raphael is the sociable angel, and if we read his red smile as a blush, we can see most fully Milton's vision of what that means. The blush is an involuntary gesture of self-consciousness; as such, it signifies a submission to a broader social world. To blush is to acknowledge that one belongs to a larger collective. In Aristotle's traditional opinion, "no one feels shame before babies and small beasts"; shame is only possible in reference to those "whose opinion he takes account of," those "who admire him and whom he admires and by whom he wishes to be admired."[50] Adam is not a beast or a baby, of course, but neither is he Raphael's equal. Yet Adam's question about angelic sexuality subjects Raphael to a kind of scrutiny that produces a unique moment in *Paradise Lost* of what we could call angelic self-consciousness. Raymond argues that the angels of *Paradise Lost* are not *mere* machinery, and though I agree that they are not merely machinery, they are machinery. Raphael's contracted brow demonstrates this fact; the angels fulfill their roles most easily — most legibly — when their actions are shadowed by the legacy of epic tradition. His rosy red smile, however, momentarily disrupts that legibility. Indeed, it is only when Raphael must confront the similarities and differences between the erotic lives of beasts, humans, and angels in his own "person" that he transcends his status as a machine. Adam's question and his own response challenge him with what it means to be an angel *as* an angel in a cosmos that includes the embodied, divided beings who are men and women.

PART FOUR

MILTON'S MATERIALISM REDUX

CHAPTER 7

Orson Pratt, Parley Pratt, and the Miltonic Origins of Mormon Materialism

JOHN ROGERS

No single writer has had a greater impact on the boldest and most original aspects of the theological component of America's nineteenth century religion, Mormonism, than John Milton. Milton's theology, as presented in the newly discovered and translated *De doctrina Christiana*, and his poetry, especially *Paradise Lost*, left an indelible imprint on the conceptual and imaginative structures of early Mormon doctrines of Creation, the Fall, and redemption. Elsewhere I have considered the specific Miltonic influence on Mormonism's prophetic founder, Joseph Smith.[1] Smith's Miltonic leanings will necessarily be of some concern to the present essay. But my goal here is to broaden the horizon of our understanding of Milton's influence on the Church of Jesus Christ of Latter-day Saints. I wish in particular to emphasize the surprising extent to which *Paradise Lost* figured in some of the new religion's earliest forays into theological speculation. Two early Mormon leaders, both appointed apostles by Smith himself, show every sign of having followed the prophet in devoting themselves to the project of mining Milton's epic and his *Treatise on Christian Doctrine* for theological and philosophical inspiration. More specifically, the interpretive community of early Mormon readers turned to the seventeenth century poet for assistance in the urgent project of developing the new faith's metaphysically inclined theology, the earliest attempts to unfold discursively and logically the religious meanings bound up in the prophet Joseph Smith's oracular utterances near the end of his life concerning the relation of matter to spirit. Ultimately, I hope to show, the evidence we have of the early Mormon reading of Milton suggests that the Latter-day Saints, writing after William Blake but well before William Empson, were engaged in one of literary history's most impressive antithetical — we can also call it satanic — interpretations of Milton's epic.

Smith died at the hands of approximately 150 men who mobbed the jail in Carthage, Illinois, where he and his brother were being held in June 1844. Less than three months before his death, Smith delivered in Nauvoo, Illinois, what was surely his most distinctive and compelling sermon, an extemporaneous address delivered before a crowd of 20,000 followers at the funeral of a Mormon elder, King Follett. It is this sermon, fortunately transcribed by a handful of disciples on the occasion of its delivery, and known now as the "King Follett Discourse," in which Smith seized the occasion to venture some of the Christian tradition's boldest theological speculations. Smith articulated his belief that the spirit of man, man's "intelligence," not only pre-exists his birth as a mortal human, but is actually eternal and "self-existent," dependent for his creation on no one, not even God. In addition to this idea that God doesn't "create" human beings or their universe, but merely "organizes" preexisting materials, Smith also proclaimed, no less shockingly, on the human origin of God and on the divine origin, and divine end, of humanity. The sermon's oracular pronouncements on the origin of matter, of humanity, and even of God, were at once so exciting and so perplexing that Smith's followers' eventual attempts at explication in the more familiar forms of theological and philosophical reasoning were surely inevitable. Also inevitable was the crisis, following Smith's death, involving the question of the prophet's successor. How would the church be organized in the absence of its founder? If Smith were to be replaced as president of the Church of Jesus Christ of Latter-day Saints, how could it be determined who would follow him? The immediate political question of church government and succession, on the one hand, and the deeper question of the meanings of the metaphysical and cosmogonal speculations Smith delivered near the end of his life, on the other hand, are both implicated in the emergence shortly after Joseph Smith's death of what we can identify as Mormon theology.

Early Mormonism's chief theologians were two of Smith's closest disciples. One was Parley P. Pratt, who in 1830 sought baptism into the Mormon faith almost immediately upon reading *The Book of Mormon*, first published that year, and who would be honored as one of the first members of the church's Quorum of the Twelve Apostles in 1835. A missionary and a historian, Parley was also one of Mormonism's most important theologians: his *Voice of Warning* and *Key to the Science of Theology* have long been considered among the most influential religious writings in nineteenth-century Mormonism.[2] The second of the movement's two great theologians was Parley's younger brother Orson Pratt, baptized a Mormon by Parley himself a few weeks after Parley's own entry into the church, and also honored in 1835 as a member of the Quorum of the Twelve Apostles. Orson's contribution has proven nearly as central to the new religion's beginnings. His work "On the Divine Authenticity of the Book of Mormon" and his pamphlet on "Celestial Marriage," the movement's first serious theological defense of polygamy, were crucial early contributions to the mission to spread the church's Restored Gospel throughout the United States and beyond. Orson's labor, later in life, editing the scriptural *Book of Mormon* and *Doctrine and Covenants*, which he was the first to divide into chapter and verse, was key in imposing on those otherwise unruly works of divine revelation a striking graphic affinity with the standardized print format of the Old and New Testaments; it was largely owing to Pratt's editorial efforts that the *Book of Mormon* could present itself as a newer New Testament. If Joseph Smith can be seen as the Jesus of Mormonism, then each of the Pratt brothers can be viewed a reasonable candidate for the role of Saint Paul, the figure celebrated by the Christian church for having taken the new religious sensibility aroused by the prophet Jesus and invested it with something like a systematic philosophical rigor. The question of which brother would come to inherit the title that one scholar has called the "St. Paul of Mormondom" will be one of the considerations of this essay.[3] To be sure, it was Parley (favored by Brigham Young, and, perhaps worth noting, the great-great-grandfather of former Massachusetts Governor Mitt Romney) who led the more obviously dramatic life: most famously, he would be murdered at age 49, after a cross-country pursuit by the estranged husband of one his 12 wives.[4] But given that it is so often the case, in life as in literature, that the younger is the more interesting of a pair of brothers, the focus of this study will rest, though not exclusively, on the younger of the two theologically minded Pratts. Both Pratt brothers were students of their prophet, Joseph Smith, and both show every sign of having been avid readers of the poet-prophet Milton. But it would be Orson, in the care and the zeal with which he attempted to interweave the truths he gleaned from both of those teachers — especially in his metaphysical treatise, *Great First Cause, or the Self-Moving Forces of the Universe* — who would most fully ascend to the imaginative heights scaled by the prophet Smith and the poet Milton.

Let us consider first the succession crisis that shook the church, lasting for at least three years after the founder's death.[5] Who in the wake of Joseph Smith's assassination would be promoted to lead the Mormon church? Would it be the two surviving members of the First Presidency — the uppermost tier of leaders in the church's hierarchy, originally consisting of the president (initially Smith) and his two chief counselors? Would it be the aggregate triumvirate of a reorganized First Presidency, with a new president installed? Might it be the larger, senatorial gathering of the Quorum of the Twelve Apostles, who could through power of consensus guide the infant faith? Or, more broadly, would the church's Presidency devolve to the even more representative body of the Council of Fifty, or the Quorum of the Seventy, wider groupings that stood beneath the Quorum of the Twelve? The crisis was intensified in part by the confusion surrounding one of the divine revelations concerning ecclesiastical organization that Joseph Smith had shared with his followers, around the time of the establishment of the Quorums, in 1835. We read, for example, in Smith's revelation as transcribed in *Doctrines and Covenants* 107:23–26, that the Twelve Mormon Apostles "form a quorum, equal in authority and power to the three presidents" who constitute the church's First Presidency. The Quorum of the Seventy, furthermore, is "equal in authority to that of the Twelve." Just a few lines down, however, in verse 33, we learn that it was also revealed to Smith that "the Twelve are a Traveling Presiding High Council, to officiate in the name of the Lord, *under the direction of the Presidency of the Church*" (italics mine).[6] On the one hand, the Quorum of the Seventy is equal to the Quorum of the Twelve, which is itself equal to the Presidency. On the other hand, the Quorum of the Twelve serves "under the direction of the Presidency." Given what could be viewed as a conflictive revelation about church organization, reasonable arguments were made for the original Mormon prophet's anticipation of his succession either by the Quorum of the Seventy, by the Quorum of the Twelve, by the three leaders of the First Presidency, or by a single, newly named president himself.

The succession crisis was long and drawn out, spanning much of the time in which the Saints marched westward to Utah in their exodus from Illinois following Smith's death. The three-man First Presidency under Smith had been dissolved shortly after Smith's assassination. Almost immediately the chief governing body of the church became the Quorum of the Twelve Apostles, of whom the charismatic Brigham Young was president. As Gary James Bergera explains, although officially it was the 12-man Quorum that served collectively as the faith's governing authority, Brigham Young "had assumed *de facto* presidency of the church by virtue of his position as president of the Quorum."[7] In the period following Smith's death, Young "wanted to consolidate his position by reconstituting the highest governing council," the First Presidency. And it would appear that Young labored to make as manifest as possible his fitness to lead the church, citing "Joseph Smith's example, his revelations, and the practical realities of church governance, all of which, he felt, mandated" his own assumption of the Presidency. Brigham Young claimed, much as Joseph Smith had, that his entitlement to his position had been divinely revealed to him. And it was on the authority of that revelation that Young could assert that he now held the Sealing Keys of the Priesthood, the presidential rights formerly assumed by Joseph Smith, which include but are not limited to the keys of the knowledge of God, the keys of salvation, the keys to minister the ceremony of a marriage on earth that could be acknowledged and sealed in heaven, and the right to "give a revelation" permitting a man to marry more than one wife.[8] In November and December 1847, the crisis came to a head when Brigham Young made a bid in a conclave of the Apostles for a formal reorganization of the First Presidency, with himself at the helm. Orson Pratt argued the most strenuously for the ongoing governance of the church by the Quorum of Twelve Apostles, while Brigham Young continued to assert what he took to be the self-evident eminence of his position. In one of the debates held by these elders of the church in late 1847, Young boldly asserted his position above the Quorum by denying that body its apparent right to authorize, or deauthorize, his Presidency: "You can't make me President," he explained to Orson Pratt, "because I am already President. You can't give me power, because I have it."[9]

Milton among the Mormons

On the basis of what evidence can we say that the seventeenth-century English poet Milton played an important role in the thinking of the church's earliest members? For some it may be sufficient merely to point out Joseph Smith's direct engagement with one of the most famous lines of *Paradise Lost* when he writes of the Mormon practice of the baptism of the dead that it "justifies the ways of God to man."[10] But the evidence of the ties that Smith and some of his closest Apostles had to Milton is much deeper than that simple citation might suggest. It has long been established that Milton was one of the most widely read and passionately revered poets in eighteenth and early nineteenth century America.[11] That a significant number of educated

U.S. readers in that period were intimately familiar with *Paradise Lost* has been amply demonstrated. What scholars haven't yet sufficiently acknowledged, however, is the zeal with which passionate but less educated readers in the late eighteenth and early nineteenth centuries approached the work of England's premier epic poet. I have discussed elsewhere the many aids to reading Milton that had been widely available since the eighteenth century: readers whose goal was to expose themselves to the stories of disobedience and redemption treated so scantily in the Bible had several ways of reading *Paradise Lost* for the plot. There were, all in print form, prose versions of Milton's poem; abridgments that removed from the flow of narrative the similes and other challenging but inessential ornaments; versions of the poem that straightened out Milton's syntax, rendering the epic "into grammatical construction"; and, perhaps most popular of all, a version, approved by the Methodist church, intended to help parents read the epic to their children.[12] And we must assume that many devout readers, inured through years of Bible study to the pain of wrestling with seventeenth century English prose, would have gone out of their way to extract what they could from Milton's poem, especially if they felt, as surely many participants in America's Second Great Awakening did after the news hit of Milton's newly published religious beliefs, that the poet's heterodox views meshed closely with their own.

Any of these avenues to the study of Milton's *Paradise Lost* might account for the degree to which many aspects of early Mormon culture resound with the poetry of *Paradise Lost*. Some of the church's earliest instantiations of the Mormons' temple ceremony of "Endowment," the script for which is attributed variously to Joseph Smith and to Brigham Young, echo, sometimes verbatim, several passages from *Paradise Lost*.[13] Milton's self-conscious embrace of Hebraism in both *Paradise Lost* and *Paradise Regained* resonated powerfully with early Mormons, as Smith's *Book of Mormon* was steeped to an unusual degree in an Old Testament scriptural mode. "Shakespeare, Byron, Shelley, Burns," wrote one of the Saints in 1869, "are both Gentile and modern in their variety and tone; ... there is only one of the great English poets who stands boldly as an example of that peculiar poetic genius manifested in the inspired writings of the prophets and psalmists of ancient Israel, and that one is the 'divine Milton.'"[14] The popular Mormon writer Eliza R. Snow, celebrated as "Zion's Poetess," was praised by nineteenth century Mormons for the Hebraic, and implicitly Miltonic, cast of her epic and other poems (though non-Mormons derided her as a "Milton in petticoats").[15] Snow certainly earned her reputation as a Miltonic poet: her 1877 "Epic Poem in Five Chapters," titled "Personification of Truth, Error, Etc.," hews closely in tone and structure to book 2 of *Paradise Lost* and relies heavily both on that book's allegory of Sin and Death and on the "Great Consult" in Pandemonium.

Among the earliest systematic theologians among the Mormons, Milton's Hebraic mantle was said at the time to have fallen on "the apostle, Parley P. Pratt, whose very prose works are poems with the prophetic cast and quality."[16] Like his younger brother Orson, as we will see below, Parley was fully immersed in the poetry of *Paradise Lost* and in the heterodox speculations comprising Milton's newly discovered *Treatise on Christian Doctrine*, whose notoriety as a heretical document accompanied its much-publicized U.S. printing in 1826. Parley's 1842 *World Turned Upside Down*, written two years before the death of Joseph Smith, begins with a rhapsodic account of the Creation, Fall, and redemption that resounds with the prophetic grandeur of, as well as a tissue of echoes from, Milton's epic.

It has naturally been suggested before that Joseph Smith was moved by Milton's vigorous defense of polygamy's ongoing favor in the eyes of God in chapter 10 of book 1 of Milton's theological treatise *De doctrina Christiana*.[17] The manuscript of Milton's treatise had been unaccounted for until its discovery in 1823, but it was quickly edited and translated by Bishop Charles Sumner and published as *A Treatise on Christian Doctrine* in London in 1825, and Boston in 1826. The treatise's shocking heresies produced a scandal among many of Milton's polite nineteenth-century readers on both sides of the Atlantic. The poet's approval of polygamy became widely known throughout Protestant America by 1826, through the best-selling pamphlet heralding Milton's newly discovered heresies by the distinguished Boston Unitarian William Ellery Channing, and through the numerous local newspapers and church periodicals that treated as scandalous not merely the great poet's heterodoxy but Channing's seeming approbation of Milton's defense of polygamy.[18] While we have every reason to believe that Joseph Smith himself was familiar with Milton's writing on polygamy, the fact that some of his early apostles were also familiar with the *Treatise on Christian Doctrine* cannot be doubted. Orson Pratt published the church's first intellectual defense of polygamy in 1853.[19] Many of the arguments concerning polygamy among the patriarchs in "Celestial Marriage" can only have been drawn from Milton's treatise; without any apparent concern that Mormonism could be taken as a faith indebted to "Miltonism," Orson Pratt's overseas periodical, the *Latter-day Saints' Millennial Star*, would offer a verbatim reprint of Milton's long argument about polygamy in two successive issues in 1854.[20] "We have much pleasure," the *Millennial Star*'s editor reports, "in presenting before our readers the extract on Polygamy, from a *Treatise on Christian Doctrine* by the author of *Paradise Lost*, and we have no doubt that they will be highly gratified in perusing the article."[21] A couple of decades later, the Mormon readers of the *Millennial Star* would be urged further to read not only the discussion of polygamy in Milton's *Christian Doctrine* but also "the whole work itself, believing they will find much matter therein for serious contemplation, as being the earnest convictions of so learned and so respected an authority."[22]

The whole of Milton's *Christian Doctrine* would indeed have been a matter of contemplation for many early Mormons, who would have found in the learned and respected poet's doctrinal work a striking validation of, not to mention a possible source for, some of Mormonism's most distinctive heterodox beliefs. These readers would have found themselves in sympathy with Milton's surprising account of the millennium, by which we are instructed to look ahead to Christ's imminent return as our king here on earth, the universe on which he will literally reside for the duration of a thousand-year trial.

They would have been gratified, too, by Milton's minority position on an exclusively lay ministry, and, perhaps especially by Milton's Arian conviction in the createdness of the Son of God.

Most important, Mormon readers of Milton's *Christian Doctrine* would have been drawn to the learned and authoritative poet's account of Creation in chapter 7 of the treatise's first book. Thanks especially to William Ellery Channing's *Remarks on the Character and Writings of John Milton; Occasioned by the Publication of His Lately Discovered Treatise on Christian Doctrine,* readers could not help but be familiar with the fact that Milton had in his theological account of creation recast the relation of matter to spirit, and that he had pressed for an understanding of the liberatory potential of a belief in a seamless continuum between a material earth and a spiritual heaven. But more influential even than Milton's prosaic doctrine of an *ex deo* creation in *Christian Doctrine* was the corresponding poetic treatment of his radical materialism that filled the lines of *Paradise Lost*.[23] Like all early nineteenth-century readers of Milton's theology, Joseph Smith, like his apostles Parley and Orson Pratt, encountered in Bishop Charles Sumner's impressive edition of Milton's *Christian Doctrine* a careful coordination of Milton's theology with his poetry. The complex, sometimes even scholastic, arguments for material monism in the learned treatise were carefully collated in the edition's footnotes with their far more inviting, often more daring, poetic reformulation in the blank verse of *Paradise Lost*. In the footnotes of his edition, Sumner had quoted nearly in full all the epic's key figurations of matter's inextricability from spirit, the role of that spiritualized matter in the potential exaltation of the unfallen Adam and Eve, and the identity of an original, divinely derived spiritualized substance that Raphael in *Paradise Lost* would call the "one first matter" (5.472). William Ellery Channing, in the popular pamphlet introducing Milton's heresies to the poet's American readers, would cite all those passages *again,* singling out with italics the phrase "one first matter all" in his long block quotation of Raphael's speech, and clearly marking a passage that may once have seemed merely ornamental poetry as Milton's wholly invested statement of doctrinal truth: "We learn here that a passage in *Paradise Lost*, which we have admired as poetry, was deemed by Milton sound philosophy." In devoting far more space to the epic's metaphysics of matter and spirit than to many of the more familiar or celebrated aspects of the poem, Channing had attempted a significant reorientation of the general understanding of *Paradise Lost*. He labored to make Milton's readers appreciate both the boldness and the "reverence" with which Milton argued, in both poetry and prose, for the divine derivation of what modernity considered base, inert substance. Milton, we learn in reading Channing, was profoundly invested in "tracing matter to the Deity as its fountain."[24]

One Elementary Simple Substance

The prolific Pratt brothers had put themselves in conversation with some of the most notable metaphysicians of the late eighteenth- and early nineteenth-centuries. Their attempts to offer intellectual justification for Joseph Smith's unmistakable theory of divinized matter and the spiritualized human body led Orson, in particular, to engage openly with the theories of the English astronomical and metaphysical polymaths Roger Joseph Boscovich (1711–87), William Paley (1743–1805), John Herschel (1792–1871), and William Whewell (1794–1866). But Pratt's appreciation of and disputations with these relatively contemporary cosmologists were always mediated by what we can only assume was his total immersion in the poetry, theology, and metaphysics of Milton's *Paradise Lost* and *Christian Doctrine*. The metaphysics of Creation in Orson Pratt's *Great First Cause, or the Self-Moving Forces of the Universe* emerges as a complex engagement with Milton's account of Raphael's description for Adam, in book 5 of *Paradise Lost*, of the monistic continuity between the material substances of heaven and those of earth. Struck by the heavenly angel's willingness to eat earthly food, Adam notes that "these earthly fruits" cannot "compare" to "Heav'n's high feasts" (5.464–67). Raphael takes Adam's interest in a comparison of earth with heaven as an invitation to spell out the metaphysics of Milton's poem. The universe is not structured by a strict division of heavenly spirit and earthly matter, he explains. Spirit is material, just as some matter is spiritual, and the ontologically unified spiritualized matter constitutive of both heaven and earth has its ultimate origin in God:

> O Adam, one Almightie is, from whom
> All things proceed, and up to him return,
> If not deprav'd from good, created all
> Such to perfection, one first matter all,
> Indu'd with various forms, various degrees
> Of substance, and in things that live, of life;
> But more refin'd, more spirituous, and pure,
> As neerer to him plac't or neerer tending.   (PL 5.469–76)

The substance constitutive of both heaven and earth derives from the same source of original substance: "one first matter all" is the remarkable phrase Raphael uses to identify the origin of all things earthly and all things heavenly in the original substance from which the "one Almightie" created both earth and heaven. What we call spirit is but an elevated form of matter, "more refin'd, more spirituous, and pure," and the whole of creation can be imagined as spanning a vertical continuum from the least refined, least spirituous substance on the bottom and the most refined, most spirituous substance at the top.[25]

The unarticulated implication of this philosophy of substance, for Adam, as for all humans, is extraordinary and, the poem wants us also to know, potentially dangerous. The idea that humans are made of the same stuff as angels has the potential, if drawn out logically to an extreme, to ennoble all human actions, supplying an almost metaphysical foundation for any aspiration human beings might have to godhead. This passage, after all, follows Eve's distressing account of the transgressive dream in which an angel encouraged the fantasy of a human's ascent of the scale of nature from earth to heaven: "be henceforth among the Gods / Thy self a Goddess, not to Earth confin'd, / But sometimes in the Air, as we" (PL 5.77–79). And the passage looks forward to Raphael's speculative suggestion to Adam and Eve, that their bodies "may at last turn all to Spirit, / Improv'd by tract of time, and wing'd ascend / Ethereal, as we" (5.497–99). Perhaps it is with an eye to checking the full liberatory potential of a monistic metaphysics that Milton takes care to articulate the limits of matter's ascent to the purer height of spirit. All matter, Raphael insists, isn't equally poised to ascend the scale from base substance to airy spirit. It's true that all things, at least theoretically, proceed upward to God. But objects and beings in the natural world are nonetheless ontologically differentiated. The baser things on the low end of nature's scale are endued more with substance, and the purer and more refined things on the higher end endued more with spirit and life. All things, regardless of purity, may well share a *general* tendency to move upward, but the extent of any particular thing or being's upward ontological mobility is limited by some form of predetermination, as Raphael explains just after identifying the origin of all things in the "one first matter": "Each in thir several active Sphears assignd, / Till body up to spirit work, in bounds / Proportiond to each kind" (5.476–78). Raphael concludes his paean to the monistic continuum of Miltonic creation with this limiting insistence on what is ultimately creation's ontological circumscription: all created things, we learn in these final three lines of Raphael's metaphysical disquisition, have been assigned by their creator specific, hierarchically segregated, spheres of being, appointed specific "bounds / Proportion'd to each kind."

As noted above, early nineteenth century America had been alerted to the import of Raphael's vision of the origin of all things in the "one first matter." Raphael's is the poem's account of the relation of matter to spirit to which in 1825 Charles Sumner drew the attention of the readers of chapter 7 of Milton's *Treatise on Christian Doctrine*, in which Milton the theologian explains that "man is a living being, intrinsically and properly one and individual, not compound or separable, not, according to the common opinion, made up and framed of two distinct and different natures, as of soul and body, — but that the whole man is soul, and the soul man, that is to say, a body, or substance individual, animated, sensitive, and rational."[26] Raphael's account of spiritualized matter in book 5, and Milton's account of spiritualized matter in the treatise, are both cited and praised by William Ellery Channing for their elevation of material substance to the status of divinity. Mormonism's visionary founder, Joseph Smith, followed Sumner's and Channing's lead and attended closely to Raphael's account of nature, explaining in 1843 that "all spirit is matter": "There is no such thing as immaterial matter. All spirit is matter, but it is more fine or pure." Taking from Milton's poem the idea of spirit's identity as "more refined, more...pure" matter, Smith adds yet another Miltonic touch, though not one introduced in this particular passage by Raphael: as if in deference to the younger Milton's Pythagorean interest in the "heav'nly tune, which none can hear / Of human mould, with gross unpurged ear," Smith points out that the physical particles of matter we call "spirit" "can only be discerned by purer eyes; we cannot see it; but when our bodies are purified we shall see that it is all matter."[27]

Apostle Orson Pratt takes from Smith the use of Milton's poem as a seedbed of language and ideas about the metaphysics of the purer, more refined material substance known as "spirit": "there is another material substance called spirit, of a more refined nature, possessing some properties in common with other matter, and other qualities far superior to other matter."[28] Further yet, Pratt, while modernizing Milton's metaphysics with references to post-Miltonic discoveries such as that of electricity, takes Raphael's phrase "one first matter" and transmutes it into (the admittedly homelier) phrase, "one elementary simple substance": "all the ponderable substances of nature, together with light, heat, and electricity, and even spirit itself, all originated from one elementary simple substance, possessing a living self-moving force, with intelligence sufficient to govern it in all its infinitude of combinations and operations, producing all the immense variety of phenomena constantly taking place throughout the wide domains of universal nature."[29] Pratt clearly goes further than Milton when he calls the "one elementary simple substance" a "living self-moving force, with intelligence sufficient to govern it in all its infinitude of combinations and operations, producing all the immense variety of phenomena."[30] Milton, we know, would himself never stretch his monistic materialist vision as far as would his younger contemporary Margaret Cavendish, who preceded Pratt in attributing all material phenomena to the self-moving capacity of matter that only appears to be inert and inanimate.[31] But Pratt can be seen nonetheless to be indebted to Milton for his organization of matter into hierarchical categories, although Pratt uses "intelligence" rather than Raphael's concept of "purity" as the main criterion of distinction separating inferior from superior matter.

So how did, for Orson Pratt, the "one elementary simple substance" produce "all the immense variety of phenomena" of creation? Pratt's version of Milton's "one first matter" populated the world with the diversity of creation, I want to suggest, in imitation, at least in part, of Raphael's explanation of the boundaries and constraints by which the spiritually hierarchized matter is organized: "There is a law given to all things according to their capacities, their wisdom, their knowledge, and their advance in the grand school of the universe." But while Pratt follows Milton in his mention of the constraints limiting the upward mobility of different forms of being, he clearly exceeds Raphael's vision of the universe when he insists on matter's capacity to overleap those hierarchically assigned boundaries when that matter virtuously and intelligently "keeps the law": "To every law there are *bounds* and conditions set, and those materials that continue within their own *sphere* of action, and keep the law, are exalted to new *spheres* of action." In stark violation of the ontological limitations Raphael describes in *Paradise Lost* when noting the assignment of all things to their differentiated "active spheres," Orson Pratt permits materials in *his* metaphysical vision to be "exalted to *new* spheres of action when they have served their appointed times."[32]

What for Pratt permits this remarkable exaltation from one seemingly segregated rung of the ladder of nature to another is the capacity of matter to "keep the law." As he writes in his essay on "The Pre-Existence of Man," if the spiritual particles of matter "abide the laws and conditions of its several states of existence, who shall say that it will not progress until it shall gain the very summit of perfection, and exist in all the glorious beauty of the image of God?"[33] This image of the conditions attached to upward ascent also has an origin in Milton's poem. Raphael, we know, would go on to explain to Adam, no more than 20 lines after his account of the "one first matter," that Adam and Eve's bodies may "at last turn all to spirit" and even "wing'd ascend / Ethereal," on the condition that the happy pair "be found obedient." Pratt lights on this later Miltonic detail of obedience, removing it from the ethical human register of Raphael's warning to Adam and Eve, and returning it to the metaphysical register of the preceding discussion of the "one first matter." The process of the self-organization of spiritualized matter is thus attuned to the obedience and disobedience of the different degrees of matter. All matter in general has the capacity to become increasingly refined and pure, but its exaltation to these more spirituous states is strictly contingent on its obedience to the laws of nature: "those materials," explains Pratt, "that have been refractory or disobedient will either remain stationary or be lowered and abased in the scale of being, till they learn obedience by the things they suffer."[34] Baser matter is not consigned as it is in Milton's poem to remain within its appointed sphere. Base, more substantial, matter for the American Pratt is eminently educable and capable of advancement, though its exaltation to higher spheres of being will require a period of suffering in something like a metaphysical purgatory.

It would be reasonable to assume that Orson Pratt intended us to imagine God having imposed on the world of spiritualized matter the physical laws that his conscious, conscientious, and surprisingly ethical matter is expected to obey. But Pratt hastens to correct any such assumption, since in his vision the elements of matter, which only move when they move themselves, don't just obey but actually prescribe the physical laws by which they willingly bind themselves. In refuting the notion embraced by the majority of his nineteenth century metaphysical contemporaries that matter is inert and implicitly "unintelligent," Pratt explains the logical necessity of matter's fundamental intelligence, and then accounts for the process by which the "conscious, intelligent, self-moving particles" of matter produce in their obedient and orderly fashion all the immense variety of creation's phenomena:

[They] prescribe laws for their own action.... An unintelligent particle is incapable of understanding and obeying a law, while an intelligent particle is capable of both understanding and obedience. It would be entirely useless for an intelligent cause to give laws to unintelligent matter, for such matter could never become conscious of such laws, and therefore would be totally incapable of obedience.... It is evident that each particle must have not only perceived the utility of such laws, but must have mutually consented to obey them in the most strict and invariable manner.[35]

It is their obedience to these physical laws of their own design for which the intelligent particles of matter are rewarded with exaltation from sphere to sphere. The study of physics, then, for Pratt, is but a testimony to the intelligence and virtue of the elements of matter, as in his truly remarkable account of how and why it is that matter obeys Newton's law of gravity:

All these self-moving materials must be possessed of a high degree of intelligence, in order to obey with such perfect and undeviating exactness the innumerable laws which obtain in the universe. There is no disobedience on the part of the materials. Under the same circumstances they invariably act alike. What depth of knowledge, for instance, is requisite in order for particles to obey the single law of "Gravitation." Each particle must not only know of the exact quantity of matter existing in all directions from itself, but must also know its exact distance from every other particle, that it may know, during every moment, how to regulate the intensity and direction of its own motions, according to the law of the "inverse square of the distance." Obedience to this one law on the part of material particles requires in them a degree of intelligence far beyond our utmost comprehension.[36]

It is by just such an account of a physical law — far wilder, surely, even than Sir Isaac Newton's own most outlandish alchemical or apocalyptic musings — that Pratt articulates his powerful rejection of "the philosophy of modern times," which "does not admit that material particles possess intelligence or knowledge."[37] Matter can in no way be seen as inert, inanimate, or, in Pratt's words, "unintelligent." Even an unswerving law such as Newton's of gravity functions for Orson Pratt as proof of the intellectual self-possession and moral probity of every particle of matter. Humanity may be fallen, but the elemental world of matter in which fallen humans find themselves is a state of perfect prelapsarian innocence, wisdom, and obedience.

"Doctrine Which We Would Know Whence Learned"

Joseph Smith, we noted earlier, had insisted near the end of his life that God had not created the elements comprising the material universe; rather, says Smith, God "organized" the elements already existing. For Smith, the most important preexisting element was the spirit of humanity, over which Smith's God could assert no rights as creator. In the 1844 King Follett discourse, Smith makes clear that every human being, or at least his spirit, is as old as God himself. "God found himself," Smith explains, in his own account of the origins of the divine being as we know it, "in the midst of spirits and glory." If for Smith the coeternity of God and the material spirit of humanity was a belief to be asserted with oracular certainty, for Orson Pratt it was a doctrine to be argued for with the tools of logic. And in his shocking midrash on Smith's King Follett discourse, Pratt outpaces in conceptual courage the prophet's already daring sense of God's creation as little more than the organization or rearrangement of preexisting spiritual matter. In *Great First Cause*, the organization of preexisting matter wasn't necessarily the work of any creator God. "All the organizations of worlds, of minerals, of vegetables, of animals," Pratt tells us, were the product not of God's creating hand; they came about, rather, as the result of the "self-combinations and unions of the preexistent, intelligent, powerful, and eternal particles of substance."[38] The eternally existent elements themselves, having moved on from a mastery of the basics of self-motion to the higher learning of cohesion and repulsion, united and combined themselves into the material world as we know it. And why stop there? Pratt presses his case yet further, denying God any claim to the creation, or organization, of "men, of angels, of spirits," which, he explains, were also themselves but the product of the unions and self-combinations of eternal matter.

Smith's King Follett discourse has long, and rightly, been held up as one of the most exuberant visions of heavenly existence ever proposed. But, as I hope I have made clear, Orson Pratt's *Great First Cause* of 1851 has to be viewed as outstripping Smith's own account of the origin of things, at least in terms of what it permits itself to picture and explain. If not the Follett sermon, what, then, could have inspired Pratt not only to imagine but actually to assert as a formal point of belief the idea that men and angels emerge as the consequence of the glorious self-motion of preexistent matter? We can find no such imagining in Boscovich, Paley, Herschel, and Whewell, the late eighteenth and early nineteenth century natural philosophers Pratt was reading as he prepared *Great First Cause*, and with whom he argues throughout his pamphlet. Nor could Milton's radically monistic, but nonetheless theocentric *Christian Doctrine* have offered Pratt anything like an understanding of the mystery of *self*-creation. In the discussion of angels, Milton makes no mention of any belief, modern or ancient, that the angels were not created by God: angelic createdness is a given in the treatise, and the only question Milton takes up there is *when* they were created (245–46).

But the treatise's nineteenth century editor and translator, Bishop Charles Sumner, nonetheless takes the opportunity to cite, in relation to the treatise's insistence on God's creation of the angels, the literary epic's account of Satan's extraordinary claim that the angels in effect created themselves. Let us turn now to that episode of *Paradise Lost*, featuring a debate about Creation that, I would like to suggest, helps shape some of Orson Pratt's most startling theological speculation. In the epic's book 5, in Milton's wholly original account of the crisis of authority in the celestial polity that preceded the war in heaven, the Father calls to assembly all the sons of heaven and announces the anointing of his vicegerent and successor, the being "whom I declare," the Father says, "My *only* Son...whom ye now behold / At my right hand" (5.603–04). A still sinless Satan, however, "could not bear / Through pride that sight, and thought himself impaired" (5.664–65). It is with this wounded sense of impairment that Satan resolves to "leave / Unworshipped, unobeyed the throne supreme" (5.669–70), and to call his followers to reject what he characterizes as the Son's unjustifiable usurpation of power: "by decree / Another now hath to himself engrossed / All power, and us eclipsed under the name / Of King anointed" (5.774–77).

The Father and the newly anointed Son of *Paradise Lost* are not without their angelic supporters, loyalists who clearly reject Satan's interpretation of the Son's "exaltation" as an unjust assumption of authority by a hitherto inconsequential heavenly being. Chief among the loyalists is the zealous angel Abdiel, who takes Satan to task for daring to question

> The just decree of God, pronounced and sworn,
> That to his only Son by right endued
> With regal scepter, every soul in Heav'n
> Shall bend the knee, and in that honor due
> Confess him rightful King.   (5.814–18)

On what grounds, Abdiel asks, does Satan dare to question the creator Father, "who made / Thee what thou art, and form'd the pow'rs of Heav'n / Such as he pleas'd?" (823–25). On what grounds, Abdiel continues, can Satan question the authority of the Son, the being

> by whom,
> As by his Word, the Mighty Father made
> All things, even thee; and all the Spirits of Heaven
> By him created in their bright degrees,
> Crowned them with glory?   (5.835–39)

It is difficult to tell whether Abdiel, in claiming not only that the Father "form'd" or "made" the angels but that he did so by means of the Son, is sharing with Satan information already widely understood in heaven, or whether he is making a pronouncement hitherto unarticulated. But we can know with certainty how Satan responds to Abdiel's claim that the angels are dependent for their creation on both the Father and the Son:

> That we were formed then sayest thou? and the work
> Of secondary hands, by task transferred
> From Father to his Son? strange point and new!

> Doctrine which we would know whence learned: who saw
> When this creation was? rememberest thou
> Thy making, while the Maker gave thee being?
> We know no time when we were not as now;
> Know none before us, self-begot, self-raised
> By our own quickening power.   (5.853–61)

This is the speech of Satan's to Abdiel that Bishop Sumner cites in a lengthy footnote to the passage concerning the creation of the angels in chapter 7 of the *Christian Doctrine*. Aware that the passage from the poem has no direct correspondence with any argument in the treatise, Sumner simply notes that "the opinion that angels were not created, but self-existent, is with great propriety attributed to *Satan* in *Paradise Lost*."[39] What is for Sumner, and surely also for Milton, the satanic antithesis of any proper assertion of God's direct responsibility for the existence of his creatures, is the audacious creaturely claim of ontological independence from God. It is Milton's God, and he alone, who supplies the foundation of being for all of creation. Any claim to the contrary must be dismissed as the hyperintellectualism of a resentful and brooding fellow creature. But it is just such a claim that Satan makes. On the evidence either of sight or of memory (5.856–57), he asserts, it cannot be proven that the angels did *not* create themselves, that they are *not* "self-begot, self-raised / By [their] own quickening power."

It is this very assertion of Milton's Satan, the denial of angelic createdness and the assertion of self-creation, that plants itself at the conceptual foundation of Orson Pratt's theologico-metaphysical account of origins in *Great First Cause; or, The Self-Moving Forces of the Universe*. To be sure, Pratt doesn't situate Satan's woefully unamplified claim directly in the treatise. A better logician than Satan, Pratt knows he cannot tell us that the angels are "self-begot, self-rais'd." He has already exposed the weakness of such a claim in his implicit critique of Milton's *ex deo* theory of Creation, which, he argues, presumes falsely that "the Deity must have created the elements, or parts of which he himself consists, which would be the very height of absurdity."[40] What "self," or coherent unit of identity and subjectivity, could possibly exist to *precede* an act of creation responsible for laying the very foundation of that "self"? Pratt's version of the satanic denial of God's responsibility for the creation of angels clears up that lapse into absurdity and posits a creative agent, or, rather, *innumerable* creative agents, distinct from the angelic "self" that emerges fully formed from the creative process performed by the infinitesimal particles of matter. It is a myriad of "preexistent, intelligent, powerful, and eternal particles of substance" who at some particular point in time decided consensually to apply their newly acquired capacities for cohesive union and combination to constitute, through aggregation, the joint venture that becomes each individual angel. Each angel, human being, and spirit in Pratt's vision is a fundamentally corporate entity, an elaborate unit not conjured magically by an omnipotent God, nor even "organized" from preexisting materials as by the creator God of the prophet Joseph Smith, but by what we have to assume is the more politic, perhaps more democratic, means of the innumerable decisions, movements, and actions undertaken by each of the fully distinct and individuated atomic particles participating in a massive group effort of consensual will.

In offering his own, more logically sustainable, version of the satanic myth of angelic "self-creation," Pratt can be seen to redeem, or at least reconsider the value of, the central ontological heresy providing the intellectual justification for the disastrous rebellion in the heaven of *Paradise Lost*. Could this mid-nineteenth-century American theologian possibly go any further, we have good reason to ask? The answer is yes. Orson Pratt completes his sweeping reconfiguration of our understanding of the material universe with a final, yet more shocking, extension of his vision of creation as the product of the decentered consensual congregation of distinct material particles. God, he avers, is himself a creature. God himself is but a belated effect of matter's capacity to combine and unite itself into meaningful formations: "the spiritual personages of the Father, of the Son, and of the Holy Ghost, must, if organized at all, have been the result of the self combinations and unions of the preexistent, intelligent, powerful, and eternal particles of substance. These eternal Forces and Powers are the Great First Causes of all things and events that have had a beginning."[41]

The "personage" of the Father in heaven, along with the personages of the Son of God and the Holy Ghost, are, in the end, denied anything like a stable, self-sufficient ontology. Orson Pratt offers an account of the origin of the "spiritual personages of the Father, of the Son, and of the Holy Ghost," which emerge in this account as the glorious consequence of the "wise adaptations and arrangements of the different portions of substance of which they consist."[42] Surely there are not many such instances in the Judeo-Christian tradition in which a major theologian denies the eternity of God. It could likely be said that for most Christian belief systems God's priority over creation emerges logically from his status as *uncreated*, or, to use Milton's term in *Paradise Lost,* "increate" (3.6). No such eternal deity exists for Pratt, as the figure known as "God" is but a historically contingent union of the "most intelligent material particles of the universe." The Deity is demoted from cause to effect, an entirely contingent consequence of the "anterior and eternal powers of each individual particle" comprising a "God"-like being. Pratt's God is less a deity than what we can think of as a "deity effect," a non-necessitated union — a union with a beginning and, too, very likely with an ending[43] — of the powers embodied in what are for him the only truly eternal beings in the universe, the preexistent, intelligent, powerful particles of substance.

In *Great First Cause*, Orson Pratt treats literally Raphael's claim of the origin of all things in the "one first matter" in a manner that could only have shocked the affable archangel and the poet who created him. The "one... matter" from which all things sprang, in Pratt's amplification of Raphael's speech, was truly, literally "first." It was not, for Pratt, as we have seen, the first thing God created. Nor was it, from the perspective of Milton's *ex deo* theory of Creation, a portion of the divine matter that the deity contributed to Creation from his own material being. Orson Pratt's "one elementary simple substance" was not in fact a product of divinity at all. "First," in a radical sense never intended by Milton, the "one elementary simple substance" didn't simply predate God. It was that God's creator.

We do not have in Orson Pratt's *Great First Cause* a treatise that anticipates later developments in nineteenth or twentieth century theology or metaphysics. If anything, Pratt looks to the late twentieth century work of young adult science fiction that shares with Pratt a powerful and unmistakable origin in the metaphysical speculation that comprises *Paradise Lost*, Phillip Pullman's fantasy trilogy, *His Dark Materials*. A seeming stepchild of Pratt's theology, Pullman's Miltonic arabesque likewise privileges Satan's implicit theology of self-creation and sketches a universe whose contingent God had begun as a mere angel, who, like all of Pullman's angels, came into existence by means of the "condensation" of the infinitesimal "particles of consciousness" known as "Dust."[44] If we ask of the imaginative systems produced by Pratt and Pullman the question Satan poses in *Paradise Lost*, book 5, concerning Abdiel's theory of angelic createdness — "Doctrine which we would know whence learned" — the answer would be the same: the doctrine of the contingent and created God was learned by means of a rigorously antithetical, satanic reading of *Paradise Lost*.

To some extent we could consider Pratt's affirmative engagement with Satan's great heresy in *Paradise Lost* as a late contribution to an earlier generation's emotional and intellectual investment in Milton's fallen angel. Thomas Jefferson would in the late eighteenth century copy in the Commonplace Book he kept between the ages of 15 and 30 some of the most rousing of Satan's speeches, invariably wrenched out of context, from the epic's first two books. A few decades later, William Ellery Channing, aligning himself with some of the English Romantic poets, would give readers of his *Remarks* on Milton an explicit model of the readerly practice of disentangling a pious fear of satanic evil from an intellectual appreciation of the magnificence of satanic genius: "We gaze on Satan with an awe not unmixed with mysterious pleasure, as on a miraculous manifestation of the *power of mind*. What chains us, as with a resistless spell, in such a character, is spiritual might made visible by the racking pains which it overpowers. There is something kindling and ennobling in the consciousness, however awakened, of the energy which resides in mind; and many a virtuous man has borrowed new strength from the force, constancy, and dauntless courage of evil agents."[45] Virtuous men may actually borrow strength from the likes of Milton's Satan, who for

Channing could be safely admired once his italicized *"power of mind"* is dissociated from his status as an "evil agent." It might be tempting to write off Orson Pratt's *Great First Cause* as just a belated manifestation of this Romantic approval of Milton's Satan. But Pratt has gone infinitely further than a Jefferson or a Channing, who could only admire a Satan whose intellectual courage and zeal for liberty could be carefully cordoned off from his unequivocal status as an enemy of God. Instead of finding, as Channing did, the redemptive quality of mind resident in a metaphysically evil Satan, Pratt works to rewrite Milton's theology so as to redeem Satan and his fallen metaphysical vision *tout court*. All Gods, in Orson Pratt's version of Joseph Smith's vast Mormon cosmology, had originally been fallen men: "as their world was exalted from a temporal to an eternal state, they were exalted also, from fallen men to Celestial Gods to inhabit their Heaven forever and ever."[46] Just as Satan's seemingly irredeemable state of fallenness doesn't preclude his ultimate redemption, so too, perhaps, Satan's seemingly irredeemable theory of angelic self-begetting might likewise find reevaluation. Far from being a source of worry, the satanic origin of Pratt's key theological argument for the createdness of God may well serve for Pratt as *proof* of the Mormon concept of the eternal progress of all beings and all things — perhaps we could add all ideas — from lower states to higher ones.

War in Heaven

As noted above, in face of the strong opposition of Orson Pratt himself, Brigham Young was in 1847 striving to establish himself as the president of the church, the holder of the keys of the priesthood, including the key of salvation itself. It was in the same year, at the height of the succession battle with Young, that Orson Pratt first publicly speculated, in a sermon, about the role of the infinitesimal particles of intelligent matter in the original organization of the being who became God.[47] Gary James Bergera, the great historian of the rift between Brigham Young and Orson Pratt, is careful not to assert any formal, or even informal, link between the political struggle of the succession, on the one hand, and the doctrinal struggle about the nature of God and the cosmos, on the other. But I take his impressive study, *Conflict in the Quorum*, as an attempt to intimate, however gently, that such a link might be valid. I suggest that we take seriously the possibility that Orson Pratt turns to the discursive world of metaphysical and theological speculation as a privileged language in which decidedly nonmetaphysical, nontheological matters of political ecclesiology can be questioned and proposed. We can certainly find in the statements of Brigham Young an implicit confirmation of the idea that theology could function for this first generation of Mormons as a politically resonant field of symbolic expression. In response to Orson Pratt's suggestion of the temporal finitude of the almost makeshift "personhood" of the Gods, Young only worked harder to affirm the eternity of Deity, coming close at times to an unlikely formulation almost akin to orthodox Christianity, with its grounding vision of an eternal creator God: "there never was a time or Eternity but what a God did exist."[48] Likewise, as Pratt pushed for the disintegration of the newly orthodox Mormon godhead into its constituent parts of divinized particles of matter, Brigham Young only increased his investment in the idea of God's status as a fully individuated, self-sufficient "person," an anthropomorphism so strong that Young eventually developed the theory that God was none other than Adam, and Adam God: "both the father of all humankind and, in the pantheon of gods, its reigning deity."[49] The concept of the eternal personhood of God supplied the conceptual basis for Young's implicit justification of his own authority to preside over the church and, eventually, to preside in heaven as well: "I was begotten by the God I worship who reigns in the heavens and I shall also in my turn reign as a God & so will you."[50] In a manner surely impossible for him to acknowledge, Young responded to Pratt's politicized theology with a politicized theology of his own.

Offering President Young his services as a writer and theologian, Orson Pratt's brother Parley would provide a philosophical defense of the new Mormon Presidency by countering Orson's *Great First Cause* with a metaphysical theology designed to champion, rather than disintegrate, the God who had personally called Brigham Young to his position of power in the Church of Jesus Christ of Latter-day Saints. Within two years of Orson's publication of *Great First Cause*, Parley had written the *Key to the Science of Theology*, in which many of Orson's most corrosive philosophical positions were countered with a much less unsettling, more comfortably "orthodox," Mormonism.[51] It must be said that Parley never embraces the traditional Christian, indeed Western, understanding of an almost oppositional divide between body and soul, matter and spirit. Both of the Pratt brothers are always attuned to Joseph Smith's powerful commitment to Milton's monistic spiritual materialism. As noted above, Smith had proclaimed in 1843, echoing both Raphael's "one first matter" speech and a key passage from chapter 7 of Milton's *Christian Doctrine*, that "all spirit is matter, but it is more fine and pure." Parley is as keen as Orson to honor and amplify the prophet's animist materialist philosophy. "Gods, angels and men," Parley would declare in his *Key*, in explanation of the unity of all things in Milton's "one...matter," "are all of one species, one race, one great family widely diffused among the planetary systems."[52] The universal kingdoms, Parley writes, in his own version of Raphael's account of matter's ascending scale in book 5 of *Paradise Lost*, "present every variety and degree in the progress of the great science of life, from the lowest degradation amid the realms of death, or the rudimental stages of elementary existence, upward through all the ascending scale, or all the degrees of progress in the science of eternal life and light, until some of them in turn arise to thrones of eternal power."[53] Like Orson, Parley invests all intelligent particles with the "power of self motion," explaining as well that such a power "implies an inherent will, to originate and direct such motion."[54] But Parley is unequivocal in his implicit rejection of Orson's vision of an almost libertarian, decentralized cosmos in which Gods, angels, and men are all utterly free and self-determining. He comes down especially hard, it would seem, on Orson's ecstatic claim that "all...Gods are equal in power, in glory, in dominion, and in the possession of all things."[55] The Gods were by no means equal in Parley's defense of President Brigham Young's vision of cosmological hierarchy. "Over them all," Parley will insist, in what strikes me as an unmistakable, though quite possibly inadvertent, exposure of the political subtext lurking beneath the surface of the early Mormon theological speculation we have been examining, "there is a *Presidency* or Grand Head, who is the Father of all. And next unto him is Jesus Christ, the eldest born, and first heir of all the realms of light."[56]

Parley has accepted much of Orson's fundamentally liberal physical universe: the material elements that make up "all things" are intelligent and self-moving, and most of the discernable phenomena of the material world can be explained in terms of the language of this intelligent self-motion. But Parley's elementary particles, just like the deities in Parley's decidedly unequal pantheon of Mormon Gods, must perform their actions only "by consent and authority of the head."[57] In fact, Parley has fashioned the symbolic structure of his theological science in such a way as to resound analogically with Brigham Young's claim to have been divinely authorized, by a personal God, to assume the Mormon Presidency. Orson had, much to Young's dismay, argued for the almost utter lack of integrity in the "person" of that deity known as the Holy Spirit: the eternally wise particles that filled the personal "tabernacle" of the Holy Spirit were indistinguishable from the particles that filled the personal "tabernacle" of *any* human being. Parley agrees that the Holy Spirit is "composed of individual particles," and in that respect "differs nothing from all other matter."[58] But he dissociates himself most pointedly from his younger brother's controversial liberation of the Holy Spirit's matter from his divine "person" or "personage." For Parley, the Holy Spirit is "under the control of the Great Eloheim," Eloheim being the Mormon God who sits above the God of our world, Jehovah.[59] The Spirit, in fact, performs a governmental function as the Great Eloheim's vicegerent, laboring to consolidate and maintain that chief God's control over creation: "His Holy Spirit centres in [the Great Eloheim's] presence, and communicates with, and extends to the utmost verge of His dominions, comprehending and controlling all things under the immediate direction of His own will, and the will of all those in communication with Him, in worlds without end!"[60]

The particles of the Holy Spirit may be, for Parley, as they were for Orson, "widely diffused among the other elements of space," but they are not left entirely on their own to cohere and unite at will to produce new organized creations. The work of creation, according to Parley, must be left to a "General Assembly, Quorum, or Grand Council of the Gods." It is that assembled body, acting not independently as brother Orson might have speculated, but "with their President at their head," that "constitute[s] the designing and creating power" of Parley Pratt's universe.[61]

Despite Parley's metaphysical efforts at reconsolidating the power of the one presidential God in his *Key to the Science of Theology*, President Young would continue to feel the threat of the libertarian ecclesiological energies unleashed by Orson Pratt's speculative metaphysics in the *Great First Cause* and other writings. As late as 1865, Young would take the time to print in both the *Deseret News* and the *Millennial Star* a formal "PROCLAMATION of the First Presidency and the Twelve" in a stern rebuke of Orson's then 15-year-old theory that each individual atomic particle of God's material being was "allwise and all-powerful, possessing the same knowledge and the same truth." The *Great First Cause* and other publications by "brother Orson," Young proclaimed publicly, "contain doctrines which we cannot sanction, and which we have felt impressed to disown, so that the Saints who now live, and who may live hereafter, may not be misled by our silence, or be left to misinterpret it." Immediately following the 1865 rebuke was a formal printed retraction by a downcast Orson himself, who "embrace[d] the present opportunity of publicly expressing my most sincere regret, that I have ever published the least thing which meets with the disapprobation of the highest authorities of the Church."[62]

CONCLUSION

We recall that in book 5 of *Paradise Lost*, it was an apparent succession crisis that spurred the thrilling speculative energy fueling the debate between Satan and Abdiel concerning the creation of the angels. In that section of Milton's epic poem, so important, I believe, not only for Orson and Parley Pratt, but for Joseph Smith before them, the pressing political matter at hand was the obligation in heaven to acknowledge and obey a newly exalted heavenly authority, the Son of God. In the end, the debate between the loyalist angel Abdiel and the rebel angel Satan did not center itself exclusively in a direct or unmediated language of political obligation or resistance. The question of the *political* obligation to obey the Son moved quickly to a question of the *ontological* obligation to obey him. God had *formed* the angels, Abdiel insisted, and he had done so by means of the Son. In the face of Abdiel's seemingly undeniable ontological justification of the creaturely obligation to obey not only the Father but now his Son as well, Satan brilliantly, and of course self-destructively, conjured a competing ontological vision that denied the Father's agency in his creation. The angels were "self-begot, self-raised / By [their] own quickening power." Crucially, what Satan didn't go on to envision was the corollary political structure logically entailed by a doctrine of angelic self-creation. Satan, we know, was eager to establish himself as a supreme heavenly authority. Given his own aspirations to glory, he understandably declined to represent the liberal universe of self-directed equals that one might reasonably extrapolate from the premise of universal angelic self-creation.

But it was a version of the radically liberal political structure logically entailed by the satanic metaphysics of self-creation that Orson Pratt labored not just to represent but actually to champion in his cosmogonal, theogonal masterpiece, *Great First Cause*. Having suffered a number of rebukes and reprimands from Brigham Young for pressing his critique of Young's reestablishment of the First Presidency, Orson Pratt had no room by 1851 in which to continue the fight with Young and his supporters on anything like explicitly political or ecclesiological grounds. Brigham Young had unequivocally won the succession battle. The president, and not the Quorum of the Twelve, would function as the church's chief governor. The more straightforward discursive realm of politics and ecclesiology closed to him, Orson Pratt turned to cosmology, with what degree of self-consciousness we cannot know, and fashioned with the tools of a materialist metaphysics an almost fantasy world of creaturely self-determination, a world liberated from impingement by anything that smacked of authoritarian control.

As if in uncanny recognition of his brother's assumption of Satan's intellectual subject position in book 5 of *Paradise Lost*, Parley Pratt seems almost effortlessly to have fallen into the role of Satan's authoritative foil, Satan's "brother," or fellow Son of God, Abdiel. Loyal to Brigham Young, Parley, in what must be read as his pointed response to *Great First Cause*, makes an Abdielian ontological argument in his *Key to the Science of Theology* for the necessity of political allegiance to the new regime. The presidential God of the cosmos, the God who stands as president even of the powerful quorum of angels, is firmly in charge, and not simply because he is the strongest of the candidates for heavenly leadership. He is the Creator. The "individual, spiritual body" that Orson had so recklessly conjectured was able to form itself from the diffused particles of all-wise and all-knowing matter can in no way for Parley justify a claim to self-determination, or independence from God or his authoritative representatives on earth. That "individual, spiritual body" in the unyieldingly theocentric *Key to the Science of Theology* was definitively, in Parley's words, "begotten by the heavenly Father, and placed under certain laws, and was responsible to its great Patriarchal Head."[63]

The metaphysical speculations of the first generation of Mormon theologians could not be disentangled from the political, ecclesiological questions that pressed themselves on the Saints after the death of Joseph Smith. To justify the ways of God's church was to justify the ways of God, and to justify the ways of God in the heady intellectual climate of early Mormonism was to justify the ways of matter and spirit. Surely it was at least in part Parley's political loyalty to Young, as well as his corresponding metaphysical vision of a theocentrically governed cosmos, that explains his ascendancy as the new religion's chief theologian. "Servant of God, well done," Milton's God tells Abdiel upon the angel's rejection of Satan's apostasy and his reaffirmation of God's supremacy (*PL* 6.29). The Abdiels of the world inherit the earth, or at least the heavens, as surely both Pratt brothers came to recognize upon Brigham Young's blessing of the superior loyalty of Parley, who, in Milton's words, "fought / The better fight" (*PL* 6.29–30), by affirming with the tools of theology and metaphysics the authority by which his leader ruled.

Orson Pratt's *Great First Cause* would be denied the new President's benediction (and, as we have seen, would need in 1865 to be retracted altogether), while the more dutiful *Key to the Science of Theology* would establish itself as a central work of Mormon doctrine, going through nine editions, and selling 30,000 copies, by 1884.[64] It was Parley, we have to assume, who would in the end, by means perhaps of his superior caution and loyalty, make the strongest claim for the official title of "Apostle Paul of Mormonism." But it was Orson who must earn our respect as the bolder thinker. Fueled by the exuberant heresies to which Milton gave voice in *Paradise Lost*, the younger brother went furthest in pursuing the logical implications of Joseph Smith's final envisionings of the birth of the cosmos and the birth of the gods.

CHAPTER 8

"The Scanning of Error"
Areopagitica *and* 3-D–Printed Guns

DAVID A. HARPER

> I'm not stupid, Lanie.... I'm not going to print none of that rubbish, never again... let me tell you the thing that I decided when I spent ten years in lockup. I'm going to print more printers. Lots more printers. One for everyone. That's worth going to jail for. That's worth everything.
> — Cory Doctorow, "Printcrime"

Long before 3-D printers were cheap and readily available, Cory Doctorow's very short story "Printcrime" imagined how this technology might reinvent manufacturing and destabilize the world economy. Inspired in part by the recording industry's "great and hysterical spasm" in reaction to the proliferation of digital music and music sharing sites, Doctorow envisions a dystopia in which jack-booted "coppers" fight a futile battle to stem the flow of bootleg 3-D–printed pharmaceuticals and brand-name knockoffs.[1] The climax of the story comes when the protagonist realizes that widespread distribution of the technology (through 3-D printers infinitely replicating themselves) may radically privatize production and render regulation, monopoly, and patents obsolete.

In 2013, when I belatedly read Doctorow's story, it was shortly after Cody Wilson and his company, Defense Distributed, managed to successfully fire the first working 3-D–printed gun. The punchline of Doctorow's story — "printers.... Lots more printers" — combined with footage of Wilson proudly firing his plastic weapon to evoke Neo from *The Matrix* requesting "guns, lots of guns" as he prepared to liberate humanity through an orgy of gun violence.[2] Doctorow's thought experiment implies that regulation of manufacturing will become impossible once 3-D printers can print more 3-D printers. Wilson, conversely, proclaimed cheerfully that this technology will ensure that "they can never eradicate the gun from the earth."[3] In interviews, he repeatedly invoked Milton's *Areopagitica* as justification for distributing free, downloadable plans for the print-at-home gun he named "The Liberator." In fact, for some time in 2013, clicking on the "our manifesto" link on the Defense Distributed website would take one directly to the Dartmouth Reading Room copy of *Areopagitica*. Defense Distributed provided no commentary about this. Their manifesto simply was *Areopagitica*, and the connection between Milton's 1644 plea against prepublication licensing and 3-D–printed guns was apparently supposed to be self-evident. Meanwhile, on the opposite end of the seemingly interminable American gun control debate, following the horrific mass murder of elementary schoolchildren in Newtown, Connecticut, Gary Wills invoked *Paradise Lost* on behalf of gun control proponents when in the *New York Review of Books* he argued that guns are America's Moloch, demanding child sacrifice at a horrific rate.[4]

Milton's involvement in recent gun control debates might be unexpected, but his appropriation on both sides of an increasingly intractable political schism presents Milton scholars with an opportunity and a challenge. We are invited once again to suggest why Milton continues to matter in his fifth century, and simultaneously challenged to interrogate this latest (and perhaps unwelcome) political use of Milton's work. Cody Wilson's deployment of *Areopagitica* to justify the endless, unregulated production of guns using the latest in printing technology demands that we consider how Milton's pamphlet, the last of his political prose works designed to advance "personal liberty," might actually apply to these twenty-first century issues.[5]

Wilson, then a law student at the University of Texas, Austin, dropped names promiscuously when defending his decision to freely distribute designs for his print-at-home plastic guns. References to Camus, Foucault, and Fukuyama pepper his interviews. But it is his take on Milton that should most grab our attention. I quote Wilson here without customary cosmetic editing. I think it is important to see him as a young man working through the issues as he talks, usually in an interview setting: "*Areopagitica* is essentially the spiritual analogue that I'm holding out for people. Which is more to do not about like why guns are good. It's more about why like speech and information is good. Why like you must reckon with, you must be free to reckon with whatever ideas that you can. It isn't enough that a society can just withhold things. That doesn't benefit you as a moral agent. That doesn't allow you to exist or to, that doesn't allow you to fully exercise your capacity as a human being, a moral agent."[6] As a self-described "(like) principled anarchist,"[7] Wilson also summarized his stance on printed guns in a more direct way: "What this project's really about, fuck your law.... It's being able to go, you know what, I don't like this legal regime [so] I neatly step outside of it."[8] While Wilson's less-than-eloquent summary of *Areopagitica* might not seem to demand an academic response, his schematic for using a 3-D printer to produce a working gun was still propagating on popular media-piracy websites even after Defense Distributed was ordered to remove it from their website. As with ill-thought-out tweets or high school yearbook photos, the design is, for better or worse, irrevocably in the public domain. Wilson might not be clear about what or whom he is resisting, but he is certain that this new technology means that they — whoever "they" are — "can never eradicate the gun from the earth."[9] His invocation of *Areopagitica* suggests that Milton would be okay with that.

Wilson's use of *Areopagitica* as justification and "manifesto" for Defense Distributed applies Milton's plea against licensing to a very different sort of printing than Milton imagined. As Stephen Dobranski aptly reminds us, Milton's concept of authorship and printing was of a profoundly collaborative process.[10] In *Areopagitica*, Milton describes it as such more than once: "When a man writes to the world, he summons up all his reason and deliberation to assist him; he searches, meditates, is industrious, and likely consults and confers with his judicious friends" (YP 2:532). As Dobranski suggests, Milton's description captures only a portion of the collaboration involved in seventeenth century authorship. More collaborators become involved as the text wends its way through the publisher, to the print shop and on to the bookseller. Milton could not envision the sort of authorial control that would be exerted by Blake in his printing house, much less my ability to conceive, print, and (should I so wish) publish this text from the splendid isolation of my office. Wilson's and Defense Distributed's application of *Areopagitica* to 3-D printing is yet more complicated because the item that Wilson demands freedom to print and distribute is not a text but, instead, a tool, an implement. Wilson seems to recognize that *Areopagitica* is concerned more with ideas than with material objects when he emphasizes that Milton's pamphlet demands that (in Wilson's paraphrase) "you must be free to reckon with whatever ideas you can."[11] This is a fair gloss on Milton's famous declaration that he could not abide a "cloistered virtue" and his belief, evident throughout his works, that one cannot be virtuous without temptation and trial. In *Paradise Lost*, the Father's exaltation of the Son, and his prohibition against tasting of the tree of knowledge, are arbitrary acts introducing trial into otherwise perfect conditions in order to exercise virtue and avoid having a "mere artificial Adam" (YP 2:527) or, for that matter, a mere artificial Satan. But are guns "ideas" to be reckoned with? Before wrestling with that key question, let us first reexamine Milton's heretical understanding of materiality and his resulting understanding of authorship and printed texts.

Milton's understanding of the nature of texts must be understood within the context of his monist materialism. As put forth in *Paradise Lost*, Milton's theodicy requires that everything in the universe be composed of the same material foundation: everything is "one first matter all," from the roots of a plant to the smell of it, and from the corrupt body to the soul itself. Consistent with this worldview, *Areopagitica* proposes that books are more than inanimate objects (or that as inanimate objects in a monist-materialist universe they are not incapable of containing the matter of spirit). Thus, Milton declares that good books "preserve as in a vial the purest efficacie and extraction of that intellect that bred them" (YP 2:492). This process of quasi-metempsychosis that preserves the spirit of an author in his books grants those books a humanlike status; to destroy them is, as Milton says, to commit homicide.

Milton does not, however, mean simply to suggest that the works of authors are labors of love that deserve respect in common with the respect accorded to other crafts. The special, protected nature of books is a result of their unique property as texts that preserve the author's agency in the world even after death. Milton's argument in *Areopagitica* is specific to texts not only because his aim is specifically to counter Parliament's prepublication licensing scheme but also because "he who destroys a good Book, kills reason itself, kills the Image of God, as it were in the eye" (YP 2:492). Most important here is Milton's employment of "reason," always a key word in any Miltonic context. In the order of created works, good (and that qualifier is important) books are nearer to God than even many human beings are because good books convey pure, unsullied reason. Books have value to Milton as material objects and even as commodities and property, but they deserve special protections because they are uniquely capable of preserving and conveying that *quintessence*, the "ethereall and fifth essence" of reason (YP 2:493). This ability of the printed word to transmit reason is what makes prepublication licensing a threat to virtue. While certain artworks might be argued to convey reason in a manner similar to the printed word, it is certainly a stretch to imagine that manufactured utilitarian objects such as sporks, designer hats, or plastic guns have the same beneficial bent toward the restoration of truth and forwarding of virtue. And, as we shall see later, 3-D–printed plastic guns may be in a category quite separate.

It would be unwise, however, to consider the distinction between objects and speech acts or between objects and ideas as the clincher in this argument. Milton's monism allows him to hint at least toward the interchangeability of these categories. Prepublication licensing will be ineffective in reforming manners, Milton claims, simply because vice will find other avenues. "If we think to regulate Printing, thereby to rectifie manners, we must regulate all recreations and pastimes, all that is delightful to man. No musick must be heard, no song be set or song, but what is grave and Dorick. There must be licensing dancers, that no gesture, motion, or department be taught our youth but what by their allowance shall be thought honest.... And who shall silence all the airs and madrigals, that whisper softness in chambers?" (YP 2:523–24). The emphasis here on the reformation of manners suggests that, again, it is the content of these arts, their ability to convey ideas, that grants them a similar status to texts. As Seth Herbst suggests in his essay in this volume, Milton conceived of music itself as no less material than printed texts, imbued with a similar ability to convey reason and effect real, lasting (physical) change upon listeners and their morals.[12] The airs and madrigals that play softly in private chambers appear a means to propagate reason that is, if less efficient, also less vulnerable to the type of suppression threatened by the licensing order.

However, there are still wider implications for Milton's capacious expansion of the very definition of "book": "Albeit what ever thing we hear or see, sitting, walking, travelling, or conversing may be fitly call'd our book, and is of the same effect that writings are, yet grant the thing to be prohibited were only books, it appears that this order hitherto is far insufficient to the end which it intends" (YP 2:528). This reference to the proverbial "nature's book" and what Milton in *Paradise Lost* would call the "contemplation of created things," seems to work in the favor of those who, like Wilson, would suggest that *Areopagitica* is concerned with more than simply printing and advocates a radical freedom from government regulation, be it of books or printed guns. But in context, this portion of *Areopagitica*'s argument is concerned with the practicalities of licensing and seeks to demonstrate that prohibiting books alone would be insufficient to enact reform. Milton posits that books are the purest mode for transmitting reason, that quintessence of an author's meaning, to other people separated by distance or time. As such, texts are privileged by extraordinary protections in Milton's tract. Even bad books are not to be suppressed prior to their chance to compete in the marketplace of ideas because the risk to human salvation is simply too high should good ideas be accidently suppressed or if human reason were denied the spiritual development afforded by grappling with contrary and tempting evils.

Even if we grant that Milton's argument against licensing may reasonably extend beyond the special protections afforded to printed texts to apply to other creative productions, we should recall that Milton was not opposed to postpublication censorship. Ultimately, bad books may be disposed of once they have had their day in the light. Defense Distributed's use of *Areopagitica* as manifesto suggests an interpretation that ignores this aspect of the tract, representing it as a proposal for radical freedom from government regulation on printing and manufacturing.[13] However, while the bulk of *Areopagitica* argues against Parliament's new order reinstating prepublication licensing, Milton does have a specific proposal for how that body *should* regulate printing. He argues that they can do no better than to revert to the licensing order of January 1642 that required "no book be Printed, unless the Printer's and the Author's name, or at least the Printer's be register'd" (YP 2:569). While registration is clearly not as restrictive as requiring the approval of a licenser before printing, it is hardly an allowance for unregulated printing. Registration imposes accountability for productions, allowing the Stationers' Company and (in theory) the state to find and, as necessary, punish those who produce harmful works. The order of 1642 has often been misinterpreted as providing for authorial copyright, but as Joseph Loewenstein points out, the order tethers authors to texts only in order to establish responsibility for any criminality in the text.[14] The register is not a protection of authorial rights but, instead, a mechanism of accountability. In *Paradise Lost*, Milton suggests the potential uses of a register to mete out punishment when he describes how the long sequence of monarchs between David and the kingdom of the messiah

> shall be registered
> Part good, part bad, of the bad the longer scroll,
> Whose foul idolatries and other faults
> Heaped to the popular sum, will so incense
> God. (12.335–39)

Here, the register acts as a balance book that allows a magistrate to take the measure of virtue or corruption, and ultimately serves to mete out just punishment. Despite the regulatory intent for identifying authors and printers, the "good" order of January 1642 was concerned with establishing the authorship of the text, ordering, "that the Master and Wardens of the Company of Stationers shall be required to take especiall Order that the Printers doe neither print, nor reprint any thing without the name and consent of the Author."[15]

We shall return to the 1642 order's apparent provision that the author must give "consent" for the printing of the text. It is enough to note here that establishing an "Author," in all the ambiguity of that word and function, demarcates a person responsible for the text's behavior. Identifying such a figure (be it the publisher, printer, or author) as associated with and responsible for a text provides accountability to the Company and establishes the printer's (not the author's) rights to the publication. Milton's advice that Parliament revert to the 1642 order is not to be confused with repealing all controls on texts but, instead, as an effort to avoid the evils of prepublication censorship while in theory ensuring accountable parties could be identified *after* publication.[16]

Milton is explicit about the consequences for publications found lacking after printing: "Those which otherwise come forth [lacking an author's or printer's name], if they be found mischievous and libelous, the fire and the executioner will be the timeliest and most effectual remedy, that man's prevention can use" (YP 2:569). Milton's meaning here is ambiguous in relationship to Parliament's prior orders attempting to regulate printing. Even under the order of 1642, publishing mischievous and libelous texts (anonymous or not) was an offense, as was publishing anonymously even those texts that were innocuous. In Milton's ambiguous construction, anonymous printing alone may or may not be sufficient grounds for punishment. However, even under Milton's less strenuous controls on the press, libel and mischief clearly *are* grounds for books to be called in and burnt by the common hangman. Milton ominously hints toward the real possibility that the same hangman might enact corporal punishment to correct the offending author or printer. No "principled anarchist" like Wilson, Milton suggests that government's role is to govern and mete out justice, but only once a book has been found troublesome in the marketplace of ideas where "the State shall be my governours, but not my criticks; [for] they may be mistak'n in an author" (YP 2:534). Milton doesn't suggest how a postpublication "trial" determining a publication's guilt or innocence might work, for he seems most concerned to establish in *Areopagitica* that a text must have its day of trial before the public and not in the private chambers of some dubiously qualified licensor.

Despite failing to provide a method for the state to adjudicate a book's propriety once printed, Milton suggests that all books, even those properly inscribed with the printer or author's name, may be policed. Milton's first point in the argument proper of *Areopagitica* is to allow that the state has an interest in the influence of books, and the ability to discipline them. It is with this ominous note that Milton inaugurates the extended metaphor of books as men that will reoccur throughout the pamphlet. Like men, books may be punished if found bad. Milton states, "I deny not but that it is of greatest concernment in the church and commonwealth to have a vigilant eye how books demean themselves as well as men, and thereafter to confine, imprison, and do sharper justice on them as malefactors"

(YP 2:492). In Milton's proposed regime of print control, one may print what one will, but if that printed text behaves badly, the text (and its author/printer) must be prepared to accept the consequences. The church and commonwealth are allowed — even encouraged — to judge how books impact society and to "confine" and "imprison" them, at least if they do not wish to burn them as one method of "sharper justice."

One wonders about this notion of imprisoning and confining books. Are these books suppressed, but archived? Are they only available to a fit audience whom even the worst books and ideas will not corrupt? Milton could have had such a scheme in mind (and clear ideas about those "elect above the rest" who might have access to the incarcerated books). He could not, of course, imagine a world in which a text becomes irrevocable, viral in minutes, and essentially beyond recall no matter how pernicious it might be. Even so, Milton's limits on free speech have implications for Cody Wilson's application of *Areopagitica* to guns, and cannot be wished away by those appropriating *Areopagitica* as manifesto. Just as printing libel or mischief has consequences despite Milton's relatively permissive vision to encourage human advancement through trial and temptation, so producing and possessing an unlicensed, untraceable gun must have consequences, whether that gun is cobbled together from supplies available at a local hardware store or printed on a 3-D printer.

Milton's plea for freedom of conscience, inextricably entwined with the freedom of the press throughout *Areopagitica*'s argument, is limited even as it advances toleration. Milton takes great pains to show that he does not intend to promote "license," but liberty only:

> I mean not tolerated Popery, and open superstition, which as it extirpates all religions and civil supremacies, so itself should be extirpate.... that also which is impious or evil absolutely either against faith or manners no law can possibly permit, that intends not to unlaw itself: but those neighboring differences, or rather indifferences, are what I speak of, whether in some point of doctrine or of discipline, which though they may be many, yet need not interrupt the *unity of Spirit*, if we could but find among us the *bond of Peace*. (YP 2:565)

There is little agreement on how limited Milton's toleration is here and throughout *Areopagitica*. Allowing for "neighboring differences, or rather indifferences" and "moderate varieties and brotherly dissimilitudes" seems hardly to suggest anarchic license (YP 2:555). Catholicism is exempt from Milton's toleration because he claims it is itself intolerant of other beliefs. To preserve the principal of toleration itself, Milton must be intolerant to Catholicism to ensure that the law (of tolerance) be not so permissive as "to unlaw itself." From Milton's perspective, allowing the unlimited dissemination of Catholicism would be like printing the end of printing. It is perhaps not too much of a stretch to imagine an analogous situation if one allowed printed guns to end all arguments about the printing of guns.

Because 3-D printing is better considered a revolution in manufacturing rather than a revolution in "printing," those employing *Areopagitica* as a manifesto for freedom from restrictive controls on production of "things" ought to examine closely how *Areopagitica* might apply in that specific context.[17] In Cory Doctorow's short story discussed above, 3-D printers and counterfeit printed items are confiscated by "coppers," a quaint nickname for police, but also perhaps hinting at the creation of a new enforcer, not of conscience, but of copyright in a world where material objects are printed "copy" no less than texts are.[18] Attending to issues of monopoly and copyright, Blair Hoxby and others have analyzed the language of commerce and trade employed throughout *Areopagitica*. Hoxby suggests that Milton "identifies books as the 'living labours' of authors so that he may make his charge of monopoly clear: licensors and Stationers attack the livings of men and in doing so become *vir sanguinis*."[19] However, Milton's objection to monopoly is consistent with his support of an author's general right to intellectual property. Parliament gave lip service to problems of ownership and profit in the problematic 1643 Licensing Order, demanding that "no person or persons shall hereafter print, or cause to be reprinted any Book or Books, or part of Book, or Books heretofore allowed of and granted to the said Company of Stationers...without the license or consent of the Master, Wardens and Assistants of the said Company; Nor any Book or Books lawfully licensed and entered in the Register of the said Company for any particular member thereof, without the license and consent of the Owner or Owners thereof" (YP 2:798). Even though Milton charges that "the just retaining of each man his severall copy," was merely a dissembling reason for the reintroduction of licensing, he is quick to insert in the same breath an editorial gloss defending copyright itself, "which God forbid should be gainsaid" (YP 2:570). Milton may decry the chilling effect that prepublication licensing would have on authors, but he supports the rights of the Stationers' Company that the 1643 order protects. In conjunction with the 1642 order, a chain of consent from author to Stationers' Company is permissible here and allows a degree of surveillance and control, at least within the book trade.

As Dobranski notes, Milton "is acknowledging in 1644 that the book trade would benefit from limited governmental regulation as a safeguard from inaccurate reprints in small, cheaply made editions and as a protection for printers against the unlawful publishing of their copies."[20] Parliament's onerous imposition of prepublication licensing might make the "living labours" of authors too difficult as they trudge to and fro to get the permission of the licensor, but Milton recognizes that *some* degree of regulation is necessary to protect those labors, just as the state must be allowed some recourse against slanderous and libelous works.

Milton's distinction between the virtue of creation and the proliferation of copies is key if one is to apply *Areopagitica* to a manufacturing process. What Cody Wilson and Defense Distributed attempted to envision as "printing" protected by *Areopagitica*'s assertion of a "free press," is actually a form of mass production. The computer code distributed by Wilson's website would allow unskilled laborers (anyone with access to a 3-D printer) to reproduce Wilson's design with the push of a button and some assembly. Reading the code, the machine produces the kit on command. Compared to the conditions of the early modern book trade that produced *Areopagitica* and all the political pamphlets laboriously produced by the "mansion house of liberty" Milton described in the heady days of the English civil wars, 3-D printing allows for remarkably consistent reproduction of objects.[21] Consider that each run of an early modern press usually resulted in various corrected and uncorrected states of the text, that each was bound variously at the whim of the owner and often in nonce collections containing other texts. Any texts produced in a single print run at an early modern printing press would have more in common with a unique, crafted item than with the faithful reproduction of a gun from downloaded 3-D printer instructions.

The free marketplace of ideas that Milton describes promotes virtue and the continued pursuit of Truth through trial and error. *Areopagitica* thus privileges original ideas, not the proliferation of mere copies. Milton's use of the metaphor of childbirth to describe the labor of authors highlights creative birth rather than mechanical copying: "Till then [the inquisition] books were ever as freely admitted into the world as any other birth; the issue of the brain was no more stifled than the issue of the womb; no envious Juno sat cross-legged over the nativity of any man's intellectual offspring, but if it proved a monster, who denies but that it was justly burnt or sunk into the sea?" (YP 2:505). In this passage, books are again compared to human beings, and postpublication censorship is once more affirmed as just. Thus, the "nativity" of new ideas cannot be regulated, but if the intellectual offspring that comes forth from one's forehead proves evil, it may justly be destroyed. In an imaginative scene worthy of Swift's *Battel of the Books*, Milton imagines these original ideas competing as on a field of battle, some faring well, some falling in a duel with opposing ideas: "When a man...calls out his adversary into the plain, offers him the advantage of wind and sun, if he please; only that he may try the matter by dint of argument, for his opponents then to sculk, to lay ambushments, to keep a narrow bridge of licencing where the challenger should passe, though it be valour anough in shouldiership, is but weaknes and cowardise in the wars of Truth" (YP 2:562). Ambushing a text or idea before it can be fairly tried by opponents is simply uncivilized conduct. But those ideas tried and found harmful may be left to litter the field of battle or (if need be) burnt. It is not the material object of the book itself that has special status for Milton but, rather, its ability to transmit in pure form ideas and reason — the "quintessence" of immortality. Bad texts birthed into the world still forward virtue, for "the knowledge and survey of vice is in this world so necessary to the constituting of human virtue, and the scanning of error to the confirmation of truth," but once scanned and found wanting they aren't guaranteed prolonged existence or further propagation (YP 2:516).

Let us imagine with Cody Wilson and Defense Distributed that Milton's pamphlet, according special status to texts as repositories and transmitters of reason, is equally applicable to manufactured objects, especially guns. As we've seen, Milton's limits on the freedom of the press in *Areopagitica* are somewhat vague. Suggesting that Catholicism cannot be tolerated lest it end toleration itself, Milton continues, "that also which is impious or evil absolutely either against faith or manners no law can possibly permit, that intends not to unlaw it self" (YP 2:565). We must decide, then, whether Milton would consider a gun "evil absolutely against faith or manners." Any attempt to determine Milton's stance toward guns and somewhat anachronistically toward "gun control" will require that we move beyond *Areopagitica* and survey the breadth of Milton's career, to include his earliest poetry and his last-hour pleas to save the commonwealth. It may be helpful to start with Robert Fallon's 1984 assertion that "Milton...always supported the rights of citizens to bear arms, as a safeguard against tyranny."[22] Fallon's claim comes in the context of his tracing Milton's changing opinion of the trained bands, an attitude that moved from enthusiasm to guarded respect and even suspicion. Fallon's wording here suggests that Milton's stance would favor those like Wilson, America's National Rifle Association (NRA), and others who advocate an armed citizenry and interpret the Second Amendment to the U.S. Constitution to guarantee all citizens a right to firearms. This interpretation requires Milton to have determined that an armed citizenry poses less of a threat then a tyrannical government (a favorite suggestion of gun rights activists today). As Fallon notes, in the first edition of *Eikonoklastes* Milton characterized this militia as "our Train'd Bands, which are the trustiest and most proper strength of a free Nation," but in a later edition added the qualification "not at warr within it self" to modify "free Nation" (YP 3:448). The change suggests that on reflection Milton had determined that in times of civil strife, armed militias may indeed be a danger rather than an asset to a free nation. In fact, even when faced with an absolute threat to freedom and the return of tyranny, Milton had significant qualms about the status of guns and the rights of citizens to them. A deep-rooted disdain for modern weaponry and gunpowder, rooted in the traditions of his literary forbearers, led Milton to view guns and gunpowder as evil rather than good.

Milton's association of gunpowder with evil, and absolute evil at that, began with his youthful poems on the Gunpowder Plot, likely composed for academic observances of Guy Fawkes Day. These poems make gunpowder the tool of hellish Catholic plots against James I, and the substance is referred to as "infernal powder" (*inferni pulveris*) in the poems. The conceit of each of these juvenile Latin poems is that the diabolical plotters attempted to use the "hellish powder" to blast James to up heaven, while (unlike the Catholics) he could get there through his own volition — it is only "loathsome cowls" and "Rome's profane gods" that require the assistance of explosive powder to ascend.[23] Gunpowder is, in these poems, an unholy tool of evil plotters. Even in "On the Inventor of Gunpowder," where Milton compares Prometheus unfavorably with the inventor, he suggests that the theft of Jove's "triple thunder" is greater and requires a greater man to do the deed. Perhaps it was a job for Satan rather than Prometheus?

In *Areopagitica*, Milton seizes a chance to compare the intellectual production of books to the mechanical production of armaments. Milton exhorts his readers to observe God's preparations for a "reforming of the Reformation it self" and declares his city of London: "the mansion house of liberty, encompast and surrounded with his [God's] protection; the shop of warre hath not there more anvils and hammers waking, to fashion out the plates and instruments of armed Justice in defence of beleauer'd Truth, then there be pens and heads there, sitting by their studious lamps, musing, searching, revolving new notions and ideas wherewith to present, as with their homage and their fealty the approaching Reformation: others as fast reading, trying all things, assenting to the force of reason and convincement" (YP 2:554). The "pens and heads" writing in service of an "approaching Reformation" produce a force that differs in type from that produced in the shops of war, but one that seems the more powerful, consisting as it does of the force of "reason." Milton alludes here to the wartime surge in arms production that progressed parallel to the surge in printing that was encouraged by the increased freedoms of the press that Milton defends in *Areopagitica*. Milton's comparison of these two very dissimilar ways of waging and preparing for political warfare highlights that the transmission of reason is the heart of reformation, unattainable by warfare alone.

Milton's apparent disdain for modern weaponry goes beyond a nice preference for more civilized means of achieving reformation. He is no pacifist, after all. As Milton's political prose (especially *Tenure of Kings and Magistrates*) makes abundantly clear, he is not adverse to violent means to resist tyranny. Nonetheless, his somewhat conventional association of gunpowder with hellish forces in the Gunpowder Plot poems matures into a fully realized scorn for modern warfare, a scorn fully realized in *Paradise Lost*.

Satan's invention of gunpowder in book 6 marks a significant change in the rhetorical tone of the war of heaven.

> Which of us who beholds the bright surface
> Of this etherous mold whereon we stand,
> This continent of spacious Heav'n, adorned
> With plant, fruit, flow'r ambrosial, gems and gold,
> Whose eye so superficially surveys
> These things, as not to mind from whence they grow
> Deep under ground, materials dark and crude,
> Of spirituous and fiery spume, till touched
> With Heav'n's ray, and tempered they shoot forth
> So beauteous, op'ning to the ambient light.
> These in their dark nativity the deep
> Shall yield us pregnant with infernal flame,
> Which into hollow engines long and round

>   Thick-rammed, at th' other bore with touch of fire
>   Dilated and infuriate shall send forth
>   From far with thund'ring noise among our foes
>   Such implements of mischief as shall dash
>   To pieces, and o'erwhelm whatever stands
>   Adverse, that they shall fear we have disarmed
>   The thunderer of his only dreaded bolt.[24]   (PL 6.472–91)

Satan's exhortation to look beyond the superficial surface of things demarcates a change in the nature of both the war in heaven and Milton's style. Prior to this, the war has been a series of rather straightforward acts (Abdiel's simple courage and his ability to literally force knee tribute from Satan, Michael and Satan's sword play). The climax of the performance of heroism and the height of the book's very literal battle is when Michael shears off Satan's entire right side, leaving him all *sinister* (6.325–30). Satan's exhortation to his followers that they must look beyond the superficial also marks a shift in Milton's language, which becomes no longer trustworthy. In these passages, words quite conspicuously have double meanings, as here begins the series of rapid-fire puns bemoaned since Addison as marring the beauty and gravitas of the epic.

With the invention of gunpowder, the battle becomes, as many have suggested, reminiscent of mock epic. Not only does the ridiculous action of the artillery bombardment suggest disdain for modern weaponry, but once the rebels tear open the surface of heaven meaning itself becomes unmoored:

>   None arguing stood, innumerable hands
>   Were ready, in a moment up they turned
>   Wide the celestial soil, and saw beneath
>   Th' originals of nature in their crude
>   Conception; sulfurous and nitrous foam
>   They found, they mingled, and with subtle art,
>   Concocted and adjusted they reduced
>   to blackest grain, and into store conveyed.   (6.508–15)

The soon-to-be fallen host *finds* the materials of creation under the placid surface of heaven (and at the same time invents the art of *foundry*). The sulfurous and nitrous foam so readily at hand, so we've been told in the previous passage, releases generative and creative energy when touched with "Heav'n's ray." As Satan describes it, these are the

> materials dark and crude,
> Of spirituous and fiery spume, till touched
> With Heav'n's ray, and tempered they shoot forth
> So beauteous, op'ning to the ambient light. (6.478–81)

These dark materials are the engine of creation, still churning with potential to produce the plants, fruits, flowers ambrosial, gems, and gold that adorn the surface of heaven. The "originals of nature" that the rebels mine are a source of energy and change that actively contribute to the ongoing miracle of growth and development in heaven.[25] The sulfurous and nitrous foam is not (as some have suggested) dangerous construction material carelessly left over from creation and rife with chaos. The structure and throne of heaven is not already mingled with infernal fire. It is the life-giving potential of ongoing creation that Satan and his host *pervert* to create the "infernal powder" of the gunpowder poems.

The inherently good, creative nature of the raw materials used in Satan's invention of gunpowder makes this Satan's most emblematic act of rebellion. He and his crew dig beneath the surface of things and take what had "open'd to the ambient light" and would normally "shoot forth so beauteous," and by "concocting and adjusting" they metamorphose it into something "blackest" in hue and purpose. Satan turns the "nativity" of creation against itself to give birth to evil, converting the generative power of creation into a destructive force. Well before Satan promised to make "evil" his "good," he was turning good into evil, an archetypal representation of his relationship with God and man.

Satan's invention of gunpowder and his exhortation to his followers that they must look beyond surface meaning and turn things against their purpose destabilize language in the epic. The new weapons crafted by the rebel host are introduced deceitfully, fraud itself hidden behind ranks of rebel angels until ready to fire, just as Satan's speech to the loyal angels hides his meaning behind puns about treaty and negotiation. Upon their discharge, the cannons belch fire and smoke in a manner that evokes flatulence or recalls the imagery of rape and bodily violation associated with Sin and Death in book 2.[26] The string of bodily puns degrades not only the epic's language but also serves to denigrate the stature of the black powder, turning it from "infernal powder" to something akin to rank wind. Satan's invention, although fearsome when first revealed, turns out to be ultimately ineffective as a weapon of war. As they uproot entire mountains and toss them upon rebel host and cannon, the loyal angels show that, without having to pervert creation, they are capable of far more sublime force than the "devilish engines" of Satan's artillery. Guns and gunpowder not only undermine heroism and heroic language; they reveal war as mockery.

In his most courageous late prose works, Milton's stance toward arming the citizenry reflects the maturation of a distrust and scorn of guns and gunpowder that we traced in his earliest poetry on the Gunpowder Plot and in his late masterpiece. However, when Robert Fallon suggested that Milton "always supported the rights of citizens to bear arms, as a safeguard against tyranny," he pointed readers toward Milton's *The Ready and Easy Way* as evidence.[27] Milton's pamphlet, published in two editions when the Reformation was certain, is a jeremiad in which Milton once again assumes the persona of the *vates* to warn his wayward people. The mode requires Milton perform at his most outspoken, that he speak truth to power. Considering the certain repercussions of putting his name on the publication, this was easily Milton's bravest performance in print, more so even than his divorce tracts, *The Tenure of Kings and Magistrates*, or his *Defenses* of regicide. Self-sacrifice is inherent in the rhetorical strategy, a fact that Milton acknowledges and embraces as he explains how "with all hazard I have ventur'd what I thought my dutie, to speak in season, & to forewarn my country in time" (YP 7:387). John Milton, Englishman, was willing to martyr himself in order to warn the people away from their own folly.

Despite its courage, *The Ready and Easy Way* is conspicuous for moments when Milton holds back, when his mistrust of the masses wins out over his desire to preserve the commonwealth. Despite modern reinventions of Milton by those such as Cody Wilson, who would cast him as some sort of proto-libertarian, Milton feared the poorly educated commoners, and would not propose a government or elections "committing all to the noise and shouting of a rude multitude" (YP 7:442). His concept of a permanent senate, a mitigating strategy to limit the diffusion of power, was softened only as a necessity in the light of a political landscape that had changed even as the first edition went to print in February 1660. By April's second edition, Milton found it necessary to at least acknowledge Harrington's model of a rotating senate, renewed by periodic elections that replace a third of the senate. Even so, Milton makes it very clear that he prefers a perpetual body, and that less frequent elections are better. A rotating senate, Milton complains, is like a "wheel of fortune" that may (through the ill choosing of the masses and the vagaries of fate) expel the best and elect less suitable replacements.

In his defense of a perpetual senate, even as certain tyranny was returning to renew its yoke upon English necks, Milton was not willing to trust most of his countrymen with the levers of government, nor with firearms. Recognizing that some might fear the growing central authority and potential corruption or despotism of a perpetual senate, Milton sought to reassure his readers that a tyrannical senate would not stand. As he put it, "Neither do I think a perpetual Senate, especially chosen and entrusted by the people, much in this land to be feard, where the well-affected either in a standing army, or in a setled militia have thir arms in thir own hands" (YP 7:435). The key terms here are "well-affected" and "settled militia." Despite pressures to the contrary in 1659, Milton had supported the standing army and proposed that the officers would be appointed for life, advancing their careers as superior positions fell vacant. In *Proposalls of Certaine Expedients*, he suggested that the army "from the highest to the lowest souldier of them take an oath of obedience to the supreme authority" of the perpetual (Rump) Parliament, unless the Parliament was not upholding the two highest principles of "liberty of conscience" and the abjuration of single rule (YP 7:337). His mention of a "settled militia" in *The Ready and Easy Way* is likely a move to mollify the significant numbers who opposed the standing, professional army. In any case, the intimation is that those bearing arms do so in the context of an organized, trained force such as the professional army or the trained bands. The antecedent requirement that these armed citizens be "well-affected" stipulates that these armed citizens be "right thinking" or "loyal" (that is, loyal to those key principles Milton requires the Parliament and the army to uphold). Together, these qualifications do not endorse an armed citizenry in the manner that Robert Fallon suggests but, instead, impose the Miltonic equivalent of a background check to ensure arms are in the hands of the *fit though few*.

While this doesn't provide any certainty that Milton would consider a printed gun "evil absolutely," which may thus be suppressed similar to the suppression of Catholic pamphlets permitted in *Areopagitica*, we should consider this a strong possibility given the consistently satanic associations of gunpowder in his later writings and his willingness to put strict limits on who can bear arms even in the face of impending tyranny.

What Wilson and Defense Distributed propose, using *Areopagitica* as a cloak, is not liberty for creative expression but, rather, the ability to download a file and press a button to produce a gun. This is neither printing nor authorship as Milton might define it, but mere copying. While there may be powerful ideas and philosophies associated with the resulting plastic gun warm from the goo of the printer, a gun itself is not an idea and does not forward virtue. Guns are useful when reason fails; unlike books, they aren't reason themselves.

NOTES

Notes to Introduction / Donovan and Festa

1. For an overview of the implications of materialism for seventeenth century literature, see John Rogers's groundbreaking study, *The Matter of Revolution: Science, Poetry, and Politics in the Age of Milton* (Ithaca, NY: Cornell University Press, 1996). See also, on Spenser, Donne, and Cavendish, Thomas Festa, "Spenser's Thaumaturgy: 'Mental Space' and the Material Forms of *The Faerie Queene* (1590)," in *The Book in History, the Book as History: New Intersections of the Material Text*, ed. Heidi Brayman, Jesse M. Lander, and Zachary Lesser (New Haven, CT: Beinecke Library, 2016), 151–83; Anthony Low, "The 'Turning Wheele': Carew, Jonson, Donne and the First Law of Motion," *John Donne Journal* 1 (1982): 69–80; Victor Harris, *All Coherence Gone: A Study of the Seventeenth-Century Controversy over Disorder and Decay in the Universe* (London: Frank Cass, 1949); Bruce Thomas Boehrer, *Animal Characters: Nonhuman Beings in Early Modern Literature* (Philadelphia: University of Pennsylvania Press, 2010), 192–98.

2. See, for example, *The Oxford Handbook of Shakespeare and Embodiment*, ed. Valerie Traub (Oxford: Oxford University Press, 2016); *Knowing Shakespeare: Senses, Embodiment and Cognition*, ed. Lowell Gallagher and Shankar Raman (New York: Palgrave Macmillan, 2010); *Materialist Shakespeare: A History*, ed. Ivo Kamps (London: Verso, 1995).

3. Gilles Deleuze, *Spinoza: Practical Philosophy*, trans. Robert Hurley (1988; repr., San Francisco: City Lights, 2001); Bruno Latour, *Politics of Nature: How to Bring the Science into Democracy*, trans. Catherine Porter (Cambridge, MA: Harvard University Press, 2004); Quentin Meillassoux, *After Finitude: An Essay on the Necessity of Contingency*, trans. Ray Brassier (London: Continuum, 2008); Jane Bennett, *Vibrant Matter: A Political Ecology of Things* (Durham, NC: Duke University Press, 2010); and Timothy Morton, *Hyperobjects: Philosophy and Ecology after the End of the World* (Minneapolis: University of Minnesota Press, 2013). For the debate over Kant's interpretation of his predecessors, see *Kant and the Early Moderns*, ed. Daniel Garber and Béatrice Longuenesse (Princeton, NJ: Princeton University Press, 2008).

4. See Jane Bennett, "The Force of Things: Steps toward an Ecology of Matter," *Political Theory* 32 (2004): 349.

5. Ibid., 364.

6. Leah S. Marcus, "Ecocriticism and Vitalism in *Paradise Lost*," *Milton Quarterly* 49 (2015): 96–111, eloquently calls for a more detailed account of the relations among seventeenth century vitalism, modern vitalism, and ecocriticism.

7. John Milton, *Paradise Lost*, ed. Barbara K. Lewalski (Oxford: Blackwell, 2007), 6.176. Subsequent quotations of the epic in this introduction are taken from this edition.

8. John Milton, *Paradise Lost*, 2 vols., in *The Poetical Works of John Milton*, 8th ed., ed. Thomas Newton (London, 1778), 1:391 (note on 5.478).

9. Samuel Johnson, "Life of Milton" (1779), in *Lives of the English Poets*, 3 vols., ed. George Birbeck Hill (Oxford: Clarendon Press, 1905), 1:184–85.

10. Augustine, *Confessions*, trans. Henry Chadwick (Oxford: Oxford University Press, 1991), 12.7.7.

11. Augustine, *The City of God against the Pagans*, trans. R. W. Dyson (Cambridge: Cambridge University Press, 1998), 12.6.

12. John Milton, *De doctrina Christiana*, in *The Complete Works of John Milton*, vol. 8, parts 1 and 2, ed. and trans. John K. Hale and J. Donald Cullington, gen. ed. Gordon Campbell and Thomas N. Corns (Oxford: Oxford University Press, 2012), 1.7.

13. William Kerrigan, *The Sacred Complex: On the Psychogenesis of "Paradise Lost"* (Cambridge, MA: Harvard University Press, 1983), 230, 231, 234–35, and 258. It's worth noting that the chapter is itself called "'One First Matter All': Spirit as Energy," in order to give due focus to this central passage.

14. Stephen M. Fallon, *Milton among the Philosophers: Poetry and Materialism in Seventeenth-Century England* (1991; repr., Ithaca, NY: Cornell University Press, 2007), 105–06.

15. A point first made by John Leonard in a note to 5.478 in John Milton, *The Complete Poems*, ed. John Leonard (Harmondsworth: Penguin, 1998), 781.

16. Fallon, *Milton among the Philosophers*, 202.

17. Marcus, "Ecocriticism and Vitalism," 104–05.

18. Leonard, *Complete Poems*, 782 (note to 5.497–500).

19. Rogers, *Matter of Revolution*, 111.

20. Ibid., 112.

21. See Abraham Stoll, *Milton and Monotheism* (Pittsburgh: Duquesne University Press, 2009).

22. Gordon Teskey, *The Poetry of John Milton* (Cambridge, MA: Harvard University Press, 2015), 2–3.

23. Augustine, *Confessions*, 12.7.7; italics added.

24. Spinoza, *Ethics*, IP15, in *A Spinoza Reader*, ed. and trans. Edwin Curley (Princeton, NJ: Princeton University Press, 1994), 94.

Notes to Chapter 1 / Shohet

1. All quotations of Milton's poetry are from *The Complete Poetry of John Milton*, ed. John T. Shawcross (New York: Doubleday, 1971); hereafter cited in the text.

2. I take "all sadness but despair" to indicate that some of Satan's sorrow *can* be mitigated. Hence I differ somewhat from Holly R. Dugan's reading that Edenic scents "contain *only* painful reminders of his own lost Paradise." Dugan, *The Ephemeral History of Perfume* (Baltimore: Johns Hopkins University Press, 2011), 172; emphasis added.

3. Jonathan Gil Harris, *Untimely Matter in the Age of Shakespeare* (Philadelphia: University of Pennsylvania Press, 2009); Dugan, *Ephemeral History of Perfume*; Holly Crawford Pickett, "The Idolatrous Nose: Incense on the Early Modern Stage," in *Religion and Drama in Early Modern England*, ed. Jane Hwang Degenhardt and Elizabeth Williamson, 19–38 (Farnham, Surrey: Ashgate, 2011).

4. Bruce R. Smith, *The Acoustic World of Early Modern England: Attending to the O-Factor* (Chicago: University of Chicago Press, 1999).

5. Karen Edwards astutely notes that Edenic fragrance is present to the reader even before the garden is visited by Raphael or indeed the narrative itself: "Long before *Paradise Lost* represents it to our sight," "Beelzebub metaphorically wafts" fragrant balm "under the nose of the fallen angels at the conclusion of the great consult" in book 2. Karen Edwards, *Milton and the Natural World: Science and Poetry in "Paradise Lost"* (Cambridge: Cambridge University Press, 1999), 182.

6. John R. Knott, "Milton's Wild Garden," *Studies in Philology* 102, no. 1 (Winter 2005): 68. David Reid suggests another way that scent in this passage dissolves boundaries by asking whether angels might themselves generate perfumed smells. I do not agree with Reid's adducing the word "distilled" in this passage as necessarily indicating the production of fragrance (rather than, say, liquor), but his overall discussion of the copious emanation/distillation dynamic of angelic and divine fragrance is illuminating, and consonant with my argument. David Reid, "Spirits Odorous," *Milton Quarterly* 25, no. 4 (December 1991): 140–43.

7. Physiologically, the indistinction of smell may derive from the fact that, as recent research from Bochum University has revealed, odor receptors are not confined to the nose but, rather, dispersed throughout the body, "in the liver, the heart, the kidneys and even sperm." "Smell Turns Up in Unexpected Places," *New York Times*, October 13, 2014, D3. Washington University biologist Yehuda Ben-Shahar suggests that olfactory receptors may not have their evolutionary origins in the nose: "They're called olfactory receptors because we found them in the nose first" (ibid.).

8. Gilles Deleuze, *The Fold: Leibniz and the Baroque*, trans. Tom Conley (Minneapolis: University of Minnesota Press, 1993). This technique is part of what aligns Milton's Baroque aesthetic and his monism, according with the "Baroque solution" to "multiply principles and in this way change their use" as a response to the potentially catastrophic contradiction among principles (67).

9. I thank Eric B. Song for suggesting I consider the sensory profile of the prohibition.

10. A study by Rachel Herz and Mary Carskadon shows that we cannot smell when asleep, and that dreams do not include scent experiences: "none of our other sense are cut off so completely while we sleep." Quoted in Rachel Herz, *The Scent of Desire: Discovering our Enigmatic Sense of Smell* (New York: William Morrow, 2007), 87. Other studies have found subjects who report smelling in dreams, but this appears to be rare.

11. Joe Moshenska, "'Transported touch': The Sense of Feeling in Milton's Eden," *ELH* 79, no. 1 (Spring 2012): 3.

12. The Trinity's symposium in ambrosial heaven participates in a tradition of scent both characterizing and underwriting the blurring of interpersonal boundaries in deep relationship. In Plutarch, the souls of the dead gather around the river Lethe, from which "wafted a soft and gentle breeze that carried up fragrant scents, arousing wondrous pleasures and such a mood as wine induces in those who are becoming tipsy; for as the souls regaled themselves on the sweet odours they grew expansive and friendly with one another." Plutarch, *Moralia*, 15 vols., trans. Phillip H. DeLacy and Benedict Einarson (Cambridge, MA: Harvard University Press, 1959), 7:285–87.

13. See esp. J. Hillis Miller, "How Deconstruction Works," *New York Times Magazine*, February 9, 1986, 25, rpt. in Miller, *Theory Now and Then* (Durham, NC: Duke University Press, 1991), 293–94; Catherine Belsey, *John Milton: Language, Gender, Power* (Oxford: Blackwell, 1988), 66; John Guillory, "From the Superfluous to the Supernumerary: Reading Gender into *Paradise Lost*," in *Soliciting Interpretation: Literary Theory and Seventeenth-Century English Poetry*, ed. Elizabeth D. Harvey and Katherine Eisaman Maus, 68–88 (Chicago: University of Chicago Press, 1990), 87; Stephen B. Dobranski. "Clustering and Curling Locks: The Matter of Hair in *Paradise Lost*," *PMLA* 125, no. 2 (March 2010): 337–53.

14. Constance Classen, David Howes, and Anthony Synnott, *Aroma: The Cultural History of* Smell (London: Routledge, 1994), 4.

15. Alain Corbin, *The Foul and the Fragrant: Odor and the French Social Imagination* (Cambridge, MA: Harvard University Press, 1988), 6.

16. Classen, Howes, and Synnott, *Aroma*, 89.

17. Plato, *Timaeus*, in *The Collected Dialogues*, ed. Edith Hamilton and Huntington Cairns, 1151–1211 (Princeton, NJ: Princeton University Press, 1961), 1190.

18. Richard Brathwaite, *Essaies upon the Five Senses* (London, 1620), 57.

19. Immanuel Kant, *Anthropology from a Pragmatic Point of View*, trans. Mary J. Gregor (The Hague: Nijhoff, 1974), 33–34.

20. Classen, Howes, and Synnott, *Aroma*, 4–5.

21. Cornelius Agrippa von Nettesheim, *Three Books of Occult Philosophy*, trans. J. F. (London, 1651), 549.

22. *The Natural History of Diodorus the Sicilian*, trans. George Booth (London, 1700), 107.

23. Avery Gilbert, *What the Nose Knows: The Science of Scent in Everyday Life* (New York: Synaesthetics, 2014), 200–01.

24. Ibid.

25. For a classic discussion of this problematic, see Dennis Danielson, *Milton's Good God: A Study in Literary Theodicy* (Cambridge: Cambridge University Press, 1982); for a recent important consideration, see Samuel Fallon, "Milton's Strange God: Theology and Narrative Form in *Paradise Lost*," *ELH* 79, no. 1 (Spring 2012): 33–57.

26. If Reid ("Spirits Odorous") is correct that angels emanate as well as transport good smells, this passage would link the unfallen Eve with angelic capacity.

27. Herz, *Scent of Desire*, 74.

28. Johan Willander and Maria Larsson, "Olfaction and Emotion: The Case of Autobiographical Memory," *Memory and Cognition* 35, no. 7 (October 2007): 1659–63, quoted in Natalie Angier, "The Nose, an Emotional Time Machine," *New York Times*, August 8, 2008, F1.

29. Larsson, quoted in Angier. "The Nose," F1.

30. Herz, *Scent of Desire*, 63.

31. Ibid.

32. Oliver Sacks, *The Man Who Mistook His Wife for a Hat* (London: Duckworth, 1987), 159.

33. Angier, "The Nose," F1.

Notes to Chapter 2 / Herbst

1. See Gordon Teskey, *Delirious Milton* (Cambridge, MA: Harvard University Press, 2006), chap. 5, "God's Body: Concept and Metaphor," 86–106.

2. See Stephen M. Fallon, *Milton among the Philosophers* (Ithaca, NY: Cornell University Press, 1991), chap. 3, "Material Life: Milton's Animist Materialism"; for more extended treatment of the development of monism in the divorce tracts, see Fallon's "Metaphysics of Milton's Divorce Tracts," in *Politics, Poetics, and Hermeneutics in Milton's Prose*, ed. David A Loewenstein and James Grantham Turner, 69–84 (Cambridge: Cambridge University Press, 1990). For discussion of the contemporary philosophical debate involving the Hobbesian mechanist universe and its threat to the concept of free will, see Fallon, *Milton among the Philosophers*, chaps. 1–3 and 8. In *The Life of John Milton*, rev. ed. (Oxford: Blackwell, 2003), Barbara Lewalski integrates Fallon's argument about monism into a broader assessment of Milton's intellectual development, including the evolution of his views on Trinitarianism, Arianism, and Arminianism (see, e.g., 414–15).

3. Although Fallon does note that in the relatively early *Comus* (*A Mask*, 1634) "the seeds of change are already present," he classifies earlier poems both Latin and English — including "In obitum Praesulis Eliensis" (1626), the Nativity ode (1629), *Il Penseroso* (1631?), and *Arcades* (1632) — as unambiguously dualist: "In all these poems, the material body is both the relatively unreal shadow of spirit and the grossly substantial barrier between the incorporeal soul and its heavenly home" (Fallon, *Milton among the Philosophers*, 81, 80).

4. I am indebted to Barbara Lewalski for this suggestion, which was the basis for this essay. Professor Lewalski further suggested to me in private conversation that the early poetry might demonstrate aspects of monist thinking even though Milton had not yet arrived at or fully articulated that concept.

5. Fallon, *Milton among the Philosophers*, Milton's phrases quoted on 88; italics are Fallon's.

6. Ibid., 88–89.

7. All references to *Paradise Lost* are to John Milton, *Paradise Lost*, ed. Barbara K. Lewalski (Oxford: Blackwell, 2007); hereafter cited in the text.

8. Raphael explains:

> And from these corporal nutriments perhaps
> Your bodies may at last turn all to Spirit,
> Improv'd by tract of time, and wingd ascend
> Ethereal, as wee. (5.496–99)

9. "Suspension" refers to a particular technique of musical harmony whereby a pitch, consonant in one chord, is carried over, or *suspended*, so that it becomes dissonant in a new chord. The *suspension* is then resolved in the new chord by stepwise motion from the dissonant pitch to a triadic, consonant pitch. The OED notes the first usage of "suspension" as a technical harmonic term only in the nineteenth century, however, so Milton may not have known the term in its modern technical musical sense. Given the context, however, and Milton's tendency to use punning language when depicting music, I suspect that the term had musical meaning in the seventeenth century, even if it was not precisely what we now take it to mean.

10. "Partial" is also a pun evoking the egotism of the demons, whose abiding interest is in personal contentment rather than the welfare of the group — again in contrast with their unfallen peers.

11. John Milton, *Christian Doctrine*, trans. John Carey, ed. Maurice Kelley, in *Complete Prose Works of John Milton*, vol. 6 (New Haven, CT: Yale University Press, 1973), 318–22. For helping me to understand God's speech in book 7, I am grateful to Teskey's account in *Delirious Milton* (chap. 5, "God's Body: Concept and Metaphor," 86–106).

12. See Lewalski, *Paradise Lost*, 10, Milton's note on "The Verse."

13. John Milton, "Ode on the Morning of Christ's Nativity," in *Complete Shorter Poems*, ed. Stella Revard, 126–40 (Oxford: Wiley-Blackwell, 2009). All of Milton's poetry except for *Paradise Lost* is from this edition, hereafter cited in the text.

14. Fallon, *Milton among the Philosophers*, 80.

15. "Fancy" has many denotative possibilities, but all of them imply a function of the mind, and the mind, or spirit, is a category of the soul rather than of the body. This reading of *fancy* is confirmed earlier in the ode, where the speaker declares that music "all their souls in blisfull rapture took" ("Nativity," 98). The enwrapping of fancy is logically equivalent to the taking of souls in rapture, which in turn implies the qualified logical equivalence of "fancy" and "souls" — the qualification is that "fancy" corresponds to a specific operation of the soul, its imaginative capacity.

16. The *Oxford English Dictionary* notes that "fantasy" had a particular meaning in the context of scholastic psychology, a meaning the well-educated Milton almost certainly would have known: "Mental apprehension of an object of perception; the faculty by which this is performed" (OED 1.a). In this particular denotation, the OED entry indicates, "fantasy" is precisely equivalent to "fancy." This meaning was current through at least 1669.

17. The libretto for Handel's oratorio *Samson*, written by Newburgh Hamilton, lifts these lines in slightly altered form for the Israelite Woman's closing aria:

> Let the bright Seraphim in burning row,
> Their loud, uplifted angel-trumpets blow.
> Let the Cherubic host, in tuneful choirs
> Touch their immortal harps with golden wires.

See George Frideric Handel, *Samson*, libretto by Newburgh Hamilton, printed in compact disc booklet notes for Handel, *Samson*, the Sixteen, conducted by Harry Christophers, Coro 16008, 2002, p. 19.

18. The most powerful use of allegory in *A Mask* occurs at its close, with the entrance of Sabrina. Whereas Silence is merely a figure of rhetoric in "Thyrsis's" speech, Sabrina is a character in the mask — technically a representative of chastity, but also, as Barbara Lewalski suggested to me in conversation, the allegorical embodiment of moral art, and most particularly, of moral music. She enters the stage while singing, and her verse as she frees the Lady is in a catalectic tetrameter meant to express musicality in contrast to the speech of other characters. Sabrina's appearance brings the material agency of music in *A Mask* to its apotheosis. Despite her Brothers' intervention and the temporary defeat of Comus, the Lady is still imprisoned in his chair, "In stony fetters fixt" (819). Only Sabrina can release the Lady, which she does, saying,

> this marble venom'd seat
> Smeared with gumms of glutenous heat
> I touch with chaste palms moist and cold,
> Now the spell hath lost his hold.   (*A Mask*, 916–19)

Sabrina's touch succeeds where military force fails. Since Sabrina herself is an embodiment of good music centered on an ethos of chastity, the liberating touch of her chaste palm emerges as a vivid means of dramatizing the material agency of *good music*.

19. See Fallon, *Milton among the Philosophers*, chap. 6, "Sin and Death: The Substance of Allegory," 168–93. Fallon's stimulating discussion of the interplay between ontology and allegory is an important account of a fascinating subject meriting further study.

20. Ibid., 168, 171.

21. While space does not here permit, in another essay, "Milton and Music," I trace in detail the development of this model and its significance in Milton's thought. See Seth Herbst, "Milton and Music," *Essays in Criticism* 66, no. 1 (2016): 96–116.

22. Milton, *Christian Doctrine*, 318.

23. Fallon, *Milton among the Philosophers*, 102.

Notes to Chapter 3 / Hackenbracht

I am indebted to David Boocker, William Shullenberger, and other audience members at the 2013 Conference on John Milton in Murfreesboro, Tennessee, for their insightful comments on a version of this essay, as well as Kevin Donovan, Charles Durham, and Kristin Pruitt for organizing the conference. I am also thankful to Garrett Sullivan and Paul Zajac for reading early drafts and providing me with helpful suggestions. All Greek and Latin translations are my own.

1. John Milton, *Paradise Lost*, ed. Barbara K. Lewalski (Malden, MA: Blackwell, 2007), 11.175–80. References to Milton's text are to this edition and are hereafter cited in the text.

2. Jennifer Nichols, "Milton's Claim for Self and Freedom in the Divorce Tracts," in *Milton Studies*, vol. 49, ed. Albert C. Labriola, 192–211 (Pittsburgh: University of Pittsburgh Press, 2009), proposes that Milton believed "inward choices can effect physiological, humoral changes" (194), so strong was the power of the human will over the body.

3. Ovid, *Metamorphoses*, Books 1–5, ed. William Anderson (Norman, OK: University of Oklahoma Press, 1997), 1.86; on the literary tradition of the Christian pilgrim, see *Pilgrimage: The English Experience from Beckett to Bunyan*, ed. Colin Morris and Peter Roberts (Cambridge: Cambridge University Press, 2002).

4. Michael Schoenfeldt, *Bodies and Selves in Early Modern England: Physiology and Inwardness in Spenser, Shakespeare, Herbert, and Milton* (Cambridge: Cambridge University Press, 1999), 2; and *Environment and Embodiment in Early Modern England*, ed. Mary Floyd-Wilson and Garrett Sullivan (Basingstoke, UK: Palgrave Macmillan, 2007). Similarly, Susanne Scholz, *Body Narratives: Writing the Nation and Fashioning the Subject in Early Modern England* (New York: Macmillan, 2000), notes that bodily demeanor was integral to early modern constructions of inwardness (17–20).

5. David Quint, *Inside "Paradise Lost": Reading the Designs of Milton's Epic* (Princeton, NJ: Princeton University Press, 2014), 63–92. See also Colin Burrow, *Epic Romance: Homer to Milton* (Oxford: Oxford University Press, 1993), who explores Satan's wandering in books 2–3 as a rewriting of Odysseus's travels (244–89).

6. Mandy Green, *Milton's Ovidian Eve* (Farnham, UK: Ashgate, 2009); and Jonathan Post, "Footloose in Paradise: Masaccio, Milton, and Renaissance Realism," *Huntington Library Quarterly* 69, no. 3 (2006): 409.

7. Lara Dodds, "Dark Looks and Red Smiles: Homeric Gesture and the Problem of Milton's Angels," chap. 6, this volume. See also Timothy Harrison, "Adamic Awakening and the Feeling of Being Alive in *Paradise Lost*," in *Milton Studies*, vol. 54, ed. Laura L. Knoppers, 29–57 (Pittsburgh: Duquesne University Press, 2013), who observes that Milton's idea of vitality derives also from Aristotle, and he notes that in the seventeenth century, "even those thinkers who undermined the principles of Aristotle's thought [e.g., Milton] continued to link life and motion" (41). On Milton's engagement with Aristotelian vitality, see Garrett Sullivan, *Sleep, Romance and Human Embodiment: Vitality from Spenser to Milton* (Cambridge: Cambridge University Press, 2012), 99–132.

8. Anne Wallace, *Walking, Literature, and English Culture: The Origins and Uses of Peripatetic in the Nineteenth Century* (Oxford: Clarendon, 1993), promotes a literary approach that she calls "thinking peripatetically," which I find useful as a critical apparatus for interpreting how Milton rewrites epic striding (16).

9. Studies on Milton's materialism include Stephen Hequembourg, "The Poetics of Materialism in Cavendish and Milton," *SEL* 54, no. 1 (2014): 173–92; Hequembourg, "Monism and Metaphor in *Paradise Lost*," in *Milton Studies*, vol. 52, ed. Laura L. Knoppers, 139–67 (Pittsburgh: Duquesne University Press, 2011); N. K. Sugimura, *"Matter of Glorious Trial": Spiritual and Material Substance in "Paradise Lost"* (New Haven, CT: Yale University Press, 2009); Rachel Trubowitz, "Body Politics in *Paradise Lost*," *PMLA* 121, no. 2 (2006): 388–404; John Rogers, *The Matter of Revolution: Science, Poetry, and Politics in the Age of Milton* (Ithaca, NY: Cornell University Press, 1996), 103–43; and Stephen Fallon, *Milton among the Philosophers: Poetry and Materialism in Seventeenth-Century England* (Ithaca, NY: Cornell University Press, 1991).

10. C. S. Lewis, *A Preface to "Paradise Lost"* (Oxford: Clarendon, 1942), 35; and David Quint, *Epic and Empire: Politics and Generic Form from Virgil to Milton* (Princeton, NJ: Princeton University Press, 1993), 8.

11. On the act of striding in Homer, see Kalliopi Nikolopoulou, "Feet, Fate, and Finitude: On Standing and Inertia in the *Iliad*," *College Literature* 34, no. 2 (2007): 174–93.

12. Michael Clarke, *Flesh and Spirit in the Songs of Homer: A Study of Words and Myths* (Oxford: Oxford University Press, 1999), notes the importance of bodily motion (as opposed to the body alone) in Homeric constructions of selfhood, and he points out that in the *Iliad* and the *Odyssey*, for instance, σῶμα (the body) always signifies an inanimate corpse, and that Homer "does not apply this word to the living human body" (116–17).

13. *A Greek-English Lexicon*, ed. Henry George Liddell, Robert Scott, and Henry Stuart Jones (Oxford: Clarendon, 1940), s.v. μένος (A.I, II); hereafter cited as LSJ. Michael Clarke discusses the word's significance in "Manhood and Heroism," in *The Cambridge Companion to Homer*, ed. Robert Fowler, 74–90 (Cambridge: Cambridge University Press, 2004).

14. LSJ, s.v. μακροβάμων (A.I). On μακροβάμων in classical epic, see Donald Lateiner, *Sardonic Smile: Nonverbal Behavior in Homeric Epic* (Ann Arbor, MI: University of Michigan Press, 1995), 93; and Jan Bremmer, "Walking, Standing, and Sitting in Ancient Greek Culture," in *A Cultural History of Gesture: From Antiquity to the Present Day*, ed. Jan Bremmer and Herman Roodenburg, 15–35 (Cambridge: Polity, 1991).

15. Homer, *Iliad*, in *Homeri opera*, 5 vols., ed. David Munro and Thomas Allen (Oxford: Clarendon, 1920), 3.22.

16. Ibid., 7.213, 13.809.

17. Ibid., 16.534.

18. On the Homeric idea of material selfhood, see Damian Stocking, "Res Agens: Towards an Ontology of the Homeric Self," *College Literature* 34, no. 2 (2007): 56–84; Clarke, *Flesh and Spirit*, 115–26; and Bruno Snell, *The Discovery of the Mind: The Greek*

Origins of European Thought, trans. T. G. Rosenmeyer (Cambridge, MA: Harvard University Press, 1953), 4–22.

19. Homer, *Odyssey*, in *Homeri opera*, 5 vols., ed. David Munro and Thomas Allen (Oxford: Clarendon, 1920), 11.489–91.

20. Ibid., 11.539.

21. Virgil, *Aeneid*, in *P. Vergili Maronis Opera*, ed. R. A. B. Mynors (Oxford: Clarendon, 1969), 12.683, 684–85.

22. Ibid., 12.715–17.

23. Ibid., 12.746–48.

24. Ibid., 12.946–47.

25. Recent ecocritical studies that address walking in relation to gardening include Todd Borlik, *Ecocriticism and Early Modern English Literature: Greener Pastures* (New York: Routledge, 2011); Ken Hiltner, ed., *Renaissance Ecology: Imagining Eden in Milton's England* (Pittsburgh: Duquesne University Press, 2008); Diane Kelsey McColley, *Poetry and Ecology in the Age of Milton and Marvell* (Aldershot, UK: Ashgate, 2007); and Ken Hiltner, *Milton and Ecology* (Cambridge: Cambridge University Press, 2003).

26. Stephen Blake, *The Compleat Gardeners Practice, Directing the Exact Way of Gardening* (London, 1664), sigs. M2^v, X^v.

27. Jean de la Quintinie, *The Compleat Gard'ner; or, Directions for Cultivating and Right Ordering of Fruit-Gardens and Kitchen-Gardens*, trans. John Evelyn (London, 1693), sigs. B^r and G3^r.

28. John Richardson, "Life of the Author," in Richardson, *Explanatory Notes and Remarks on Milton's "Paradise Lost,"* 3 vols. (London, 1734), 1:vii.

29. John Aubrey, "John Milton," in *Brief Lives*, 2 vols., ed. Andrew Clark (Oxford: Clarendon, 1898), 2:68.

30. Barbara K. Lewalski, *The Life of John Milton: A Critical Biography* (Malden, MA: Blackwell, 2000), 279.

31. On self-knowledge and the mutability of personhood in *Paradise Lost*, see Albert Fields, "The Creative Self and the Self Created in *Paradise Lost*," in *Spokesperson Milton: Voices in Contemporary Criticism*, ed. Charles Durham and Kristin Pruitt, 153–64 (Selinsgrove, PA: Susquehanna University Press, 1994); and Fields, "Milton and Self-Knowledge," *PMLA* 83, no. 2 (1968): 392–99.

32. Susan Wiseman, "Eve, *Paradise Lost*, and Female Interpretation," in *The Oxford Handbook of Milton*, ed. Nicholas McDowell and Nigel Smith, 534–46 (Oxford: Oxford University Press, 2009), maps the parallels between physical flight and social aspiration in Eve's dream.

33. Quint observes that Eve is presented with the same choice Icarus and Phaethon faced: an opportunity to remain grounded, or "to flight and to the godhood that such flight would prove" (*Inside "Paradise Lost,"* 86).

34. Critics have long noted that Eve bears a closer connection with the geography of Eden than Adam does; see Shannon Miller, *Engendering the Fall: John Milton and Seventeenth-Century Women Writers* (Philadelphia: University of Pennsylvania Press, 2008), 28; Julia Walker, *Medusa's Mirrors: Spenser, Shakespeare, Milton, and the*

Metamorphosis of the Female Self (Newark, DE: University of Delaware Press, 1998), 160–62; and Diane Kelsey McColley, *Milton's Eve* (Urbana, IL: University of Illinois Press, 1983), 110–13.

35. On the Fall as a loss of place, see John Gillies, "Space and Place in *Paradise Lost*," *ELH* 74, no. 1 (2007): 27–57.

36. Katherine Calloway, "'His Footstep Trace': The Natural Theology of *Paradise Lost*," in *Milton Studies*, vol. 55, ed. Laura L. Knoppers, 53–85 (Pittsburgh: Duquesne University Press, 2014), observes that the activity of tracing God's footsteps, metaphorically speaking, was "the central question of natural theology," and that in Adam's response to Raphael, Milton engages contemporary debates on the topic (72).

37. *OED Online*, s.v. "trace," II.5.a (Oxford: Oxford University Press, 2014), accessed August 12, 2016.

38. Louis Martz, *The Poetry of Meditation: A Study in English Religious Literature of the Seventeenth Century* (New Haven, CT: Yale University Press, 1954), documents the Augustinian nature of Milton's idea of self-knowledge (118–52); see also Lee Jacobus, *Sudden Apprehension: Aspects of Knowledge in "Paradise Lost"* (The Hague: Mouton, 1976). On Augustinian self-knowledge, see Brian Stock, *Augustine the Reader: Meditation, Self-Knowledge, and the Ethics of Interpretation* (Cambridge, MA: Harvard University Press, 1996); and Edward Booth, *Saint Augustine and the Western Tradition of Self-Knowing* (Villanova, PA: Villanova University Press, 1989).

39. Gregory Machacek, *Milton and Homer: "Written to Aftertimes"* (Pittsburgh: Duquesne University Press, 2011), points out that in his revision of Homeric and Virgilian subjects, Milton resists the "martial ideology of pagan epic" (118), and I suggest that Milton's denunciation of striding as prideful is part of his endeavor to supplant classical virtues with Protestant virtues. On Milton's revision of Achilles's heroic virtues, see also Stella P. Revard, "Milton, Homer, and the Anger of Adam," in *Milton Studies*, vol. 41, ed. Albert C. Labriola, 18–37 (Pittsburgh: University of Pittsburgh Press, 2002).

40. *OED Online*, s.v. "vain," I.1.a and I.4.a, accessed August 12, 2016.

41. Milton's reworking of epic imperialism when Satan arrives at earth is explored by David Armitage, "John Milton: Poet against Empire," in *Milton and Republicanism*, ed. David Armitage, Armand Himy, and Quentin Skinner, 206–26 (Cambridge: Cambridge University Press, 1995); and Quint, *Epic and Empire*, 253–56, 264–66.

42. Anthony Low, "The Fall into Subjectivity: Milton's 'Paradise Within' and 'Abyss of Fears and Horrors,'" in *Reading the Renaissance: Ideas and Idioms from Shakespeare to Milton*, ed. Marc Berley, 205–32 (Pittsburgh: Duquesne University Press, 2003), 209.

43. Matthew 7:14.

44. Elizabeth Sauer, "The Partial Song of Satanic Anti-Creation: Milton's Discourses of the Divided Self," in *Agonistics: Arenas of Creative Contest*, ed. Janet Lungstrum and Elizabeth Sauer, 226–39 (Albany, NY: State University of New York Press, 1997) describes the conquest of Sin and Death as an "imaginative" act of colonization resulting from a lack of self-awareness (229).

45. *A Latin Dictionary*, ed. Charlton Lewis and Charles Short, s.v. *expedio, -ire* (I) (Oxford: Clarendon, 1962).

Notes to Chapter 4 / Murphy

1. William Slatyer, "To the Noble and Generous Lovers of Venrable Antiquity," in *Genethliacon* (London, 1630).
2. Slatyer's genealogy ends with Charles I's ascent in 1625.
3. *Genethliacon* joins widespread efforts to invoke the typology of kingship in this moment. See Ann Baynes Coiro, "'A ball of strife': Caroline Poetry and Royal Marriage," in *The Royal Image: Representations of Charles I*, ed. Thomas Corns, 26–46 (Cambridge: Cambridge University Press, 1999), 37. On Henrietta Maria and the cult of Mary, see Erica Veevers's *Images of Love and Religion: Queen Henrietta Maria and Court Entertainments* (Cambridge: Cambridge University Press, 1989). On this birth imagery, see Erin Murphy, *Familial Forms: Politics and Genealogy in Seventeenth-Century English Literature* (Newark: University of Delaware Press, 2011), 74–78.
4. Slatyer, "Noble and Generous Lovers," A3.
5. Elizabeth Povinelli, "Notes on Gridlock: Genealogy, Intimacy, Sexuality," *Public Culture* 14, no. 1 (2002): 235.
6. Ibid., 218.
7. John Milton, *On the Morning of Christ's Nativity*, in *Complete Poems and Major Prose*, ed. Merritt Y. Hughes (New York: Hackett, 1957), lines 149–50. All subsequent references to Milton's poetry are from this edition and will appear parenthetically in the text.
8. Murphy, *Familial Forms*, 73–92.
9. Jonathan Goldberg, "What dost thou in this world?," in *Milton Now: Alternative Approaches and Contexts*, ed. Catharine Gray and Erin Murphy, 51–68 (New York: Palgrave, 2014), 52.
10. For key examples, see David Quint, "'David's Census': Milton's Politics and *Paradise Regained*," in *Remembering Milton: Essays on the Texts and Traditions*, ed., Mary Nyquist and Margaret Ferguson, 128–47 (New York: Methuen, 1987); and Stella Revard, "Charles, Christ and Icon of Kingship," in *Visionary Milton: Essays on Prophecy and Violence*, ed. Peter E. Medine, John T. Shawcross, and David V. Urban, 215–39 (Pittsburgh: Duquesne University Press, 2010).
11. See both Goldberg's reading of the Son's "identity-in-citation" ("'What dost thou'") and Gordon Teskey's "delirious identity" in chapter 8 of *Delirious Milton: The Fate of the Poet in Modernity* (Cambridge, MA: Harvard University Press, 2009), 148–79.
12. On Milton's postdynastic vision, see Rachel Trubowitz, *Nation and Nurture in Seventeenth-Century English Literature* (Oxford: Oxford University Press, 2012).
13. Judith Butler, "Is Kinship Always Already Heterosexual?" *Differences* 13, no. 1 (2002): 34.
14. In her foundational *Milton's Brief Epic: The Genre, Meaning, and Art of "Paradise Regained"* (Providence, RI: Brown University Press, 1966), Barbara Lewalski established the importance of the question of identity to the poem: "the central issue in the dramatic encounter between Christ and Satan is the problem of determining…'In what degree or meaning thou art call'd / The Son of God' (IV.516–17)" (134).

15. Recent scholarship has shown how much more widespread the politics of family were than any reductive picture of monarchic appeals to patriarchalism, and I have discussed elsewhere the extreme subtlety of James's engagement with the varied familial foundations of his political power. See Su Fang Ng, *Literature and the Politics of the Family in Seventeenth-Century England* (Cambridge: Cambridge University Press, 2007); and Murphy, *Familial Forms*, 50–61.

16. James I, *A Meditation vpon the 27.28.29 Verses of the XXVII. Chapter of Saint Matthew* (London, 1620), 229.

17. Ibid., 230.

18. James I and VI, *Basilicon Doron* (1603), in *Political Writings, King James VI and I*, ed. Johann P. Sommerville (Cambridge: Cambridge University Press, 1994), 15, and *Meditation*, 244. In *Basilicon doron*, James seems to be thinking of 1 Timothy 1:4, which links "fables and endless genealogies, which minister questions" but does not specifically criticize any particular genealogies, so the later *Meditation* is likely following Hugh Broughton's distinction in *The Holy Genealogie of Jesus Christ* (London, 1612) between the profane genealogies condemned by Saint Paul and the genealogies of Christ (1).

19. James I, *Meditation*, 246.

20. On James I's use of genealogical versus genetic arguments, see Murphy, *Familial Forms*, 55–57.

21. John Speed, *The history of Great Britaine under the conquests of ye Romans, Saxons, Danes and Normans Their originals, manners, warres, coines & seales: with ye successions, lives, acts & issues of the English monarchs from Iulius Caesar, to our most gracious soueraigne King Iames* (London, 1614), 884.

22. Broughton was famous for his extreme belief in the chronological accuracy of the Bible. See G. Lloyd Jones, "Broughton, Hugh (1549–1612)," in *Oxford Dictionary of National Biography*, ed. H. C. G. Matthew and Brian Harrison (Oxford: Oxford University Press, 2004), May 2013, www.oxforddnb.com/view/article/3585 (accessed January 2, 2015).

23. Broughton, *Holy Genealogie*, 1.

24. John Speed, "Jesus of Nazareth, King of ye Jewes" (London, 1616), 2. Speed augmented the 1592 *Genealogies* with *A direction to finde all those names expressed in that large table of genealogies of scripture, lately gathered* (1595). In 1616, he provided context for the arbors in the King James Bible with his publication of *A Cloud of Witnesses: And They the Holy Genealogies of the Sacred* (reissued in 1620 and 1628).

25. Marshall D. Johnson, *Purpose of the Biblical Genealogies: With Special Reference to the Setting of the Genealogies of Jesus* (Cambridge: Cambridge University Press, 1988), 227.

26. Ibid., 235.

27. Ibid., 252.

28. Ibid., 235.

29. In the wake of the widespread dissemination of Speed's biblical arbors, William Cowper argued in *Three Heavenly Treatises concerning Christ* (London, 1612), that Luke offered a more universalizing vision than Matthew, showing that "all believing people hath their interest in Christ, not they who are of Abraham's posteritie only, but they, who are of Adams also" (7–8).

30. On James's lineal reading of the Norman Conquest, see *Familial Forms*, 55–57.

31. For the classic work on the Stuart typology of kingship, see Steven N. Zwicker, *Dryden's Political Poetry: The Typology of King and Nation* (Providence, RI: Brown University Press, 1972).

32. Quint, "'David's Census,'" 133, 135. Quint, however, does not mention James I's use of this image.

33. James I, *Meditation*, 233.

34. It also mirrors the moment in book 12 (lines 329–30) of *Paradise Lost*, whose significance Teskey explains: "there is no escaping the suggestion Milton is making by the phrase 'of kings / The last': that the eternity of Christ's kingdom makes every subsequent king a usurper" (*Delirious Milton*, 154–55).

35. On Restoration appeals for indefeasibility, see Howard Nenner, *The Right to Be King: The Succession to the Crown of England, 1603–1714* (Chapel Hill: University of North Carolina Press, 1995), 95.

36. John Milton, *The Readie and Easie Way*, in *Complete Prose Works of John Milton*, 8 vols., ed. Don M. Wolfe et al. (New Haven, CT: Yale University Press, 1953–82), 7:436. All subsequent references to Milton's prose are to this edition, cited parenthetically in the text as YP, followed by the volume and page number. On the tract's lineal politics, see Murphy, *Familial Forms*, 130–31.

37. John Rogers, "Introduction: Relation Regained," *Huntington Library Quarterly* 76, no. 1 (Spring 2013): 4–5.

38. On the poem's debt to Luke, see Dayton Haskin, "Milton's Portrait of Mary as a Bearer of the Word," in *Milton and the Idea of Woman*, ed. Julia M. Walker, 169–84 (Urbana: University of Illinois Press, 1988).

39. Johnson, *Purpose of Biblical Genealogies*, 252.

40. See Murphy, *Familial Forms*, chap. 4, and "Sabrina and the Making of English History in *PolyOlbion* and *A Mask Presented at Ludlow Castle*," *Studies in English Literature* 51, no. 1 (Winter 2011): 87–110.

41. Teskey, *Delirious Milton*, 177.

42. Rogers, "Relation Regained," 5.

43. Here, Satan emphasizes maternal lineage much like Luke ("By Mother's Side thy Father" [*PR* 3.155]), but uses the word "father" only in reference to David, as he does in "thy Father David's house" (3.282) and "as thy Father David did" (3.353).

44. Elizabeth Sauer, *Barbarous Dissonance and Images of Voice in Milton's Epics* (Montreal: McGill-Queen's University Press, 1996), 151.

45. Haskin, "Milton's Portrait of Mary," 169; Trubowitz, *Nature and Nurture*, 149–50.

46. Mary Beth Rose, "Why Is the Virgin Mary in *Paradise Regain'd?*," in *Visionary Milton: Essays on Prophecy and Violence*, ed. Peter E. Medine, John T. Shawcross, and David V. Urban, 193–213 (Pittsburgh: Duquesne University Press, 2010), 213.

47. Murphy, *Familial Forms*, chap. 4.

48. On the significance of the word "fulfilling," see Goldberg, "'What dost thou,'" 59–60.

49. Haskin, "Milton's Portrait of Mary," 179.

50. Trubowitz, *Nature and Nurture*, 149–50.
51. Rose, "Why Is Virgin Mary," 209.
52. Thomas Hobbes, *On the Citizen*, ed. Richard Tuck and Michael Silverthorne (Cambridge: Cambridge University Press, 1998), 108.
53. Hobbes, *On the Citizen*, 108.
54. Rose, "Why Is Virgin Mary," 204.
55. Hobbes, *On the Citizen*, 109.
56. Ibid., 109.
57. Ibid., 108.
58. As Su Fang Ng argues in "Hobbes and the Bestial Body of Sovereignty," in *Feminist Interpretations of Thomas Hobbes*, ed. Nancy Hirschmann and Joanne Wright, 83–101 (State College: Pennsylvania State University Press, 2012), "the relation between the child and the nurturing mother, for Hobbes, is a relation of contract" (96).
59. Speed, *Jesus of Nazareth*, 17, 2, 20.
60. Butler, "Is Kinship Heterosexual?," 16.
61. D. R. Woolf, *The Social Circulation of the Past* (Oxford: Oxford University Press, 2003), 134.
62. Michael Warner, "Irving's Posterity," *ELH* 67, no. 3 (2000): 777.
63. Lee Edelman, *No Future: Queer Theory and the Death Drive* (Durham, NC: Duke University Press, 2004).
64. Ibid., 12.
65. Ibid., 13, 64.
66. Quint, "'David's Census,'" 142.
67. Ibid., 143.
68. Starting in 1990, several articles have discussed homosexuality and the Son in *Paradise Regained*. See Gregory W. Bredbeck, "Milton's Ganymede: Negotiations of Homoerotic Tradition in *Paradise Regained*," *PMLA* 106, no. 2 (March 1991): 262–76; Claude J. Summers, "The (Homo)sexual Temptation in Milton's *Paradise Regain'd*," in *Reclaiming the Sacred: The Bible in Gay and Lesbian Culture*, ed. Raymond-Jean Frontain, 45–69 (New York: Haworth, 1997); Thomas Luxon, *Single Imperfection: Milton, Marriage, and Friendship* (Pittsburgh: Duquesne University Press, 2005), 181–92; John T. Shawcross, "*Paradise Regain'd* and the Second Temptation," *ANQ: A Quarterly Journal of Short Articles, Notes and Reviews* 21 (Spring 2008): 34–41; and David V. Urban, "The Homosexual Temptation of the Son in Milton's *Paradise Regain'd*: A Reply to John T. Shawcross and Claude J. Summers," *Connotations* 21, nos. 2–3 (2011/2012): 272–77.
69. Luxon, *Single Imperfection*, 192. This moment belies this groundbreaking book's critique of heteronormativity, which has helped open new paths in Milton criticism.
70. Here, my reading finds some kinship with Joseph Wittreich's striking articulation, "The story of a perfect man is also the story of humankind perfected," in "A World with a Tomorrow: *Paradise Regained* and Its Hermeneutic of Discovery," in *Visionary Milton: Essays on Prophecy and Violence*, ed. Peter E. Medine, John T. Shawcross, and David V. Urban, 109–135 (Pittsburgh: Duquesne University Press, 2010), 134.

Notes to Chapter 5 / Buckham

1. John Milton, *Paradise Lost*, ed. Barbara Lewalski (Malden, MA: Blackwell, 2007), 8.530, 8.615–17. All further references are to this edition and will be cited parenthetically in the text.

2. Jonathan Goldberg, *The Seeds of Things: Theorizing Sexuality and Materiality in Renaissance Representations* (New York: Fordham University Press, 2009), considers Milton's angels as part of a project "that hopes to suggest that there is more to Christianity than body hatred" (5).

3. In *Matter of Glory: A New Preface to "Paradise Lost"* (Pittsburgh: University of Pittsburgh Press, 1987), John Rumrich suggests that Raphael is ignorant of the pleasures of human lovemaking, which is "slower and sweeter than angelic because it must cross a gulf of difference in will and body that is relatively immaterial for the angels" (119–20)."

4. Drew Daniel, *The Melancholy Assemblage: Affect and Epistemology in the English Renaissance* (New York: Fordham University Press, 2013), 3. Daniel is interested in encounters that have a particular affective tenor — melancholy — but his attention to perceptual relations that are set up only to be withdrawn relates to my more general focus.

5. Goldberg, *Seeds of Things*, 195.

6. Jesús Rivas and Gordon M. Burghardt, "Crotalomorphism: A Metaphor for Understanding Anthropomorphism by Omission," in *The Cognitive Animal: Empirical and Theoretical Perspectives on Animal Cognition*, ed. Mark Bekoff, Colin Allen, and Gordon M. Burghardt, 9–18 (Cambridge, MA: MIT Press, 2002), 10.

7. Ibid., 13–14.

8. Robert West, *Milton and the Angels* (Athens: University of Georgia Press, 1955), 163.

9. Walter Stephens, *Demon Lovers: Witchcraft, Sex, and the Crisis of Belief* (Chicago: University of Chicago Press, 2002).

10. For the anecdote about the chimpanzee, see Vicki Hearne, *Adam's Task: Calling Animals by Name* (1987; repr., New York: Random House, 1982), 35. See the story of Pony the orangutan, who underwent rehabilitation after her life as a prostitute. "Pony's New Life," Borneo Orangutan Survival Foundation, July 25, 2013, http://orangutan.or.id/ponys-new-life-2.

11. Timothy Morton, *The Ecological Thought* (Cambridge, MA: Harvard University Press, 2010).

12. Ibid., 40–41.

13. *Areopagitica*, in *Complete Prose Works of John Milton*, 8 vols., ed. Don M. Wolfe et al. (New Haven, CT: Yale University Press, 1953–82), 2:514.

14. Joad Raymond, *Milton's Angels: The Early-Modern Imagination* (Oxford: Oxford University Press, 2010), 269–70.

15. Ibid., 282.

16. In his editorial note to "Sups" (*PL* 5.426), Thomas Luxon reads the passage as something like an interspecies food chain: "Milton refers to the classical notion that the sun feeds on the ocean. His cosmology specifies that the Moon feeds on Earth's exhala-

tions, and the Sun on the exhalations of all the other planets, in a grand cosmic pecking order." Thomas H. Luxon, ed., *The John Milton Reading Room*, http://www.dartmouth.edu/~milton.

17. See W. B. Stanford, *Greek Metaphor: Studies in Theory and Practice* (1936; repr., New York: Johnson Corp., 1972). See discussion of Aristotle's fourth kind of metaphor, analogical metaphor: "Analogy is an equality of ratios containing at least four terms," which Stanford takes to mean "equality of relations" (11).

18. Stephen M. Fallon, *Milton among the Philosophers: Poetry and Materialism in Seventeenth-Century England* (1991; repr., Ithaca, NY: Cornell University Press, 2007), qualifies the lines: "Gabriel says 'hard' and not 'impossible'" (142).

19. Robert Watson, *Back to Nature: The Green and the Real in the Late Renaissance* (Philadelphia: University of Pennsylvania Press, 2006), 36.

20. William G. Madsen, *From Shadowy Types to Truth: Studies in Milton's Symbolism* (New Haven, CT: Yale University Press, 1968), 69–70. Madsen turns to Milton's own consideration of metaphor in *Art of Logic* to suggest instead that "Milton ... is one of the company of mundane rhetoricians when he defines metaphor as 'a similitude contracted to one word without signs, which, however, are understood.'" He also aligns Milton's view of metaphor with "the same cautious, rationalistic approach to metaphor that Bacon, Hobbes, and the proponents of the Royal Society do" (70). Of course, Milton's own theory of metaphor need not constrain a more critically active account of the metaphorical work performed by his representation of angels.

21. Cited in Christine Rees, *Johnson's Milton* (Cambridge: Cambridge University Press, 2010), 146.

22. C. S. Lewis, *A Preface to "Paradise Lost"* (1959; repr., London: Oxford University Press, 1942), 105–08.

23. Ibid., 108. Echoing Lewis, West contends, "Raphael does not mean that he will speak in bodily terms of that which has no body, but that he will reduce to terms of a body known to Adam the activities of a kind of body normally above reach of human sense and so out of Adam's experience" (*Milton and the Angels*, 138).

24. William Bedell Stanford, *Greek Metaphor: Studies in Theory and Practice* (Oxford: Basil Blackwell, 1939), 101. Cited in Madsen, *From Shadowy Types*, 54.

25. Diane McColley shows the affective capacity of Milton's poetics, which elicits the reader's bodily involvement with the animals of Eden. McColley, "Milton and Ecology," in *A New Companion to Milton*, ed. Thomas N. Corns, 157–73 (Malden, MA: Blackwell, 2016), 159.

26. See Abraham Stoll's reading of the poetics of Satan's wound as similarly performative in *Milton and Monotheism* (Pittsburgh: Duquesne University Press, 2009), 154.

27. Milton uses "sanguine" to describe the hyacinth in *Lycidas*, not because it is a red-colored flower but because it grows from where the blood of Hyacinthus fell.

28. This is how Laura Lockwood takes "gross" in line 661 — "dense and coarse, contrasted with *air, spiritual substance*, etc." She does not include an entry for "gross" as shadowy or obscure, but only having meaning with respect to physical size or density of substance. See Laura Lockwood, *Lexicon to the English Poetical Works of John Milton* (1907; repr., New York: Burt Franklin, 1968).

29. In *The Soul of an Octopus* (New York: Atria Books, 2015), Sy Montgomery cites cephalopod research that has found gene sequences for sensitivity to light, "usually expressed only in the retina of the eye," to be present in the skin of cuttlefish (50).

30. Rivas and Burghardt, "Crotalomorphism," 10.

31. Ibid., 10–11. The term is Jacob von Uexküll's. See also John Andrew Fisher's distinction between "interpretive" and "imaginative" anthropomorphism in "The Myth of Anthropomorphism," in *Readings in Animal Cognition*, ed. Marc Bekoff and Dale Jamieson, 3–16 (Cambridge, MA: MIT Press, 1996), 5.

32. Lewis, Preface to *"Paradise Lost,"* 110.

33. Raymond, *Milton's Angels*, 257.

34. Ibid.

Notes to Chapter 6 / Dodds

1. John Milton, *Paradise Lost*, in *John Milton: Complete Poems and Major Prose*, ed. Merritt Y. Hughes (Indianapolis: Hackett 2003), 8.595, 616–17. All further references to *Paradise Lost* are to this edition and cited parenthetically in the text.

2. Barbara K. Lewalski, "Innocence and Experience in Milton's Eden," in *New Essays on Paradise Lost*, ed. Thomas Kranidas, 86–117 (Berkeley: University of California Press, 1969), 115.

3. Peter Lindenbaum, "Lovemaking in Milton's Paradise," in *Milton Studies*, vol. 6, edited by James D. Simmonds, 277–306 (Pittsburgh: University of Pittsburgh Press, 1974), 297.

4. G. Stanley Koehler, "Milton's Use of Color and Light," in *Milton Studies*, vol. 3, ed. James D. Simmonds, 55–81 (Pittsburgh: University of Pittsburgh Press, 1971), 65. On red as the color of the seraphim, see also Lewalski, "Innocence and Experience," 115.

5. James Grantham Turner, *One Flesh: Paradisal Marriage and Sexual Relations in the Age of Milton* (Oxford: Clarendon Press, 1987), 265.

6. Joad Raymond, *Milton's Angels* (Oxford: Oxford University Press, 2010), 282.

7. Samuel Johnson, *The Major Works*, ed. Donald Greene (Oxford: Oxford University Press, 2000), 710. For a full discussion of how Milton's angels differ from earlier Catholic and Reformed traditions, see Feisal G. Mohamed, *In the Anteroom of Divinity: The Reformation of the Angels from Colet to Milton* (Toronto: University of Toronto Press, 2008).

8. Robert H. West, *Milton and the Angels* (Athens: University of Georgia Press, 1955), 104–06.

9. Arnold Stein, "Milton's War in Heaven—An Extended Metaphor," *ELH* 18, no. 3 (1951): 207, 17.

10. Stephen Fallon, *Milton among the Philosophers* (Ithaca, NY: Cornell University Press, 1991), 165. Raymond builds upon Fallon in his discussion of the angels and natural philosophy. See Raymond, *Milton's Angels*, 277–310. See also Karma deGruy, "Desiring Angels: The Angelic Body in *Paradise Lost*," *Criticism* 54, no. 1 (2012) 117–49. N. K. Sugimura offers a different account of the balance between matter and spirit in

Milton's universe but also assumes that the representation of the angels is consistent with a coherent natural philosophy. N. K. Sugimura, "*Matter of Glorious Trial*": *Spiritual and Material Substance in "Paradise Lost"* (New Haven, CT: Yale University Press, 2009), 158–95.

11. Thomas Wright, *The Passions of the Minde in Generall* (London, 1604), 30.

12. Juan Huarte, *Examen de ingenios: The Examination of Mens Wits* (London, 1594), 266, from Brian Cummings, "Animal Passions and Human Sciences: Shame, Blushing and Nakedness in Early Modern Europe and the New World," in *At the Borders of the Human: Beasts, Bodies and Natural Philosophy in the Early Modern Period*, ed. Erica Fudge, Ruth Gilbert, and Susan Wiseman, 26–51(Houndsmills: Palgrave, 2002), 32.

13. Cited from H. T. Swedenberg Jr., *The Theory of the Epic in England, 1650–1800* (Berkeley: University of California Press, 1944), 278. Devils, however, may have passions and inclinations, but "by reason that they have no good Qualities, do not come so near to humane Nature as the infernal Gods of the Heathens; and since by reason that they have all of them infernal Rage and diabolical Malice, and bear an immortal Hatred to Man, the good as well as the bad, which the infernal Powers of the Heathens, no, not even the Furies do not; they rather appear to be horrible and odious, than they seem to be terrible" (278). For discussion of the problems faced by writers of the Christian epic with regard to the theological and literary decorum of divine action, see Tobias Gregory, *From Many Gods to One* (Chicago: University of Chicago Press, 2006).

14. Fallon, *Milton among the Philosophers*, 143.

15. Raymond, *Milton's Angels*, 220, 6.

16. In addition to Fallon (*Milton among the Philosophers*), see John Rogers, *The Matter of Revolution: Science, Poetry, and Politics in the Age of Milton* (Ithaca, NY: Cornell University Press, 1996), 103–43.

17. For a study of angels' tears and classical allusion, see Richard J. DuRocher, "'Tears such as Angels Weep': Passion and Allusion in *Paradise Lost*," in *Milton Studies*, vol. 49, edited by Albert C. Labriola, 124–45 (Pittsburgh: University of Pittsburgh Press, 2009).

18. In this essay I focus solely on facial gestures because, for the angelic characters, these show the greatest debts to Homer. Other types of gestures, particularly hand-holding, are important for the human characters of *Paradise Lost*. See Stephen B. Dobranski, "Seizures, Free Will, and Hand-Holding in *Paradise Lost*," in *Milton, Rights, and Liberties*, ed. Neil Forsyth, 277–91 (Bern: Peter Lang, 2007).

19. For a metrical and linguistic analysis of Homeric speech introductions, see Mark W. Edwards, "Homeric Speech Introductions," *Harvard Studies in Classical Philology* 74 (1970): 1–36. Gregory Machacek argues that Milton creates a similar effect through the aggregation of "meaningless allusions" that "reproduce in a written epic the aesthetic effect of the formulaic diction in which oral epics like those of Homer are composed" (89). Gregory Machacek, *Milton and Homer: "Written to Aftertimes"* (Pittsburgh: Duquesne University Press, 2011), 73–94.

20. Donald Lateiner, *Sardonic Smile: Nonverbal Behavior in Homeric Epic* (Ann Arbor: University of Michigan Press, 1995), 31.

21. Ibid., 39.

22. Homer, *The Iliad*, trans. A. T. Murray (Cambridge, MA: Harvard University Press, 1967), 24.559.

23. Lateiner, *Sardonic Smile*, 60.

24. John M. Steadman, *Milton's Epic Characters: Image and Idol* (Chapel Hill: University of North Carolina Press, 1968), 177–226; David Quint, "Ulysses and the Devils: The Unity of Book Two of *Paradise Lost*," in *Milton Studies*, vol. 49, ed. Albert C. Labriola, 20–48 (Pittsburgh: University of Pittsburgh Press, 2009).

25. Richard Strier, "Milton's Fetters, or, Why Eden Is Better than Heaven," in *The New Milton Criticism*, ed. Peter C. Herman and Elizabeth M. Sauer, 25–48(Cambridge: Cambridge University Press, 2012), 35.

26. One possible exception is the "stern regard" (*PL* 10.866) that Adam directs toward Eve before his misogynist rant.

27. Translation of "looking darkly" is from Lattimore; "glower" or "glare" is from A. Cook, cited from James P. Holoka, "'Looking Darkly': Reflections on Status and Decorum in Homer," *Transactions of the American Philological Association* 113 (1983): 1n1. Translation of "dark glance" is from Homer, *The Iliad*, trans. Robert Fagles (New York: Penguin, 1998).

28. *Chapman's Homer: Illiad*, vol. 1, ed. Allardyce Nicoll (Princeton, NJ: Princeton University Press, 1998), 4.349, 12.230.

29. *Homer His Iliads Translated*, trans. John Ogilby (London, 1660), 2.245, 5.251, 12.230.

30. *Iliad* 14.89 and *Odyssey* 2.304–05, in *The Poems of Alexander* Pope, 10 vols., ed. Maynard Mack (London: Methuen, 1967), 8:162, 9:43.

31. Holoka, "Looking Darkly," 16.

32. *Iliad* 17.141 (Ogilby).

33. Holoka, "Looking Darkly," 8.

34. *Iliad* 17.169 (Nicoll).

35. On smiles in Homer, see Daniel B. Levine, "Homeric Laughter and the Unsmiling Suitors," *Classical Journal* 78, no. 2 (1982): 97-104.

36. Lateiner, *Sardonic Smile*, 43.

37. Cummings, "Animal Passions," 33.

38. Without presuming that Adam's psychology is Cartesian here, Descartes's discussion of the relationship between the will and the passions can help explain this paradox. The strength of the soul must be allied with knowledge of truth for actions to be properly regulated. Often it appears that men have "determinate judgements according to which they regulate part of their actions"; however, in some cases these judgments may be false because they are based upon a passion that has previously defeated the soul. René Descartes, *The Passions of the Soule: In Three Books* (London, 1650), 42.

39. John Milton, *Paradise Lost*, 2nd ed., ed. Alastair Fowler (Harlow: Longman, 1998).

40. John Leonard, *Faithful Labourers: A Reception History of "Paradise Lost," 1667–1970*, 2 vols. (Oxford: Oxford University Press, 2013), 1:386.

41. Leonard includes summaries of most of the major commentary on this simile in his chapter on the epic simile (ibid., 1:327–90). Among others, this simile is discussed in Geoffrey Hartman, "Milton's Counterplot," *ELH* 25, no. 1 (1958): 10–12; Christopher Ricks, *Milton's Grand Style* (Oxford: Clarendon Press, 1963), 129–30; and William Empson, *Some Versions of Pastoral* (New York: New Directions, 1974), 171–72.

42. Stanley Eugene Fish, *Surprised by Sin: The Reader in "Paradise Lost,"* 2nd ed. (Cambridge, MA: Harvard University Press, 1998), 174-75.

43. C. S. Lewis, *A Preface to "Paradise Lost"* (London: Oxford University Press, 1961), 124.

44. Many instances of this gatekeeping are cited in the introduction above; however, this language is near ubiquitous even when critics allow that Raphael blushes. For instance, Michael C. Schoenfeldt explains that Raphael's blush is a "licit and benign version of the passion of shame that marks the moral descent of humans at the Fall." Michael C. Schoenfeldt, "'Commotion Strange': Passion in *Paradise Lost*," in *Reading the Early Modern Passions*, ed. Gail Kern Paster, Katherine Rowe, and Mary Floyd-Wilson, 43-67 (Philadelphia: University of Pennsylvania Press, 2004), 61.

45. Michael's visit to Adam in books 11–12 might be described as an instance of bodily accommodation. He appears "Not in his shape celestial, but as man / Clad to meet man" (11.239–40), as apparently befits Adam's fallen state. Raphael, however, appears to Adam in his "proper shape" (5.276), and his interactions with Adam seem to presume honesty and transparency.

46. Susan James, *Passion and Action: The Emotions in Seventeenth-Century Philosophy* (Oxford: Oxford University Press, 2000), 86.

47. Ibid.

48. *Iliad* 5.888 (Nicoll).

49. According to Levine, a smile is always a "true reflection a character's position: if he smiles in triumph or with anticipation of victory, he is always justified in doing so" ("Homeric Laughter," 104). In *Paradise Lost* the smiles and laughter of the Father and the Son follow this pattern. See John N. King, *Milton and Religious Controvery: Satire and Polemic in "Paradise Lost"* (Cambridge: Cambridge University Press, 2000), 109–32.

50. Aristotle, *On Rhetoric*, trans. George A. Kennedy (New York: Oxford University Press, 1991), 2.6.

Notes to Chapter 7 / Rogers

1. See my "Latter-day Milton," in *Immortality and the Body in the Age of Milton*, ed. John Rumrich and Stephen Fallon (Cambridge: Cambridge University Press, 2017). Let me thank Kristin Pruitt and Charles W. Durham for their invitation to speak at Murfreesboro, Tennessee, and Thomas Festa and Kevin Donovan for including me in this volume and for permitting me to substitute this piece for the paper I delivered at the conference. For invaluable scholarly advice about Mormonism, I am very grateful to William John Silverman.

2. Terryl L. Givens and Matthew J. Grow, *Parley P. Pratt: The Apostle Paul of Mormonism* (New York: Oxford University Press, 2011), 331.

3. While in the mythology of Mormonism Joseph Smith clearly played the role of Jesus, it has been a matter of disagreement as to who played the role of Paul, who reshaped Jesus's message into something like a systematic theology. Breck England, *The Life and Thought of Orson Pratt* (Salt Lake City: University of Utah Press, 1985), 299, suggests that Paul is Orson, "a Mormon Aquinas; a Mormon Aristotle; a 'philosopher apostle'—hence a Mormon Paul." Quoted from Gary James Bergera, *Conflict in the Quorum: Orson Pratt, Brigham Young, Joseph Smith* (Salt Lake City: Signature Books, 2002), 88–89. Orson likewise is the "St. Paul of Mormondom" for B. Skabelund, "Cosmology on the American Frontier: Orson Pratt's Key to the Universe," *Centaurus* 11, no. 3 (1965): 191. But Parley P. Pratt also emerged as a Pauline interpreter of Smith's visions. Givens and Grow have perhaps settled the question with the subtitle of their book, *Parley P. Pratt: Apostle Paul of Mormonism*.

4. See the gripping narrative of Parley's death in Givens and Grow, *Parley P. Pratt*, 366–92.

5. See D. Michael Quinn, "The Mormon Succession Crisis of 1844," *Brigham Young University Studies* 16, no. 2 (1976): 187–233.

6. All citations from the Scriptures of the Church of Jesus Christ of Latter-day Saints are taken from the church's official website, https://www.lds.org/scriptures. This particular section of *The Doctrines and Covenants* is https://www.lds.org/scriptures/dc-testament/dc/107.14 (accessed July 15, 2015). On the succession crisis, see J. Spencer Fluhman, "Authority, Power, and the 'Government of the Church of Christ,'" in *Joseph Smith, the Prophet and Seer*, ed. Richard Neitzel Holzapfel and Kent P. Jackson, 195–232 (Salt Lake City: Deseret Book, 2010), 195–232; and Kurt Widmer, *Mormonism and the Nature of God: A Theological Evolution, 1830–1915* (Jefferson, NC: McFarland, 2000), 27. The most powerful study of the succession crisis, and the reading of early Mormonism to which I am most indebted, is Bergera's *Conflict in the Quorum*.

7. Bergera, *Conflict in the Quorum*, 53.

8. *Seer* 1, no. 2 (February, 1853), 31.

9. Bergera, *Conflict in the Quorum*, 80. Scholars of Mormon history have every reason to be grateful to Bergera, who reproduces at considerable length the still unpublished contemporary transcripts of the succession debates in 1847. Bergera cites his source as "'Minutes of Councils, Meetings, & Journey,' 16, 30 Nov., 5 Dec. 1847" (54n) and notes in his preface that much of the research for his book had been undertaken in the LDS historical archives in the late 1970s, before the church officially blocked "access to the papers of general church officers" (x).

10. John Smith, "Baptism of the Dead," in *Times and Seasons*, April 15, 1842, 761, Brigham Young University, Mormon Publications: Nineteenth and Twentieth Centuries Collection, http://contentdm.lib.byu.edu/cdm/ref/collection/NCMP1820-1846/id/9200. This passage is cited by the Mormon historian Boyd Jay Petersen, "One Soul Shall Not Be Lost: War in Heaven in Mormon Theology," *Journal of Mormon History* 38 (2012): 2–45. But citing John Tanner's caveat that Mormonism and Miltonism must be seen as distinct, Petersen adds, as if somewhat reflexively, that "whether Joseph Smith read Milton is not certain." My own hunch is that Smith and at least a few of his Apostles began their reading of *Paradise Lost* in the period shortly

before Smith's allusion to the opening of *Paradise Lost* appeared in 1842. It is that year, over a decade after the appearance of the decidedly non-Miltonic *Book of Mormon*, in which Smith initiated the extravagantly Miltonic ritual of "Endowment," and in which Parley Pratt's Miltonic *World Turned Upside Down* appears. There were, of course, many available U.S. editions of William Ellery Channing's essay and of *Paradise Lost*. These Mormon readers also may have had available to them one of the recent English editions of Milton's works prefaced by the American Channing's essay on the poetry and theology. See, for example, *The Poetical Works of John Milton: To Which Is Prefixed the Life of the Author: Together with Dr. Channing's Essay on the Poetical Genius of Milton* (London: Allman, 1836), or *The Poetical Works of John Milton: With a memoir, and Dr. Channing's Essay on his poetical genius* (London: C. Daly, 1840).

11. George F. Sensabaugh, *Milton in Early America* (Princeton, NJ: Princeton University Press, 1964); Lydia Dittler Schulman, *"Paradise Lost" and the Rise of the American Republic* (Boston: Northeastern University Press, 1992); K. P. Van Anglen, *The New England Milton: Literary Reception and Cultural Authority in the Early Republic* (University Park: Pennsylvania State University Press, 1993); Reginald A. Wilburn, *Preaching the Gospel of Black Revolt: Appropriating Milton in Early African American Literature* (Pittsburgh: Duquesne University Press, 2014). Although not committed to a history of the reception of Milton, Keith W. F. Stavely uses a reading of Milton as a lens through which to understand early American culture, in *Puritan Legacies: "Paradise Lost" and the New England Tradition, 1630–1870* (Ithaca, NY: Cornell University Press, 1987). See Christopher Kendrick's insightful evaluation of Sensabaugh, Schulman, and Stavely's works in his "Un-American Milton: Milton's Reputation and Reception in the Early United States," *University of Toronto Quarterly* 77 (2008): 903–22.

12. See Rogers, "Latter-day Milton."

13. The Endowment rite's appropriation of certain lines of *Paradise Lost* was a common theme in some of the nineteenth century antipolygamy literature. See J. H. Beadle, *Polygamy; or, The Mysteries and Crimes of Mormonism, Being a Full and Authentic History of This Strange Sect from Its Origin to the Present Time* (1904; repr., London: Forgotten Books, 2013), 397–99; Beadle's book first appeared as *Life in Utah; or, The Mysteries and Crimes of Mormonism* (Philadelphia: National, 1970), microform, which was "an exposé of the secret rites and ceremonies of the Latter-day Saints with a full and authentic history of polygamy and the Mormon sect from its origins to the present time." An apostate wife of Brigham Young, Ann Eliza Young reveals the Miltonic content of the Endowment ritual in her *Wife No. 19; or The Story of a Life in Bondage, Being a Complete Expose of Mormonism* (Hartford, CT: Dustin, Gilman, 1876), 357.

14. *Utah Magazine*, May 15, 1869, 24.

15. W. Wyl, *Mormon Portraits; or, The Truth about the Mormon Leaders from 1830 to 1880* (Salt Lake City: Tribune Printing, 1886), 272.

16. *Utah Magazine*, May 15, 1869, 24.

17. George D. Smith, *Nauvoo Polygamy* (Salt Lake City: Signature Books, 2008), 530–31.

18. William Ellery Channing, *Remarks on the Character and Writings of John Milton; Occasioned by the Publication of His Lately Discovered Treatise on Christian Doctrine*

(Boston: Isaac R. Butts, 1826). No aspect of Channing's revelation of Milton's heresies was more shocking to the American public than his enthusiastic revelation of Milton's views on polygamy. The Congregational *Christian Magazine* 3 (1826): 178, for example, gave the simple title "Polygamy" to its article about Channing's account of Milton's *Christian Doctrine*. Channing's striking sympathy with Milton's position on polygamy is noted with even more alarm in a later article, "Milton and Channing on Polygamy," *Boston Recorder* 31 (1846): 205. See also Francis E. Mineka, "The Critical Reception of Milton's *De Doctrina Christiana*," *University of Texas Studies in English* 23 (1943): 115–47.

19. In *Seer* 1, no. 1 (January 1853), Pratt presents the treatise "Celestial Marriage" as a transcription of a divine revelation "given to Joseph Smith, The Seer, in Nauvoo, July 12th, 1843."

20. "Milton on Polygamy," part 1, *Latter-day Saints' Millennial Star* 16, no. 21 (May 27, 1854): 321–24. The second part of Milton's discussion of polygamy from chapter 10 of the *Christian Doctrine* is printed in the next issue, no. 22 (June 3, 1854): 342–45.

21. "Milton on Polygamy," part 1, 328.

22. G. S., "John Milton on Plural Marriage," *Latter-day Saints' Millennial Star* 38, no. 11 (March 13, 1876): 161–65.

23. For a discussion of Joseph Smith's borrowing of the specific language of Milton's *ex deo* theory of creation, see my "Latter-day Milton."

24. Channing, *Remarks*, 37.

25. Key accounts of Milton's monistic spiritual materialism include Stephen M. Fallon, *Milton among the Philosophers: Poetry and Materialism in Seventeenth-Century England* (Ithaca, NY: Cornell University Press, 1991), 79–110; and William Kerrigan, *The Sacred Complex: On the Psychogenesis of "Paradise Lost"* (Cambridge, MA: Harvard University Press, 1983), 193–262.

26. John Milton, *A Treatise on Christian Doctrine, Compiled from the Holy Scriptures Alone*, 2 vols., trans. Charles R. Sumner (Boston, 1825): 1:250–51.

27. Milton, "Arcades," line 73. Joseph Smith, "Doctrine and Covenants," The Church of Jesus Christ of Latter-day Saints website, 131.7–8, accessed July 4, 2016, https://www.lds.org/scriptures/dc-testament/dc/131.

28. Orson Pratt, "Figure and Magnitude of Spirits," *Seer* 1, no. 3 (March 1853): 33.

29. Orson Pratt, *Great First Cause, or the Self-Moving Forces of the Universe*, in *A Series of Pamphlets, by Orson Pratt, One of the Twelve Apostles of the Church of Jesus Christ of Latter-day Saints* (Liverpool: R. James, 1851); repr. in *The Essential Orson Pratt*, ed. David J. Whitaker (Salt Lake City: Signature Books, 1991), 196. All subsequent citations of *Great First Cause* will be taken from this edition.

30. Ibid., 196.

31. I have discussed Cavendish's theories of self-moving matter in *Matter of Revolution: Science, Poetry, and Politics in the Age of Milton* (Ithaca, NY: Cornell University Press, 1996), 177–211.

32. Orson Pratt, *Great First Cause*, 196; italics mine.

33. Orson Pratt, "The Pre-Existence of Man," *Seer* 1, no. 7 (July 1853): 103.

34. Orson Pratt, *Great First Cause*, 196.
35. Ibid., 187–88.
36. Ibid., 188.
37. Ibid.
38. Ibid., 196.
39. *Christian Doctrine*, p. 245; Sumner's italics.
40. Orson Pratt, *Great First Cause*, 176.
41. Ibid., 196.
42. Ibid., 197.
43. "[God's] person may have had a beginning" (ibid., 173).
44. For the constitution of "Dust" or "Shadows" as "particles of consciousness," see Philip Pullman, *His Dark Materials*, vol. 2 (New York: Random House Bluefire, 2011), 364. Later, in volume 3, the angel Balthamos offers this explanation of the origin of God, known primarily in Pullman's work as "The Authority":

> The Authority, God, the Creator, the Lord, Yahweh, El, Adonai, the King, the Father, the Almighty — those were all names he gave himself. He was never the creator. He was an angel like ourselves — the first angel, true, the most powerful, but he was formed of Dust as we are, and Dust is only a name for what happens when matter begins to understand itself. Matter loves matter. It seeks to know more about itself, and Dust is formed. The first angels condensed out of Dust, and the Authority was the first of all. He told those who came after him that he had created them, but it was a lie. (569–70)

45. Channing, *Remarks*, 25.
46. Orson Pratt, "Pre-Existence of Man," 23.
47. See Bergera, *Conflict in the Quorum*, 89–91, who valuably reproduces the notes taken on the sermon by Apostle Wilford Woodruff.
48. Ibid., 145.
49. Ibid., 95. Early Mormonism's now disavowed "Adam-God" theory was another feature of the religion likely indebted to Milton's *Paradise Lost*. The God Adam who comes from another world to help "organize" this one, and to become its first earthly progenitor, is identified with the Archangel Michael, the angelic being who features prominently in Milton's poem, converting Adam to Christianity shortly after the Fall. Young would make this celebrated formulation of the Adam-God, or Adam-Michael-God, theory in 1852: "When our father Adam came into the garden of Eden, he came into it with a *celestial body*, and brought Eve, *one of his wives*, with him. He helped to make and organize this world. He is MICHAEL, *the Archangel*, the ANCIENT OF DAYS! About whom holy men have written and spoken — HE is our FATHER *and our* GOD, *and the only God with whom* WE *have to do.*" See *Journal of Discourses* 1, no. 50 (April 9, 1852), cited in Bergera, *Conflict in the Quorum*, 95. There is some speculation that Young's Adam-God theory had an origin in Joseph Smith. As reproduced in *Doctrines and Covenants*, 27.11, Smith had identified Michael as "Adam...the ancient of days." See Boyd Kirkland, "The

Development of the Mormon Doctrine of God," in *Line upon Line: Essays on Mormon Doctrine*, ed. Gary James Bergera, 35–52 (Salt Lake City: Signature Books, 1989).

50. Bergera, *Conflict in the Quorum*, 146.

51. Givens and Grow, *Parley P. Pratt*, 331, note that while *Key to the Science of Theology* wasn't published until 1855, Parley had completed it by May 1853.

52. Parley P. Pratt, *Key to the Science of Theology: Designed as an Introduction to the First Principles of Spiritual Philosophy; Religion; Law and Government; as Delivered by the Ancient, and as Restored in This Age, for the Final Development of Universal Peace, Truth and Knowledge* (Liverpool: F. D. Richards, 1855), 33. Givens and Grow, *Parley P. Pratt*, 332, write usefully of Parley's materialism: "By so naturalizing Deity, Pratt furthered Smith's work of collapsing the entire universe of God and humankind, heaven and hell, body and spirit, the eternal and the mundane into one sphere." I have made a case for the presence of Milton in Parley's early pamphlet, *The Regeneration and Eternal Duration of Matter* (1840), in "Parley Pratt, the Broken Planet of *Paradise Lost*, and the Creation of Mormon Theology," forthcoming in *Milton Studies*, vol. 58, *Milton in the Americas*, ed. Elizabeth Sauer and Angelica Duran (Pittsburgh: Duquesne University Press, 2017).

53. Parley P. Pratt, *Key*, 36.

54. Ibid., 37.

55. Orson Pratt, "Pre-Existence of Man," 24.

56. Parley P. Pratt, *Key*, 35; italics mine.

57. Ibid., 35.

58. Ibid., 39.

59. Ibid., 39.

60. Ibid., 41.

61. Ibid., 45.

62. "Proclamation of the First Presidency and Twelve, October 21, 1865 (Rebuke of Orson Pratt)," from James R. Clark, comp., *Messages of the First Presidency of the Church of Jesus Christ of Latter-day Saints*, 6 vols. (Salt Lake City: Bookcraft, 1965–75), 2:235–40.

63. Parley P. Pratt, *Key*, 51.

64. Givens and Grow, *Parley P. Pratt*, 331.

Notes to Chapter 8 / Harper

Epigraph is from Cory Doctorow, "Printcrime," *Nature* 439 (January 2006): 242. Quotations of Milton's prose in this chapter are taken from *Complete Prose Works of John Milton*, ed. Don M. Wolfe et al., 8 vols. (New Haven, CT: Yale University Press, 1953–82), hereafter cited as YP. The views in this chapter are those of the author and do not reflect the opinion of the U.S. Military Academy, the U.S. Army, or the U.S. Department of Defense.

1. Doctorow explained the inspiration for "Printcrime" in the preface to his 2007 collection. Cory Doctorow, *Overclocked: Stories of the Future Present* (Philadelphia: Running Press, 2007), 1. "Printcrime" originally appeared in *Nature* 439 (January 2006): 242.

2. *The Matrix*, dir. Andy Wachowski and Larry Wachowski; perf. Keanu Reeves, Laurence Fishburne, Carrie-Anne Moss, Hugo Weaving (Warner Bros. Pictures, 1999).

3. Glenn Beck, interview with Cody Wilson, on "The Blaze," January 17, 2013, https://youtu.be/iwkX8sWSxNQ (accessed December 18, 2016). Wilson is customarily vague about who "they" are.

4. Gary Wills, "Our Moloch," *New York Review of Books*, December 15, 2012, www.nybooks.com/daily/2012/12/15/our-moloch (accessed December 18, 2016).

5. In the *Second Defense* (1654) Milton reflects on *Areopagitica* as part of a long engagement with the "three varieties of liberty without which civilized life is scarcely possible, namely ecclesiastical liberty, domestic or personal liberty, and civil liberty" (YP 4:624).

6. Elias Groll, "Meet Cody Wilson, the Anarchist behind the World's First 3-D Printed Gun," *Foreign Policy Blog*, May 6, 2013, foreignpolicy.com/2013/05/07/meet-cody-wilson-the-anarchist-behind-the-worlds-first-3-d-printed-gun (accessed December 12, 2016).

7. Beck interview with Wilson.

8. "Should We Print Guns? Cody R. Wilson Says 'Yes,'" video interview on Slashdot.org, posted by Roblimo on September 5, 2012, hardware.slashdot.org/story/12/09/04/1837209/should-we-print-guns-cody-r-wilson-says-yes-video (accessed November 15, 2016).

9. Beck interview with Wilson.

10. See Stephen Dobranski, *Milton, Authorship, and the Book Trade* (Cambridge: Cambridge University Press, 1999), and *Milton in Context* (Cambridge: Cambridge University Press, 2010).

11. Groll, "Meet Cody Wilson."

12. See Seth Herbst, "Sound as Matter: Milton, Music, and Monism," chapter 2 in this volume.

13. Given the nature of 3-D printing, one should likely consider it more as "manufacturing" than as "printing," but parallels between this technology and the rise of print culture, and later computer-aided printing and publication, are unavoidable.

14. Joseph Loewenstein, *The Author's Due: Printing and the Prehistory of Copyright* (Chicago: University of Chicago Press, 2002), 187.

15. Reprinted in ibid., 162.

16. Contrary to popular belief, the Stationers' Register is not a mechanism for state censorship or control, but instead a mechanism for regulating the business of the stationers. There is no record, even in the tumultuous years of the civil wars, that the register was used by the government to identify authors or printers of suspect texts.

17. Advances in self-publishing since the early 2000s have already far surpassed the freedoms in manufacturing promised by 3-D printers. Blogs, social media platforms, and the ability to self-produce and publish e-books provide far more freedom than those printing presses "in corners" that the Commons worried about in the 1640s.

18. Doctorow, "Printcrime," 242.

19. Blair Hoxby, "*Areopagitica* and Liberty," in *The Oxford Handbook of Milton*, ed. Nicholas McDowell and Nigel Smith, 218–37 (Oxford: Oxford University Press, 2009), 231.

20. Stephen Dobranski, "Licensing Milton's Heresy," in *Milton and Heresy*, ed. Stephen Dobranski and John Rumrich, 139–58 (Cambridge: Cambridge University Press, 1998), 147.

21. See *Areopagitica*, YP 2:554, for Milton's description of London as a "mansion house of liberty."

22. Robert Fallon, *Captain or Colonel: The Soldier in Milton's Life and Art* (Columbia: University of Missouri Press, 1984), 89n37.

23. *Works of John Milton*, ed. Frank Allen Patterson (New York: Columbia University Press, 1931), 1.224–25. Note that the ascension of "loathsome cowls" on an explosive wind finds later expression in the limbo of vanities we find in *Paradise Lost*, where Satan is the inventor of gunpowder.

24. *Paradise Lost* is quoted from *The Complete Poetry and Essential Prose of John Milton*, ed. William Kerrigan, John Rumrich, and Stephen M. Fallon (New York: Modern Library, 2007).

25. And on Earth. Raphael points out that the same materials are at hand under the surface of the earth, suggesting that the knowledge of the destructive potential that lies beneath creation is itself morally neutral. As with the promiscuous reading of books encouraged by *Areopagitica*, the knowledge that potentially dangerous minerals are available beneath the earth's surface should serve only to instruct rather than to corrupt in paradise.

26. The editors of the Modern Library edition of *Paradise Lost* point out that "shared imagery ties Satan's perverse engines of destruction to his generative history with Sin and Death (cp. 2.755–802)." The observation is more apt when one considers that it is the stuff of nativity and generation that is being used for this destruction (*Complete Poetry and Essential Prose*, 464n).

27. Fallon, *Captain or Colonel*, 89n37.

ABOUT THE CONTRIBUTORS

REBECCA BUCKHAM completed the essay in this volume while a graduate student at Johns Hopkins University, where she studied early modern literature with an emphasis on Milton.

LARA DODDS is professor of English at Mississippi State University and the author of *The Literary Invention of Margaret Cavendish*. She has also published widely on Milton and on early modern women's writing in *Milton Studies, English Literary Renaissance, Texas Studies in Literature and Language*, and elsewhere.

KEVIN J. DONOVAN, professor of English at Middle Tennessee State University, codirected with Charles W. Durham and Kristin A. Pruitt the biennial Conference on John Milton from 1991 to 2015. With Christopher J. Wheatley he coedited *Irish Drama of the Seventeenth and Eighteenth Centuries: An Anthology* and has published articles in *English Literary Renaissance, Studies in Bibliography, New Hibernia Review*, and other journals as well as in edited collections. He also wrote the "Survey of Interpretive Criticism" for the New Variorum Shakespeare *King Lear*, edited by Richard Knowles, and is associate editor of the volume.

THOMAS FESTA is associate professor of English at the State University of New York, New Paltz. He is the author of *The End of Learning: Milton and Education*; and coeditor, with Michelle M. Dowd, of

Early Modern Women on the Fall: An Anthology, which won the Best Teaching Edition Award from the Society for the Study of Early Modern Women. An article of his was given the 2009 Award for Distinguished Scholarship from the John Donne Society. His essays have appeared in *Milton Studies, Huntington Library Quarterly, Studies in Philology*, and numerous essay collections.

RYAN HACKENBRACHT is an assistant professor of English at Texas Tech University. A recipient of the Albert C. Labriola Award from the Milton Society of America in 2013, his essays have appeared in *Milton Studies, Philological Quarterly, Renaissance and Reformation, Studies in Philology*, and several edited collections. His current book project, *National Reckonings: The Last Judgment and Literature in Milton's England*, shows how Milton and other writers politicize eschatology and attempt to bring divine judgment into the present.

DAVID A. HARPER is associate professor and head of the Department of English and Philosophy at the U.S. Military Academy, West Point, where he teaches courses in literature and composition. His research has been supported by the Rare Book School–Andrew W. Mellon Fellowship in Critical Bibliography. He is currently completing a book on Milton and the rise of modern literary criticism, and is the author of numerous articles on Milton and seventeenth century literature, including "Critical Mass: Contextualizing Bentley's *Paradise Lost*," in *Milton in the Long Restoration*, edited by Blair Hoxby and Ann Baynes Coiro, as well as journal articles in *Milton Quarterly, Review of English Studies, Studies in Philology*, and the *Papers of the Bibliographic Society of America*.

SETH HERBST is assistant professor of English in the Department of English and Philosophy at the U.S. Military Academy, West Point. Herbst studies the relation between words and music in the Renaissance, as well as later musical adaptations of works by Shakespeare, Milton, and other early modern writers. Herbst's work on Milton and music has appeared in *Essays in Criticism*; his current book project examines Milton's lifelong poetic preoccupation with music alongside the poet's afterlife in music.

ERIN MURPHY is associate professor of English and Women's, Gender and Sexuality Studies at Boston University. Her publications include *Familial Forms: Politics and Genealogy in Seventeenth-Century English Literature*; several articles on Milton; and *Milton Now: Alternative Approaches and Contexts*, which she coedited with Catharine Gray. She has also coedited a special issue of *Criticism* on the work of Eve Kosofsky Sedgwick with James Keith Vincent.

JOHN ROGERS is a professor of English at Yale University. The author of *The Matter of Revolution* and many articles on the literature and culture of seventeenth century England, he is currently completing a study of Milton's relation to Antitrinitarianism, titled *Milton's Passion*, and he has begun work on a book that investigates the impact of *Paradise Lost* and *De doctrina Christiana* on nineteenth century U.S. religion.

LAUREN SHOHET is professor of English at Villanova University. The author of *Reading Masques: The English Masque and Public Culture in Seventeenth-Century England* and recent essays on Milton, Marvell, and Wroth, she is editor of *Temporality, Genre, and Experience in the Age of Shakespeare: Forms of Time* (Arden, forthcoming 2017) and is working on a monograph on Milton's Eve.

INDEX

accommodation, and angel-human relationship, 124–26, 128, 133, 150–51
Adam: sexuality of, 149–50; and smell, 22; and walking, 64–70, 80
Adam-God theory, 235n49
Addison, Joseph, 205
angels: creation of, 175–78, 180; and embodiment, 12–13, 112, 116, 120, 125–36, 137–39; facial coloring and expressions of, 111–12, 128, 137–53; and food, 113, 116, 118–20, 151, 167; Homeric heroes compared to, 141–45; humans compared to, 113–20, 127, 134–36, 139–40, 168; material nature of, 120–21; in *Paradise Lost*, 111–53; sexuality of, 111–14, 118, 135–36, 153
Angier, Natalie, 36
animals, humans in relation to, 115–16, 133–34
animist materialism: music and, 39–41, 43–45, 55; walking and, 65
Annunciation, 87, 95–96, 98–99
anthropomorphism, 114–15, 134–36
anti-Trinitarianism, 9
Aquinas, Thomas, 138, 141
Areopagitica (Milton): and authorship, 192–201, 196–97; on censorship, 195–98, 201; on freedom of conscience, 198–99; and gun control debate, 14–15, 190–92, 198–209; on prepublication licensing, 15, 192–95, 200; on reason and ideas, 193–95, 201–04; on texts, 192–97
Arianism, 9
Aristotle, 39, 152
"At a Solemn Musick" (Milton), 48–50, 53–54
Aubrey, John, 64
Augustine, Saint, 4, 9–10, 53, 68
authorship, 192–201

Bacon, Francis, 39
Bennett, Jane, 2
Bergera, Gary James, 161, 181
biblical genealogies, 82, 86–90, 92, 96, 100–02, 223n29
Blake, Stephen, 63
Blake, William, 158, 192
blushing, 111–12, 128, 137–41, 146, 149–50, 152–53
the body: hierarchy characteristic of, 121–23; motion of, 79–80; soul in relation to, 47–48, 54, 65; subjectivity and, 60. *See also* embodiment
Boscovich, Roger Joseph, 167, 175
Brathwaite, Richard, 31
Broughton, Hugh, 86
Buckham, Rebecca, 12–13
Bunyan, John, 60
Burghardt, Gordon M., 114, 134
Butler, Judith, 84

243

Calloway, Katherine, 221n36
Camus, Albert, 191
Catholicism, 199, 203, 209
Cavendish, Margaret, 1, 170–71
censorship, 195–98, 201
Channing, William Ellery, 165, 166–67, 169–70, 180–81, 233n10, 233n18
Chapman, George, 144, 151
Charles I, 84–85, 88–89
Charles II, 81, 83, 88–90, 104
Church of Jesus Christ of Latter-Day Saints. *See* Mormonism
Clarke, Michael, 218n12
Classen, Constance, 31
communion, sacrament of, 124–26
contractual relationships, 100
Cook, James, 31
copyright, 199–200
Corbin, Alain, 31
Cowper, William, 223n29
creation: *ex Deo* vs. *ex nihilo*, 9, 177; Jesus and, 9–10, 166; Mormon conception of, 158, 166, 167, 171, 174–81, 183–85; music and, 43–44, 49; in *Paradise Lost*, 9–10, 43–44, 166, 175–81, 186; in *Treatise on Christian Doctrine*, 4, 9, 177

Daniel, Drew, 112–13
dark looks, 140–41, 143–45, 147, 151–52
David, King, 85–89, 95–96, 101, 104
death/Death: as lack of substance, 52–53; motion of, 77–79; smell and, in *Paradise Lost*, 25–26
De doctrina Christiana (Milton): creation in, 4, 9, 49; materialism in, 8, 43; monism in, 54–55; on sacrament of communion, 125. *See also Treatise on Christian Doctrine* (Milton)
The Defence of the English People (Milton), 8
Defense Distributed, 190–92, 195, 200, 202, 209

Defenses (Milton), 207
Deleuze, Gilles, 2, 23
Dennis, John, 140
Diodorus, Siculus, 32
Dobranski, Stephen, 192, 200
Doctorow, Cory, "Printcrime," 189–90, 199
Dodds, Lara, 13, 28, 60
Donne, John, 1
Donovan, Kevin, 20
Dugan, Holly R., 20, 213n2

Edelman, Lee, 104, 107
Eden, walking in, 59, 61, 64–70, 74–80
Edwards, Karen, 213n5
Eikonoklastes (Milton), 202–03
embodiment, 11–13; of angels, 112, 116, 120, 125–36, 137–39; sacrament of communion and, 124–26; of Satan, 128–30. *See also* the body
Empson, William, 158
ethology, 133–34
Eve: sexuality of, 149–50; and smell, 23–24, 33; and walking, 59, 65–70, 76–77, 80
Evelyn, John, 63
evil, 4, 52–53, 203
evolutionary thought, 114–17
Exclusion Crisis, 90

Fallon, Robert, 202, 207, 209
Fallon, Stephen, 6–7, 44; on the corporeality of angels, 138, 140, 141; on development of materialist thinking in Milton, 11, 37–39, 47, 48, 52, 55, 215n3
family/kinship: consent as basis of, 101–02; in *Paradise Regained*, 91–92, 97–107; performative nature of, 90, 92–94, 106; reimagining of, 84, 103–07. *See also* sonship, Jesus's
Festa, Thomas, 20
Ficino, Marsilio, 126–27, 130, 131

figurative language, 4–5
Fish, Stanley, 149
Floyd-Wilson, Mary, 60
Follett, King, 158
Foucault, Michel, 191
freedom of conscience, 198–99
Fukuyama, Francis, 191

gardening, 63–64
genealogy, 12, 81–107; biblical, 82, 86–90, 92, 96, 100–02, 223n29; in the Gospels, 83, 85–88, 91–92, 97, 223n29; of Jesus, 86, 88, 90–91, 101–05; *Paradise Regained* and, 12, 82–84, 86, 88–107; paradoxical nature of, 82, 88, 91, 101; royal, 81–90, 105
Gilbert, Avery, 32
God: and creation, in Mormon theology, 158, 172, 174, 177–81, 183–85; creative act of, 4, 9–10, 43, 49, 158, 174; theodicy and, 32; and the Trinity, 9–10, 179
Goldberg, Jonathan, 83, 89, 113–14, 226n2
Gospel genealogies, 83, 85–88, 91–92, 97, 223n29
Green, Mandy, 60
gunpowder, 203–07, 209
Gunpowder Plot, 203, 204
guns: as ideas, 192; Milton and, 202–09; print-at-home, 14–15, 189–209; as production, not printing, 200–01

Hackenbracht, Ryan, 11–12
Haller, Albrecht von, 31
Harper, David A., 14–15
Harrington, James, 208
Harris, Jonathan Gil, 20
Harrison, Timothy, 218n7
Haskin, Dayton, 98
Henry, Prince, 84–85
Henry IV, 88

Henry V, 85
Herbst, Seth, 11, 194
Herschel, John, 167, 175
Herz, Rachel, 34–35
Hobbes, Thomas, 99–100
Holoka, James, 144, 145
Homer: facial expressions and gestures in, 13, 141–45; walking in, 60–62, 71, 79–80
Howes, David, 31
Hoxby, Blair, 199
human nature: angels compared to, 113–20, 127, 134–36, 139–40, 168; animals compared to, 115–16, 133–34; Mormon conception of, 158

ideas. *See* reason/ideas, publication and
identity: genealogy and, 12, 83; human, 115–16

James, Susan, 150
James I, 81, 84–89, 104, 203, 223n18
James II, 90
Jefferson, Thomas, 180–81
Jesus: birth of, 82–83; genealogy of, 86, 88, 90–91, 101–05; humanity of, 84, 107; Mary as mother of, 97–100; performative kinship of, 90, 92–94; sonship of, 90–97, 175–77, 222n14; Stuart genealogy's connection to, 81–83, 85, 88–90; and the Trinity, 9–10, 179
Johnson, Marshall, 87
Johnson, Samuel, 3, 125–27, 130, 138, 141
Joseph, husband of Mary, 101–02
The Judgement of Martin Bucer (Milton), 101, 105

Kant, Immanuel, 1–2, 31
Kerrigan, William, 5–6
kinship. *See* family/kinship
Knott, John R., 21

246 Index

La Quintinie, Jean de, 63
Larsson, Maria, 35
Lateiner, Donald, 142, 145
Latour, Bruno, 2
Leonard, John, 7, 148
Levine, Daniel, 152
Lewalski, Barbara, 64, 215n4, 222n14
Lewis, C. S., 61, 126–27, 135, 149
literal language, 4–5
Lockwood, Laura, 227n28
Loewenstein, Joseph, 196
Low, Anthony, 75
Lucretius, 60
Luxon, Thomas, 226n16

Machacek, Gregory, 221n39
Madsen, William, 125, 127, 227n20
Marcus, Leah, 7
marriage, alternative conceptions of, 101–02, 107. *See also* polygamy
Mary, mother of Jesus, 91, 96–103, 107
Masaccio, 60
A Mask (Milton), 11, 50–53, 217n18
materialism: angels and, 120–21, 138–39; hierarchy and, 121–23, 171–72; in Milton's works, 3–8; Mormonism and, 158, 166–74, 178–81, 183–85, 236n52; music and, 37–55; in *Paradise Lost*, 3–9, 120–24, 166–72, 193; role of intelligence in, 172–73, 185; scholarship on, 1–2; texts and, 193–94. *See also* animist materialism
The Matrix (film), 190
McColley, Diane, 29
Meillassoux, Quentin, 2
metaphor: concept of, 127–28, 132–33, 227n20; and representation of angels in *Paradise Lost*, 128–36
migration, 69–70, 80
militias, 202–03, 207–09
Milton, John: Hebraism of, 163–64; materialism and vitalism in, 3–10; monism of, 3–10, 11; politics of, 7–8, 208; walking habits of, 64

monarchy, hereditary. *See* Stuart genealogy
monism: and body/soul relationship, 47–48, 54, 65; in Milton's works, 3–10, 11, 37–40, 45, 47–49, 52–55; music and, 11, 38, 53–55
monotheism, 8–9
Mormonism, 14, 157–88; Adam-God theory of, 235n49; materialism of, 158, 166–74, 178–81, 183–85, 236n52; Milton's influence on, 157–58, 162–81, 185–88, 232n10, 233n13, 235n49; Smith's influence on, 158–61; succession crisis in, 160–62, 181–88; theology of, 159, 167–74, 177–88
Morton, Timothy, 2, 116–17, 127
Moshenska, Joe, 24
motherhood, 99–101
Murphy, Erin, 12
music, 37–55; and creation, 43–44; as matter, 37–55; monism and, 11, 38, 53–55; ontology and agency of, 39–53

National Rifle Association, 202
Nativity ode. *See* "On the Morning of Christ's Nativity" (Milton)
Nettesheim, Cornelius Agrippa von, 32
new materialism, 1
Newton, Isaac, 173
Newton, Thomas, 3
Nichols, Jennifer, 218n2

object-oriented ontology, 1
Of Education (Milton), 11, 39
Ogilby, John, 144, 145, 151
"On Creation," *De doctrina Christiana*, 4
"On the Morning of Christ's Nativity" (Milton): and monism, 11, 38, 45–47; and reproductive futurity, 105; and time, 20–21, 82–84
Ovid, 60

Paley, William, 167, 175
Paradise Lost (Milton): American reception of, 14; angels in, 12–13, 111–53; creation in, 9–10, 43–44, 166, 175–81, 186; epic antecedents of, 60–62, 71, 79–80, 141–45, 151–53; facial expressions and gestures in, 142–53, 229n18; and gun control debate, 190; gunpowder in, 204–07; Jesus's sonship in, 92; materialism in, 3–9, 120–24, 166–72, 193; Mormonism influenced by, 157, 163–64, 166–81, 185–88, 232n10, 233n13, 235n49; music in, 11; smell in, 19–36; walking in, 11–12, 59–61, 64–80; war in heaven in, 125–26, 128–33
Paradise Regained (Milton): challenges to monarchy in, 82–84, 89, 97, 103, 105; genealogy in, 12, 82–84, 86, 88–107; Jesus's sonship in, 90–97; kinship in, 91–92, 97–107; Mary in, 97–100
Parsons, Robert, 86
Petersen, Boyd Jay, 232n10
Phillips, Edward, 64
Pickett, Holly Crawford, 20
Plato, 31, 39, 40
politics, 7–8, 208
polygamy, 159, 164–65, 233n18
Pope, Alexander, 144
Post, Jonathan, 60
Povinelli, Elizabeth, 82, 103, 107
Pratt, Orson, 14, 159–60, 162, 166–67, 170–75, 177–88; "Celestial Marriage," 159, 165; Great First Cause, or the Self-Moving Forces of the Universe, 167, 174–75, 177–82, 185–86, 188; Latter-day Saints' Millennial Star, 165; "On the Divine Authenticity of the Book of Mormon," 159; "The Pre-Existence of Man," 171
Pratt, Parley P., 159–60, 164, 166–67, 182–88, 236n52; Key to the Science of Theology, 159, 183–85, 187–88; Voice of Warning, 159; World Turned Upside Down, 164, 233n10
Proposalls of Certaine Expedients (Milton), 208–09
Proust, Marcel, 35
Pullman, Philip, 14, 180, 235n44

queerness, in kinship/family relations, 84, 103–07
Quint, David, 60, 61, 89, 105–06
Quorum of the Seventy Apostles, 161
Quorum of the Twelve Apostles, 159, 161–62

Raphael (angel): and angelic nature, 12–13, 111–14, 116–36, 137–38, 140, 146, 149–53; materialism in speech of, 3–9, 113, 167–72, 179
Raymond, Joad, 119, 120, 135, 138, 141, 153
The Readie and Easy Way (Milton), 90, 207–09
reason/ideas, publication and, 193–95, 201–04, 209
Reid, David, 213n6, 215n26
reproductive futurity, 83–84, 104–07
rhyme, 45
Richardson, John, 64
Rivas, Jesús, 114, 134
Rogers, John, 7–8, 14, 90, 92, 141
Romney, Mitt, 160
Rose, Mary Beth, 97, 99
Rumrich, John, 226n3

Sacks, Oliver, 35–36
Satan: and creation, 175–77, 180, 186; embodiment of, 128–30; genealogical investigation of, 86, 90–91, 94–96, 105–06; gestures of, 143–47; gunpowder associated with, 204–07; popular fascination with, 180–81; and smell, 19–20, 23, 26–27; and walking, 66, 71–79

Sauer, Elizabeth, 96
scent. *See* smell
Schoenfeldt, Michael, 60
Second Amendment, 202
Second Great Awakening, 163
self-knowledge, walking as means to, 59, 61, 64–76, 79–80
sexuality: of Adam and Eve, 149–50; angels and, 111–14, 118, 135–36, 153; demonic, 115
Shohet, Lauren, 10–11
Slayter, William, 81–83, 85, 86, 91
smell, 10–11, 19–36; boundary-crossing character of, 21–28, 31–32; and cognition, 30–32; in Eden, 20–24, 26–27; and human–divine communication, 25; meanings and poetic functions of, 20–21; and memory, 32, 34–35; and semiotics, 28–30; and space, 22–23, 26–27; and temporality, 20–21, 26–36; in Western tradition, 31
smiling, 152
Smith, Bruce R., 20
Smith, Joseph, 157–67, 170, 174, 178, 181, 183, 186, 188, 232n10, 235n49; "King Follett Discourse", 158, 174–75
Snow, Eliza R., 163–64
Snyder, Gary, 111
sonship, Jesus's, 90–97, 175–77, 222n14
soul: Milton's conception of, 40; music's effect on, 41–43; relationship of body to, 47–48, 54, 65
space, smell and, 22–23, 26–27
Speed, John, 86–88, 92, 96, 100–02, 223n29
Spenser, Edmund, 1
Spinoza, Baruch, 10, 23
Stanford, W. B., 127–28, 132
Stationers' Company, 195, 196, 200
Stein, Arnold, 138
Stephens, Walter, 115
striding, 62, 71–72, 80

Strier, Richard, 143
Stuart genealogy, 81–90, 105
subjectivity: the body and, 60; decentering of, 2; smell and, 20. *See also* self-knowledge
Sullivan, Garrett, 60
Sumner, Charles, 164, 166, 169–70, 175, 177
Swedenberg, H. T., Jr., 229n13
Swift, Jonathan, *Battel of the Books*, 201
synaesthesia, 22, 25
Synnott, Anthony, 31

temporality: genealogy and, 83, 106; smell and, 20–21, 26–36
The Tenure of Kings and Magistrates (Milton), 8, 204, 207
Teskey, Gordon, 9, 92
Tetrachordon (Milton), 101–02
theodicy, 32
theophany, 76
thing-power materialism, 2
time. *See* temporality
transubstantiation, 124–26
Treatise on Christian Doctrine (Milton): on creation, 4, 9, 177; on the millennium, 165; Mormonism influenced by, 157, 164–66, 175; on polygamy, 164–65, 233n18
Trinity, 9–10, 179
Trubowitz, Rachel, 97, 98
Turner, James Grantham, 138

Virgil, walking in, 62–63, 79
vitalism: commonalities of modern and early modern, 2; in Milton's works, 3–8; scholarship on, 1–2

walking, 11–12, 59–80; Adam and Eve and, 64–70, 76–77, 80; in the epic tradition, 60–63; gardening associated with, 63–64; and holy migration, 69–70, 80; Satan and,

71–79; and self-knowledge, 59, 61, 64–76, 79–80; striding, 62, 71–72, 80; in Western tradition, 60
Wallace, Anne, 218n8
Warner, Michael, 104
Watson, Robert, 125, 126
West, Robert, 115, 138, 226n23
Western tradition: smell in, 31; walking in, 60

Whewell, William, 167, 175
William the Conqueror, 88
Wills, Gary, 190
Wilson, Cody, 14–15, 190–92, 197–98, 200, 202, 208, 209
Woolf, D. R., 103

Young, Brigham, 160–63, 181–88, 235n49

www.ingramcontent.com/pod-product-compliance
Lightning Source LLC
Chambersburg PA
CBHW022048290426
44109CB00014B/1021